The MANY FACES *of*
PRAYER

How the Human Family Meets
Its Spiritual Needs

Thomas Shepherd, D.Min.

Also by the Author

Nonfiction
Friends in High Places, Third Edition
Good Questions
Jesus 2.1: An Upgrade for the 21st Century

Fiction (written under the pen name *Thomas Henry Quell*)
Wrathworld
The Princess and the Prophet

The MANY FACES *of* PRAYER

How the Human Family Meets
Its Spiritual Needs

Thomas Shepherd, D.Min.

Unity Library
1901 NW Blue Parkway
Unity Village, MO 64065

Unity Village, Missouri

The Many Faces of Prayer

A Unity Books Paperback Original

Unity Books are available at special discounts for bulk purchases for study groups, book clubs, sales promotions, book signings or fundraising. To place an order, call the Unity Customer Care Department at 1-866-236-3571 or email *wholesaleaccts@unityonline.org*.

Bible quotations are from the New Revised Standard Version unless otherwise noted.

Cover design: Terry Newell
Interior design: The Covington Group, Kansas City, Missouri

Library of Congress Control Number: 2012951544

ISBN: 978-0-87159-362-7

Canada BN 13252 0933 RT

For all my students,

past,

present,

and future.

CONTENTS

FOREWORD

At a time when religious perspectives in America as well as much of the rest of the world are disagreeing, sometimes violently, *The Many Faces of Prayer* offers a path to harmony and mutual respect among all spiritual paths. Rev. Dr. Thomas Shepherd has explored the fascinating subject of prayer in a way that promotes understanding, appreciation, and reverence for the rich diversity of beliefs about and practices of prayer that humankind has evolved. Readers of *The Many Faces of Prayer* will very likely come away not only with a new appreciation of the prayer traditions of other spiritual movements, but also with a greater appreciation of and enthusiasm for the prayer practices of the spiritual tradition they follow themselves.

Helicopter pilot in Vietnam, divinity student, career military chaplain, middle-school teacher, pastor, author, broadcaster, and seminary professor, Tom Shepherd has worked professionally in all of these areas and has built a strong marriage and family at the same time. Here is a man whose life has been anything but dull!

Spiritually inquisitive from childhood, Dr. Tom shares insights from the many paths he has explored, among them the Reformed Protestant tradition, the United Church of Christ, the Baha'i Faith, and Unitarian Universalism, settling into Unity as his home base more than 30 years ago. Tom is no stranger to Eastern spirituality. He's been honored as a friend and colleague by the Venerable Bhante Y. Wimala, traveling

Buddhist monk and Chief *Sangha Nayaka* (Head Monk) to the United States from Sri Lanka.

The rich diversity of his religious experience, training, and background has given Tom extraordinary insight into the beauty and the deep spiritual meaning of prayer traditions. In *The Many Faces of Prayer*, he writes with respect and affection for all of the paths he has followed. Perhaps these words from the preface best capture the spirit of *The Many Faces of Prayer*:

> This book is not about the right way to pray; it's about the ways people pray, what they pray to, and what they pray for. One of the principles guiding my work in the theology of spiritual practice is that the discussion should never be about what is correct and incorrect in prayer and spirituality. Let me be clear: A yawning chasm separates, "You got it wrong," from "I see it differently." To my knowledge, no one has been appointed the prayer police. How to approach God—or whatever you call the content of your pantheon—is a metaphysical question with deeply personal implications ... You get to choose.

The Many Faces of Prayer guides the reader through a concise and very readable history of the God concept, beginning with the concept's prehistorical roots, and looking at the sometimes very different ways evolving cultures have conceived of Ultimate Reality—including what Shepherd calls "nontheistic options." More than other books on prayer I've discovered, *The Many Faces of Prayer* offers a comprehensive look at prayer and its meaning.

Perhaps the most significant question Tom Shepherd addresses here is what he calls the "Let It In/Let It Out Controversy." Dr. Tom asks:

1) Is the goal of spiritual growth to open your mind to the inflow of Omnipotent Holy Spirit (*let It in*)? Or ...

2) As Eric Butterworth suggests from his book title, to "discover the power within you" and release your indwelling divinity *(let It out)?*

What's unique about Tom Shepherd's approach to the question is his very obvious respect for *both* perspectives. Perhaps recalling Stephen Covey's *Seven Habits of Highly Effective People,* Shepherd seeks to understand before seeking to be understood. *The Many Faces of Prayer* will help readers from many spiritual paths grow in understanding of the sometimes very different paths their brothers and sisters follow. Perhaps this significant and readable work will inspire some who had abandoned spirituality to take up a spiritual path of their own.

Tom Thorpe, M.A.R.
Unity Village, Missouri

PREFACE

The work you are about to read flows from a lifelong interest in cross-cultural spirituality and ritual. As I think back over the decades, everything seemed so simple early in life. There was home, school, and church. Everyone sang the same music. *Hosanna, Jesus loves me, pass the Lebanon bologna.* Life was simple, until my curiosity drew me outside the cozy circle of familiarity, past a point where I began to hear the different drummers.

As a Baby Boomer growing up in a row house of an ethnically homogenous Protestant neighborhood in Reading, Pennsylvania, I was fortunate to attend Thirteenth and Union Elementary School. Not exactly diverse by today's standards—we had *one* African-American student—nevertheless, the school had a significant minority of Jewish and Catholic students. We were also blessed with vibrant faculties who exposed us to the new, postcolonial, post-World War II world. Albert Schweitzer, Gandhi, and Martin Luther King Jr. We never spoke of religions in the emerging new countries, but teachers shared an enthusiasm for a wide range of cultures, East and West. And the Jewish and Catholic students sitting around me in class represented alien worlds to a Pennsylvania Dutch kid.

Sometimes a Jewish friend would invite me to the family Shabbat meal, where I donned a skullcap and listened to readings from the sacred text, previously known to me only as the "Old" Testament. It began to occur to me that people

I cared deeply about—my friends and classmates—included those who saw the world quite differently than it had been presented to me at Zion's Reformed Church. The struggle to make sense of life always presented a spiritual dimension to me, yet here were young people who didn't believe in Jesus, and others who said they were Christians but prayed in the presence of full-sized idols. Where in the Bible did Jesus' mom get promoted to some kind of goddess? My friends, not just marching to a different drummer, but worshipping a different deity? Wasn't that the very definition of *sin*?

I loved and respected my elders at Zion's—which was a kindly place full of Townhouse Crackers and Bible stories, and nothing approaching judgment. We never spoke of *hell* at Zion's Reformed Church, because that was for bad people and we didn't know anybody like that. Oh, sure. Hell was still on the books—like a law against emptying your bedpan from a second-story window—but it just didn't apply. And these un-Protestant kids were my *friends* who just happened to believe differently. There was also my crabby, agnostic Uncle Gibb, who sneered at religion. Uncle Gibb knew I loved going to church, so he gleefully repeated the urban legend about Russian Cosmonaut Yuri Gagarin saying he had found no God up there in 1961 when he orbited the earth.

So many differences of opinion on religion. I suppose that's when I discovered I had become a universalist, even before moving away from childhood to travel the world. Travel doesn't just broaden—it deepens. I encountered ever more diversity—Baha'is, Buddhists, Muslims, Hindus, an endless array of spiritual traditions that by comparison made Jews and Catholics seem like coreligionists to a woefully ignorant Protestant like me.

The common theme I began to discover in spirituality and prayer was the need to make sense out of life and live it successfully. Different groups understood differently what "live it successfully" meant, but the impetus for a balanced, meaningful life flows horizontally through all the cultures of humanity and reflects in the religions we create to meet those needs. The central theme of this book is that humans do not share the same *answers*; we share the same *questions*, which we have answered differently.

As a theologian and teacher of graduate students, I tend to look at the questions through an analytic, cross-cultural lens, but after four decades in ministry, the residual pastor within me still loves and appreciates the practical aspects of human spirituality. My goal in writing *The Many Faces of Prayer* was to present a multicultural look at prayer, meditation, and ritual that addresses both the intellectual and devotional sides of the topic. Obviously, with a world of religious traditions to draw upon, this study cannot pretend to be exhaustive. Behind each door leading to a major faith group is another room full of doors, each with corridors full of subgroups, denominations, and geo-cultural practices.

Full Disclosure: Tossed Salad

Any serious study of world religions is likely to demonstrate that humans have evolved different answers to similar questions. *The Many Faces of Prayer* examines alternative points of view on prayer and attempts to be objective and even-handed. However, social, historical, and theological connections link every human worldview to a living culture. As a matter of full disclosure, let me place my theological cookbook face-up on the table: This study proceeds from an understanding of prayer as a tossed salad of communication and reflection. For me, *prayer is communion with the divine— One Presence/One Power—in both the inner and the outer dimensions of life.* To comply more completely with this goal of intellectual candor, I have offered a personal summary of belief, "Affirmation of Inclusive Christianity in a Multifaith World," posted as an Appendix. As a theologian, I reserve the right to modify everything as new thoughts break through. Certainly the dialogue will continue, as each new generation wrestles with the questions of life and faith.

The fun part begins when we explore new sources of nourishment. What other banquets have humans cooked up for their daily spiritual fare? How can we incorporate touches of the wide diversity of world religious traditions to add color and flavor in our devotional diet? Cross-cultural prayer, meditation, and ritual practices offer a large choice of recipes for new, tasty dishes, adding zest to our spiritual cuisine. The café of world spiritual practices requires no reservations. Save your fork and spoon—dessert courses will be offered.

See you there.

Invocation

Father Almighty! We bow before Thine infinite goodness, and invoke in prayer Thine all-merciful presence of love.

We ask, and as we ask we give thanks that Thy power and presence are here in love and that we are tightly held in Thine all-embracing arms, where our every need is supplied and where we shall ever rest secure from all the buffets of the world.

Open to us the inner chambers of peace and harmony, which divinely belong to us as Thy children.

We come as little children into the sacred and trustful presence of Thy love, knowing full well that only love can draw and hold us in peace and harmony and prosperity.

Every fear falls away as we enter into Thee and Thy glory of love and as we bask in the sunshine of love, Thy love, Thy never-failing love! [1]

—Charles and Cora Fillmore, *Teach Us to Pray*

PART
ONE

MANY PATHS, MANY GODS, MANY OPTIONS

"Lift up your hands to the holy place,
and bless the LORD."

Psalm 134:2

The greatest threat to civility—and ultimately to civilization—is an excess of
certitude. The world is much menaced just
now by people who think that the world
and their duties in it are clear and simple …
It has been well said that the spirit of liberty
is the spirit of not being too sure that you
are right. One way to immunize ourselves
against misplaced certitude is to contemplate—even to savor—the unfathomable
strangeness of everything, including ourselves.[1]

—George F. Will

1
COMMUNICATION OR REFLECTION?

"The world in which you were born is just one model of reality. Other cultures are not failed attempts at being you; they are unique manifestations of the human spirit."[2]

—Wade Davis

It is a simple act—to kneel, sit, or stand in prayer. Billions of people do it every day, observing a wide variety of culturally shaped habits. Prayer can be sounds or silence, thoughts or actions—floating flowers in the Ganges River or offering the body and blood of Jesus Christ in the Sacrament of Eucharist; contemplating the divine presence in the simplicity of the Quaker Meeting House or in the luxuriant Celestial Room of a Mormon Temple; Buddhist chanting to prepare the mind for meditation or Pentecostal Christians crying aloud in unknown tongues under the influence of the Holy Ghost.

Even a cursory glance at human religious experiences clearly indicates that spiritual practices always come with pre-existing conditions. Long before participating in daily devotions, people acquire a set of lenses that shape their experience, and the more effective the worldview, the less likely people will notice its effects. On a planet with thousands of languages and a vast multitude of cultures, intelligent life could hardly proceed otherwise. This very diversity of thought makes religious studies fascinating.

Back in the 1980s, when I was a U.S. Army Chaplain serving in Germany, I took a busload of soldiers on a weekend spiritual retreat to a guesthouse at Muggendorf, in the part of Bavaria known as Little Switzerland. The countryside was mountainous although not alpine, with architectural gems tucked here and there among the narrow valleys. One place we visited was a medium-sized basilica that rested like a house of solace under yellow, orange, and red trees.

Opening the door, I was struck with the interior size— larger than it appeared from the outside—and the wild proliferation of images. Through the centuries, European cathedrals provided a kind of religious education in stone and painting for illiterate peasants. Churches have been called the poor person's Bible, because those who could not read the sacred text could see it illustrated all around them. Devout custodians of this sacred space had carried on the tradition; they crowded every alcove with statuary and decorated every flat space above the floor with frescoes about church history and Scripture. Sections of the floor offered more imagery through inlaid mosaics.

I sat on a hardwood pew and tried to focus on the artwork, but it was like listening for a lone voice in a riot. Even the altar overflowed with statues; gleaming golden spikes exploded from the heads of the apostles and the Virgin Mary. Instead of a worship experience, I felt besieged, bombarded by figurines and murals and picture-jammed stained glass windows.

When I looked at the soldiers, I noticed two distinct reactions. Some of the troops sat quietly. Their heads traveled back and forth, wall to ceiling to altar, like they were watching invisible angels playing handball across the vaulted sanctuary. None of them seemed to be praying. Meanwhile, other soldiers were kneeling in worship. I puzzled over the radically different responses until after we emerged from the church. As we waited for the bus, a Protestant soldier said, *"Sir, I couldn't pray in that place. It was packed with idols."* A few minutes later, a young Catholic woman in the group said, *"Chaplain, wasn't that wonderful?"*

At that moment I totally and viscerally "got" an intellectual concept I had known for years. *Worship needs vary greatly for people from different backgrounds.* It isn't right or wrong, it's the lenses we wear. Spiritual needs are universal. Who hasn't craved a quiet moment by oneself? But the takeaway lesson my Protestant and Catholic soldiers taught me was that any spiritual practice must be organically right for you. As Jesus of Nazareth reportedly said:

> Ask, and it will be given to you; search, and you will find; knock, and the door will be opened for you. For everyone who asks receives, and everyone who searches finds, and for everyone who knocks, the door will be opened.[3]
>
> —Mt. 7:7

Consequently, this book is not about the right way to pray; it's about the ways people pray, what they pray to, and what they pray for. One of the principles guiding my work in the theology of spiritual practice is the discussion should never be about what is correct and incorrect in prayer and spiritual practices. Let me be clear: A yawning chasm separates *"You got it wrong"* from *"I see it differently."* To my knowledge, no one has been appointed the prayer police. How to approach God—or whatever you call the content of your pantheon—is a metaphysical question with deeply personal implications.

You get to choose.

Asking "Which religion is right?" is an adolescent distraction that adds nothing to the discussion. Besides, if pushed to answer candidly, even people who accept the maxim of *truth in all religions* would probably say, "Of course, personally I believe my religious faith is 'right,' or why would I be *here* and not *there*?" Trusting my belief system in no way requires denigration of differing views.

No one has the right to tell 1.5 billion Muslims they are wrong to pray to a single Almighty Being, *Allah* (God) *the Merciful, the Compassionate*; or tell 900 million Hindus they should not be worshipping at temples dedicated to many gods and goddesses; or tell 2.5 billion Christians their Jesus is not the Way to God; or call 400 million Buddhists mistaken when they encourage meditation rather than prayer, because they believe no Supreme Deity exists. Some people connect with neighbor and universe through a God or gods out there; others find the Divine strictly as Indwelling Spirit; still others find the Divine in both the inner and outer dimensions. Some seek salvation from eternal punishment and access to the joys of paradise or heaven; some pursue enlightenment and absorption into the Oneness; others look for nonbeing and release from the cycle of birth-death-rebirth; others hunger for blissful union with God.

You and I have our preferences—we might even think another path is a dead end, or possibly harmful—but all people have full membership in the club of humanity, and everyone may bring whatever belief system works for them to the interfaith table. The opposite attitude, intolerance of differences, too often has given people license to act with violence toward offensive points of view. As I write this book, Muslim extremists in Libya and Egypt have attacked the American embassies in those countries. At Benghazi, Libya, heavily armed attackers set fire to the compound, resulting in the death of U.S. ambassador to Libya Christopher Stevens and three other Americans. Libyan officials condemned the attackers in strong terms. Mobs in both Egypt and Libya were outraged by an Internet movie that was critical of Islam, although at this writing the lethal attack in Libya may have been executed by a band of terrorists who piggybacked their moves on the public outcry.[4]

Libya has seen more Muslim-on-Muslim attacks than assaults against infidels; for example, the bombing of Mosques by rival factions in the Islamic community. Arabic news service Al-Jazeera has condemned the lack of response by security forces when minority religious groups, like the Sufis, are attacked. Al-Jazeera says police lethargy undermines "the principle of plurality within unity in Libya and all emerging democratic transitions in the Arab Middle East."[5] It is noteworthy the key principle of tolerance which Al-Jazeera cites— "plurality within unity"—closely resembles the motto of the United States of America, *E Pluribus Unum* ("Out of Many, One," or "Unity From Diversity").

Unfortunately, scenes of religious violence have occurred with alarming regularity throughout human history, with players from various faith groups exchanging roles of victim and perpetrator. Christian crusaders boasted about God's pleasure as they shed the blood of nonbelievers to wrest the Holy Land from Muslim hands; Buddhist and Shintoist pilots attacked Pearl Harbor and flew suicide missions against enemy vessels during World War II; a Hindu extremist killed Mohandas Gandhi. George F. Will's comment, cited earlier, seems to apply here: "The greatest threat to civility—and ultimately to civilization—is an excess of certitude."[6] Surely the baseline for a civilized world must include tolerance of beliefs that individuals may find personally intolerable. Aggression in the Name of God wins no hearts, makes no friends, and was condemned by founders of all the world faiths.

Library Full of Doors

Assembling a sampler of representative studies worthy of this book's subtitle, *How the Human Family Meets Its Spiritual Needs*, requires hard choices leading to sins of omission, an occupational hazard for theologians. Teaching world religions at Unity Institute® and Seminary often feels like leading students into a vast library full of doors. Each portal represents a major faith group: *Baha'i, Buddhism, Christianity, Confucianism, Islam, Jainism, Judaism, Hinduism, Neo-paganism, Shinto, Sikhism, Tribal-Indigenous Religions, Voodoo, Zoroastrianism* — an endless parade of faiths and practices.

Step inside and what do you find? Another room of doors! Each new doorway leads to antechambers of subgroups, denominations, and schisms of the faith marked on the outer entrance. The floor upon which we stand merely represents religious traditions *today*. Think about the levels below and above, the history and potential of each faith.

Open the Christian door, for example. Inside you will find another hall with doors leading everywhere—from the snake-handling euphoria of extreme Pentecostalism to majestic rhythms of incense-cloaked Russian Orthodox worship; Quaker Silent Meeting to boisterous melodies of African-American Baptist churches. In what bizarre chemistry of faith does a Lutheran and a Jehovah's Witness share common DNA? Yet they all claim to be Christians. Who is qualified to say they are not? Every Christian group traces its family tree back to Jesus Christ and the disciples, but that was apparently the last time we all belonged to the same household. Some find this lack of continuity disturbing. For example, take the following quote from a website of a conservative church in Pennsylvania:

The New Testament condemns religious division. Christ prayed for the unity of his disciples (John 11) so that the world might believe the Father had sent him into the world. Religious division (denominationalism) is contrary to his will and defeats his purpose.[7]

Others consider the subdivisions in religious thinking as natural, even healthy. Certainly, as best-selling author and biblical scholar Bart Ehrman has demonstrated in his book *Lost Christianities: The Battles for Scripture and the Faiths We Never Knew*, Christianity has never been monolithic. Variability in doctrine and ritual dates to the period immediately after the death of Jesus. Some of the differences were so extreme that modern Christians often have difficulty accepting the variations that did not prevail as a legitimate part of the historic Church.

> The wide diversity of early Christianity may be seen above all in the theological beliefs embraced by people who understood themselves to be followers of Jesus. In the second and third centuries there were, of course, Christians who believed in one God. But there were others who insisted that there were two. Some said there were 30. Others claimed there were 365 ... there were Christians who believed that Jesus' death brought about the salvation of the world. There were other Christians who thought that Jesus' death had nothing to do with the salvation of the world. There were yet other Christians who said that Jesus never died.[8]

Multiplicity in thought and practice exists in every religious tradition on Earth, but Christianity in the United States has taken the art of diversity to a new zenith. American *denominationalism* is the new orthodoxy.

The practice of denominationalism came into being in the 18th century during the Evangelical Revival, but the idea started with the Puritans. The whole idea of denominationalism is a reaction to sectarianism. Sectarianism is exclusive, meaning that each sect of a religion believes that its way is the right way and that no other way is acceptable. Denominationalism as a concept is more inclusive, because it espouses that one particular Christian group is really just a part of a bigger religious community—the Christian Church. Denominationalism means that each subgroup is accepted and acknowledged, and no one group can represent the entirety of Christianity.[9]

Gathering as equals who are not the same, we can learn from one another by beginning with words like, *"Here's what works for me ..."* then listening with an open mind as they reciprocate. We do not need to agree on theology to get along. Besides, that will not happen in this lifetime—probably not in the lifetime of our species. We do need to disagree agreeably, which is a basic ingredient for peace in a pluralistic world.

What Am I Doing in Prayer?

Without aiming to agree on everything, let's begin our look at *The Many Faces of Prayer* with the most basic question: What am I doing in prayer? More specifically, to Whom (or what) am I praying? The power of the mountain, a river god, an honored ancestor, the Patron Saint of Editors (there is one—St. John Bosco[10]), or the solitary Creator of the cosmos, or maybe the divinity within me? Am I *communicating* with a Presence and Power beyond myself—engaging in an *I-Thou* relationship with my Higher Power—or *reflecting* upon something deep in my consciousness? Can prayer be both, or neither? What kind of link could exist between my apparently limited lifespan and the divine? For that matter, what is *the divine* anyway? How does my cultural worldview, which I inherited at birth, affect my method of prayer?

All of the following rhetorical questions represent religious worldviews *currently held* by religious traditions on this planet:

- If I am the creation of a Supreme Being, totally mortal without a shred of divinity, how will my prayer be different than if I see myself as a localized expression of God-energy?
- If many gods and goddesses roam the world, blessing and cursing at their discretion, what kind of religious duties will I create in my vigorous attempt to avoid offending while actively pleasing those whimsical divinities?
- How is my prayer affected if not all gods are good? What if the supernatural world includes malicious deities, evil spirits, or mischievous demigods who take delight in bringing chaos and ruin upon mortals?
- What if there is an ongoing struggle between the forces of good and evil, a celestial civil war in which humans are bystanders who nevertheless take collateral damage? How do I pray in a cosmic combat zone?
- How will I approach an All-Powerful Supreme Being, an Ethical God who punishes wrong and rewards the right?
- Or what if the Cosmos itself is divine, yet containing lesser components such as falling stars, tigers, human beings, major and minor gods and goddesses, heavens and hells? What kind of prayer evolves in that spiritual ecosystem?

Culture, history, geography, and longstanding tradition powerfully shape every child's worldview. Slightly different shades of belief bring significantly different results. A Roman Catholic monotheist might pray to a Saint or the Blessed Virgin Mary, which a Baptist or Methodist monotheist is not likely to do. Muslims pray facing Mecca; Mormons do not.

Many Hindus believe in reincarnation and a multitude of gods and goddesses; many Buddhists believe in reincarnation and no god whatsoever.

When children grow to adulthood, they will sometimes reject the religious tradition in which they were born. Dalton Roberts—multitalented poet, philosopher, teacher, musician, songwriter, author, newspaper columnist, and formerly the highest elected official in Chattanooga, Tennessee—took this thought to its logical conclusion in his weekly *Sunday Journal* column:

> After my early disenchantment with religion, I went through years of trying to not believe. I don't just mean to not believe in religion, but to not believe in anything so I could make sure I had an open mind. Yet all the time my thinking was leading me to make decisions on what I was thinking. Self-honesty finally made me see that I was always believing in something—tarot cards, fate, luck, the law of averages, science—you name it. I came to see it is *as impossible to not believe as it is not to think.*[11]

Even disbelief comes with a hidden program running in the background. Some children, especially in Western Europe and North America today, are raised in homes without any formal religious affiliation. However, dominant religio-ethical themes provide a cultural context in our secular world, whether people are churchgoers or not. When American or British atheists reject God, they are not usually rejecting the Hindu Preserver *Vishnu*, the Māori god of the sea *Tangaroa*, or the African storm god *Shango*. Even Satanists rely upon Jewish, Christian, and Muslim mythologies for the main characters in their anti-pantheon. An urban legend illustrates this point. During the Protestant-Catholic disturbances in Northern Ireland of the mid-20th century, a young man approaches a barricaded checkpoint and is halted by the guard.

"Catholic or Protestant?" the sentry demands.

"Atheist," the stranger replies cockily.

The guard is not impressed. "Catholic atheist or Protestant atheist?"[12]

Preset categories of thought shape the world and influence us even when we categorically deny their existence. We grope in the dark to find answers, yet it is the questions that elude them. Those who forsake Christianity seldom abandon Jesus' ethical mandate to love our neighbor as ourselves, return not evil with evil, treat neighbors and strangers with equal respect, show kindness to the poor and afflicted and gentleness toward children, and work for justice and equality for all people. The more we reflect on this "simple act" of prayer, the more we realize the complex assumptions and embedded theologies we bring to the process of seeking—or rejecting—communion with the divine.

Anyone who has studied the religions of humanity knows our species has displayed a high degree of creativity in meeting its spiritual needs. In his 1966 book, *Religion: An Anthropological View*, Anthony F.C. Wallace noted, "Even the so-called 'monotheistic' religions invariably include an elaborate pantheon." Wallace went on to list the supernatural beings in the complex mix of historic religion and pop culture of the small American town in which he grew up. The list hit all the players—God, Jesus, the Devil, Saints, and on to minor Judeo-Christian characters—then continued with less obviously "religious" but clearly present supernatural entities—ghosts, souls in some kind of afterlife, witches, Santa Claus, and fairies, plus depersonalized supernatural forces such as superstitions. Wallace added, "Not everyone 'believed in' all of these supernatural beings, at least not all at the same time ..." But the network of supernatural and supersensory phenomenon that constitutes a pantheon is much more extensive than most people credit.[13]

Other observations from the social sciences can help make sense of the complex world of religious traditions. When surveying unfamiliar territory in cross-cultural prayer studies, looking through the lens of a social science tool known as *cultural relativism* can help chart the way.

Cultural Relativism

Cultural Relativism is the view that moral or ethical systems, which vary from culture to culture, are all equally valid and no one system is really "better" than any other. This is based on the idea that there is no ultimate standard of good or evil, so every judgment about right and wrong is a product of society. Therefore, any opinion on morality or ethics is subject to the cultural perspective of each person. Ultimately, this means that no moral or ethical system can be considered the "best," or "worst," and no particular moral or ethical position can actually be considered "right" or "wrong."[14]

The religions of humanity represent an array of beliefs and practices, some quite simple, others highly complex. Although diversity of thought is unavoidable, undue emphasis on the differences among the faiths has led to mutual excommunications, crusades, holy wars, and acts of genocide, as the critics of "organized religion" have rightly observed. The history of bigotry-based violence has driven some progressive thinkers to declare parity among world religions, summarized by a charming ditty from the Baha'i Faith:

God is one, man is one
And all the religions are one.
Land and sea, hill and valley
Under the beautiful sun.
God is one; man is one
And all the religions agree.
When everyone learns the three one-nesses
We'll have world unity.[15]

It is politically correct, especially among today's Cultural Creatives, to identify points of unity and avoid mentioning the disagreements. Certainly, affable relations between faith groups require mutual respect, but there is a vast difference between accepting the principle of *cultural relativism*—which proclaims all truth is local—and declaring all religions proclaim the same message.[16] They clearly do not, and never have. Teachers of the great faiths usually addressed specific issues endemic to their times and places. They were not abstract philosophers but practical leaders who solved existential problems and answered the everyday questions of a living community. When their successors continued the faith, they adapted its ideas and practices to new circumstances.

These differences cannot be ignored without discounting the unique contributions of all communities of faith. To affirm cultural relativism—all religions are *equal*—is not the same as pronouncing all religions the *same*. There are genuine differences in the way human communities have answered basic questions about Ultimate Concerns: life, death, eternity, and humanity's place in the Cosmos. To lump all religious traditions into one amorphous "Interfaith" heap only denigrates the rich diversity of world faiths. We come to the interfaith table as members of a culture. Dialogue begins when we recognize that theological differences have as much to teach us as similarities do.

I recall the first time this idea dawned on me. It was the 1960s, during the hot days of the Civil Rights movement in the United States. I was a young soldier living in the barracks with men from all sorts of ethnic and religious backgrounds. During our many late-night, solve-the-world's-problems marathon discussions, one of my favorite contributions was to declare all people are the same, regardless of race. Although my liberal-sounding platitude usually went unchallenged, one evening an African-American soldier surprised me by disagreeing.

"No, Tom. We are not all the same," he said. "I'm *not* just a dark white guy. We're different, and it makes life more interesting."

It was another *aha* moment. Differences add, not subtract. Flower gardens need variety. In the garden of humanity, diversity in religion or ethnicity or race enhances life.

Who knows what concepts remain a mystery because of the lenses we wear, or perhaps the sounds we can't hear? Cetaceans, a group of highly intelligent marine mammals that includes dolphins and whales, communicate through complex sounds that some researchers think is language. Humpback whales sing recognizable melodies across vast stretches of sea, and their tune changes every year.

At this writing, scientists have no idea how whales in the warm waters near Mexico receive the same new music as other humpbacks swimming the cold North Pacific, or why humpbacks in different ocean basins sing different songs, even though all the whale communities update their melodies annually. The vocalizations appear to be related to mating behavior, but does the language of whale love also contain spiritual dimensions?[17]

Differences in human spiritual behavior are easier to track. For example, take Islam and Hinduism. Although they often share geographic boundaries and live in enclaves within each other's territory, Muslims and Hindus sing a different tune religiously. They share no harmony about the number of gods that may be worshipped; they disagree about the number of lives an individual may live along the path to spiritual mastery; they stand at odds over the number of sexual practices blessed by the divine; and they differ about the proper menu of dietary taboos. Nor are the differences trivial: Hindus pray in temples adorned with hundreds of idols; Muslims condemn idolatry as grievous sin. To declare these two religions in harmonious agreement is only possible if one has never encountered a Muslim or a Hindu.

Critical thinking about spiritual practice clears the underbrush and asks, *"What is actually happening here? What are religionists really saying? What points of similarity-dissimilarity are present?"* Metaphysical theology loses its credibility when it succumbs to the New Age fantasy of "all religions are the same" and attempts to homogenize ideas that are contradictory and unmixable. To comprehend Hinduism or Islam clearly—finding some points in common, others wholly incompatible—is far better than trying to make a hybrid from two very different worldviews, which does a disservice to both. To understand this dynamic better, look at ecological studies.

The natural world energetically produces creatures that simultaneously cooperate and compete. Predator and prey need each other for a balanced ecosystem to endure; insects and carrion eaters clean up the leftovers, and the grass and other plants absorb nutriments through the soil when all the mobile critters stop moving at the end of their lives. Human systems of thought are also competitive and cooperative. Religions occupy a niche in all sociocultural systems and have an important contribution to make to the health and well-being of humanity, but their specific contributions will vary with the cultural environment.

Dueling Dualisms

The question about whether effective prayer can be dualistic or not seems to underlie much of the recent hullabaloo about prayer in Metaphysical Christianity. Speakers and authors often wrestle with the demon of dualism and attempt to exorcise it from their ministry and spiritual life. I have heard seminary students fret about praying in public, because they feared someone might criticize them for "praying dualistically."

Some of the confusion comes from the fact the word *dualism*, like *spiritual* or *metaphysical*, is a technical term philosophers and theologians use differently from the generic way it is used by ordinary religionists. Dualism signifies opposites—for example, *Yin and Yang*, male and female, good and evil, truth and error, divine and human, God and the Devil. Note that not all opposites are at war. Yin-Yang, male-female, divine-human can be held in creative tension to form a greater whole. However, any sort of separating difference can technically be called dualistic. Communication between conscious minds implies dualism; you speak, and I receive your ideas through sound waves and language. Conversation, dialogue, or even talking to oneself can arguably be called dualistic.

> Dualism contrasts with monism, which is the theory that there is only one fundamental kind, category of thing or principle; and, rather less commonly, with pluralism, which is the view that there are many kinds or categories. In the philosophy of mind, dualism is the theory that the mental and the physical— or mind and body or mind and brain—are, in some sense, radically different kinds of things.[18]

The polar opposite of dualism is *monism*, which maintains diversity is at best an error-belief, because the All is indivisibly One. Since we experience the world as separated—many people, places, and events—the dance of dualism is much easier to perform than Monism, which requires a little fancy footwork. Sometimes those who hold to cosmic monism attempt to explain the variety in everyday experience by speculating about two realms—an ideal, eternal, changeless world versus the ephemeral plane of human existence, the *Absolute* and the *relative*. Some scholars find monism within the ancient Vedānta school of Hinduism in the East, although others hold the Vedic works contain both dualistic and monistic elements.[19]

Western expressions of monism go back at least to Platonic idealism of the fifth century BCE. Plato held the real world was an ideal realm of perfect forms; the everyday world was no more than a shadow on the wall by comparison. However, Plato's star pupil, Aristotle, repudiated his mentor and said all we have is the everyday world. The ideal realm of perfection is an illusion based on the concrete world we see, not the other way around.

Beyond metaphysical considerations, there are ethical dimensions to the dualism-monism discussion. Some monists denigrate the manifest world as temporary, shallow, unreal existence. For its shadowy brevity, they substitute visionary hopes for an ascension to or absorption in the eternal Absolute through spiritual and mental disciplines. While such a grand vision can help individuals cope with life, it can also trivialize human suffering and place all hope on a world of ideal existence rather than working to solve problems in the only world we know firsthand. Not surprisingly, the argument between dualists and monists over what constitutes Ultimate Reality continues to this day.

Prayer: Communication or Reflection?

Every practice humans identify as *prayer* seems to fall into one of two categories, and the way a religious faith answers this question is in some ways more important than the shape of its God concept. Either we are addressing some kind of spiritual reality *beyond* ourselves, or we are contemplating the spiritual essence that dwells *within* us. While researching this work, the only variation I discovered was among those who attempt to do *both*—to see prayer as *communication* with God in the cosmos, and also as *reflection* upon their Indwelling Divinity—which might be a third option, provided we avoid playing linguistic mind games. More about that later.

What premises underlie the acts of prayer *to God* as opposed to prayer *as God?*

Most religionists in Western traditions address their prayers to a Supreme Being, to Saints, the Virgin Mary, or to some kind of benign external Power. Prayer for them is definitely *communication*, albeit in many different forms. They pray *to* God. Other traditions, more commonly found in Asia but also in the West, see themselves as expressions of the divine, and view prayer as *reflection.*

Sometimes reflective prayer (exploring spiritual thoughts) is hard to distinguish from meditation (listening, or seeking stillness beyond words). Prayer as reflection can involve communion with Indwelling Divinity, God-self, Christ-within, the Buddha-nature, or the *I AM*, which many believe is the true identity of every sentient being. Reflective prayer can be in stillness, the Silence, or by use of affirmations and Centering. The first three verses of the 23rd Psalm, perhaps the best-known spiritual reading in the Bible, are not addressed to an external deity but represent straightforward affirmations by which the psalmist reflects on the power of God.

The Lord is my shepherd, I shall not want.
He makes me lie down in green pastures;
he leads me beside still waters;
he restores my soul.

He leads me in right paths
for his name's sake.[20]

If this is prayer, to whom is it addressed? The psalmist seems to be talking to himself about his belief in Divine Providence. Even verses 4-6, which ostensibly speak *to* God, are neither supplication nor thanksgiving but *second person declarations*, as if the psalmist is reminding himself what is true.

Even though I walk through the darkest valley,
I fear no evil;
for you are with me;
your rod and your staff—
they comfort me.

You prepare a table before me
in the presence of my enemies;
you anoint my head with oil;
my cup overflows.
Surely goodness and mercy shall follow me
all the days of my life,
and I shall dwell in the house of the Lord
my whole life long.[21]

The 23rd Psalm is undoubtedly prayer, but it's a better example of prayer as *reflection* rather than *communication*. The psalmist is not talking *to* a Supernatural Being; he appears to be talking to himself *about* the God of Israel. Historically speaking, the author of the Shepherd Psalm was not ready to evict Yahweh from His throne in the clouds or His Mercy Seat inside the veiled holy of holies in the Jerusalem Temple. Reflective prayer for the psalmist probably meant an inward consideration about outer realities, not yet an attempt to become one with an indwelling divine nature. That concept would come later in Jewish and Christian mysticism.

Yet the prayer mostly recounts what the psalmist already knew about God, rather than telling God what He (Yahweh was male) knew about Himself. Even when shifting from third person (*"He makes me lie down in green pastures ..."*) to second person (*"You anoint my head with oil ..."*), the psalmist continues to *reflect* on God's mighty deeds rather than convey new requests and wait for a response, which defines genuine *communication*.

Letters to God

Elements of a maximum-inclusive definition for prayer have sometimes appeared in the writings of mystical theologians like Charles Fillmore. For example, this passage from *Atom-Smashing Power of Mind*:

> ... prayer is the opening of communication between the mind of man and the mind of God. Prayer is the exercise of faith in the presence and power of the unseen God. Supplication, faith, meditation, silence, concentration, are mental attitudes that enter into and form part of prayer. When one understands the spiritual character of God and adjusts himself mentally to the omnipresent God-Mind, he has begun to pray aright.[22]

It is obvious Mr. Fillmore was attempting to allow for prayer as both communication and reflection. His writings are full of examples of speaking *to* God; other times, he reflects on the Divine-within. Myrtle Fillmore frequently sounds even more traditional in her published works. The following passage from *Myrtle Fillmore's Healing Letters* suggests she did not fear appearing dualistic.

> Prayer, as Jesus Christ understood and used it, is
> communion with God; the communion of the child
> with his or her Father; the splendid confidential talks
> of the son or daughter with the Father. This commu-
> nion is an attitude of mind and heart ... Sometimes I
> have written a letter to God when I have wanted to
> be sure that something would have divine consider-
> ation and love and attention. I have written the letter,
> and laid it away, in the assurance that the eyes of the
> loving and all-wise Father were seeing my letter and
> knowing my heart and working to find ways to bless
> me and help me to grow.[23]

Mrs. Fillmore was very clear that prayer, for her, involved direct "communion with God," which she described as a talk between daughter and Father. She wrote letters to God to be sure her Father got the message. This is not just looking to God-within; Mrs. Fillmore reached out to God with her mind and felt a powerful *I-Thou* connection.

Even before the Fillmores became husband and wife, Myrtle made certain Charles understood she would follow her own guidance on theological issues. In a letter dated September 1, 1878, she writes to her future spouse:

> You question my orthodoxy? Well, if I were called
> upon to write out my creed it would be rather a
> strange mixture. I am decidedly eclectic in my theol-
> ogy—is it not my right to be? Over all is a grand idea
> of God, but full of love and mercy.[24]

Myrtle Fillmore's declaration of the right to be "decidedly eclectic" in her theology necessarily allowed the same free-dom for others. Unity began as a teaching-healing movement, a way of life, not a set of doctrines. The ongoing diversity of religious thought suggests this is a good strategy for life in a multifaith world.

Communion with God ... but which god?

Swimming in the depths of consciousness, which the followers of the Baha'i Faith call *"the ocean of divine unity,"* brings its own set of challenges.[25] When someone reads the word *prayer,* culturally shaped images come into play.

Prayer as communion with the divine is difficult to characterize because it comes in so many shapes, colors, and flavors depending on the religio-cultural lenses acquired while growing up. Some people see prayer as an *I-Thou* interaction with a unitary Supreme Being (e.g., Judaism, Islam, Baha'i, Unitarianism, and the Jehovah's Witnesses), or communion with the divine as it outpictures in the form of multiple divine beings (Hinduism, Shinto, Neo-Paganism), or supplication to a Three-in-One Divine Union (Protestantism), or the same Trinitarian adoration supplemented by petitionary conversation with exalted human souls (saints) in heaven (Roman Catholicism, Eastern Orthodoxy). Prayer can attempt to awaken the enlightened nature within the individual (Buddhism), or its goal might be to guarantee the orderly transition of the seasons and keep the gods from wrecking human civilization (Aztecs, Egyptians, Greeks, Romans). Prayer could be talking or thinking or dancing or singing; it could be chanting while working a trade, or playing a musical instrument with no words involved.

Study Group Note

Our survey of prayer now looks at the struggle about finding God outside oneself or finding the divine within. We begin with a problem I call the *"Let It In/Let It Out"* Controversy, then tackle the provocative question whether praying "to" God makes sense today.

A far-reaching study of prayer is best done in small groups. Our ancestors danced their daily exploits before the community fire to a movement of Spirit within them. The hunger for group interaction continues today in the need for simple sharing time in a circle of trusted fellow seekers. To facilitate this process, each chapter concludes with six "Check Your Knowledge" questions, six "Discussion Starters" questions, and a "Suggested Activity." The activities will provide plenty of opportunities to "dance around the fire" as you reflect on ideas presented in each chapter. If you don't dance, bring a drum and make joyful noise. Or just listen in the stillness and share as guided.

Check Your Knowledge

1. What did the author learn from the Catholic and Protestant soldiers he took to the church in Little Switzerland?
2. In what way is the study of prayer from a comparative religions perspective like entering a library full of doors?
3. Explain how culture, history, and geography shape our religious thinking?
4. Does "Cultural Relativism" mean all religions are the same? Explain.
5. Describe the major two categories into which all forms of prayer seem to fall.
6. What is the author's "full disclosure" definition of *prayer*?

Discussion Starters

1. Looking at your life, what cultural factors have influenced your beliefs?
2. What are you doing when you pray?
3. How do you react when someone with a different understanding of prayer offers to pray for you?
4. Have you had any experiences that challenged your basic beliefs about God? What did you do about it?
5. Discuss the pros and cons of Cultural Relativism. Why is this principle so hard to practice among societies with different worldviews?
6. How flexible should the spiritual practices of a church be? What are the limits? (Don't pretend there are none.)

Suggested Activity:
Exploring Your Neighborhood Pantheon

Note: This can be done as an individual or group activity, or simply a meditation exercise.

Chapter 1 introduced the idea that spiritual practices are powerfully shaped by the religious culture in which you were socialized. Sometimes we take this backdrop for granted, as social scientist Anthony F.C. Wallace suggested a generation ago. To test this concept, make an exhaustive list of ALL religious or supernatural entities present in the belief systems of people in the city, town, or rural community where you grew up. Obviously, you will not personally believe in many of these beings, but their survival in the corners of your mind has colored the way you see the world. For example, in order to decide there is no Santa Claus, you need to know what part the Jolly Old Elf plays in the mythology of childhood.

Most people begin this exercise by listing God, Jesus, and the Holy Spirit, perhaps adding Catholic Saints, the Virgin Mary, and Grandma in heaven. But don't forget fairies, the Easter Bunny, and the Devil. The only requirement is that *someone* in your immediate world—old or young, no matter what religious or cultural background—must have believed in the entity sometime, past or present. Don't forget to examine your memory for the range of groups nearby. Did you have Wiccans, Hindus, or Native Americans in your immediate world?

You'll be amazed what's in your neighborhood pantheon!

If this is a group activity, start individually then compare your lists. Discuss similarities and differences. Note any surprises?

2

THE "LET IT IN/LET IT OUT" CONTROVERSY

Let nothing disturb you,
Let nothing affright you.
All things are passing.
God never changes.
Patient endurance attains all things.
God alone suffices.

—St. Teresa of Avila[1]

Deciding whether prayer is *communication* or *reflection* is part of a longstanding mêlée among theologians and practitioners about how to get spiritualized. Enlightened. Saved. Pick your word. Do we open ourselves to an inflowing Holy Spirit, or allow the Divine Spirit within to emerge in consciousness? In previous works, I have called these two choices the *Let It In/Let It Out Controversy*. The difference between *Let It In/Let It Out* is not a word game but a fundamental clash about the ultimate nature of metaphysical reality. How folks resolve the controversy shapes the way they look at God, neighbor, and themselves. The dispute can be summarized by two questions:

1) Is the goal of spiritual growth to open your mind to the inflow of Omnipotent Holy Spirit (*let It in*)? Or ...

2) In Eric Butterworth's words of his book title, to "discover the power within you" and release your indwelling divinity *(let It out)?*

After investigating these two options, we shall consider whether there is any way to bridge the apparently insurmountable gulf between prayer as *communication* with God and prayer as *reflection* upon the Divine-within.

Option 1: "Let It In"

In this paradigm, the direction of flow is Divine-to-human. *"Let It In"* religious traditions teach people to be open and receptive to the inflow of divine inspiration. Multiculturally speaking, two-way communication can come from a personal deity who is a member of a trinity of exalted beings—whether the Holy Spirit for Christians or the god Vishnu for Hindus— or from a solitary high God, like Yahweh or Allah. *"Let It In"* encompasses such diverse arrangements as divine guidance inferred from experience in daily life; direct communication from the Universal Mind; visions and dreams from angels, saints, good spirits, gods and goddesses; and a variety of premonitions based on coincidental events, natural signs, omens, fortune telling, and prophecies. Obviously, it is unlikely anyone would choose to access all the spiritual resources above; they are meant more like a grocer's inventory than a shopping list.

Statistically, most religions of humankind have looked to outer resources for spiritual assistance. The animist called upon the spirit of the river to ward off floods. Polytheistic ancient Romans sacrificed a pig, sheep, and bull to encourage the god Mars to bless and purify the land. Today, Muslims face Mecca and pray to God the Merciful and Compassionate; Sikhs invoke the presence of God-within by chanting to raise consciousness. A little less elegantly but directly to the point,

Shintoists clap their hands to alert the god of their presence, express joy for the god, and ward off evil spirits.[2]

What these diverse practices share is an orientation to prayer as communication between the individual and some sort of divine power or personality in the outer world. We have not yet discussed motivation—fear or joy, duty or delight—because these are accelerants, not factors that shape the basic concept. If I call upon a goddess because I fear she is angry with me, or because I want to thank her for the beauty of the sunset, I am in both instances *calling upon a goddess.* Even when she remains silent, the movement in consciousness is toward dialogue, not soliloquy.

Looking at prayer as communication with divine forces or an unseen Presence beyond oneself, it is easy to stigmatize the *"Let It In"* approach by illustrating the practice with examples of spiritual oppression and fear-mongering. The early life of Martin Luther is a prime example. He was raised by severe parents who whipped him until the blood flowed for stealing snacks from the kitchen. Small wonder Martin thought God, the most awesome parent-figure of all, should demand utter perfection from His children. So Luther tried to comply.

"If ever a monk got to heaven by his monkery," he wrote years later, "it was I. All my brothers in the monastery who knew me will bear me out. If I had kept on any longer, I should have killed myself with vigils, prayers, readings, and other work."[3] A sense of infinite inadequacy seized him when, as a newly ordained priest, Luther contemplated saying Mass in the presence of an All-Holy God. "Who am I, that I should lift my eyes or raise my hands to the divine Majesty?" He envisioned himself a pygmy standing before the King of the Universe.[4] Obsessed with self-doubt, Luther spent so many hours in the confession box that his confessor ran him off, advising young Martin: "Why don't you go out and commit some real sins, and come back when you have something to confess?"[5]

Luther finally discovered God was not the enemy; in fact, God was not even angry with him. God is reconciling love, not the raging disapproval of an abusive parent.

This story is an example of the potential for spiritual cruelty people can project upon any god in the Universe. However, specific examples of great harm can be counterbalanced by other examples of great good. Mistreatment at the hands of one lover does not obligate someone to a life of celibacy.

For many people, faith in God as an available Presence and Power in the outer world is the main reason they can keep living with some degree of success after tragedy, trial, or disappointment. More important, billions of human beings through history have felt a personal connection with the animating Force of the Cosmos. Intimacy with the Divine as an inflow of God-power cannot be discounted or explained away merely because it falls short of a theological formula.

When standing under the night sky and feeling the awesome, all-embracing wholeness of all things, muttering a prayer of thanks seems perfectly logical. In the words of the widely esteemed Hindu Swami Vivekananda (1863–1902), "So long as we have five senses and see the external world, we must have a Personal God."[6]

Option 2: "Let It Out"

To some metaphysical Christians, the quality Buddhists call *mindfulness* is not poured into the believer from outside but can only be accessed by an ever-increasing awareness of the divine-within. Several New Testament authors provide theological support for this viewpoint. Paul wrote to the church at Corinth:

> Do you not know that your body is a temple of the
> Holy Spirit within you, which you have from God,
> and that you are not your own? For you were bought
> with a price; therefore glorify God in your body.[7]

Other biblical passages suggest the Holy Spirit takes up
residence in our bodily temples only after we accept Jesus
Christ. When it comes to locating God within or opening ourselves to inflowing Divine Spirit from outside, Paul is rather
ambiguous. Sometimes he rhapsodizes about the indwelling
spirit, as he did in the above quote from First Corinthians.
Other times, Paul makes the Spirit sound like your second
cousin from Boston, who entered the priesthood and visits
home occasionally. Take the following passage from Romans:

> Likewise the Spirit helps us in our weakness; for we
> do not know how to pray as we ought, but that very
> Spirit intercedes with sighs too deep for words. And
> God, who searches the heart, knows what is the mind
> of the Spirit, because the Spirit intercedes for the
> saints according to the will of God.[8]

Like the apostle Paul, Metaphysical Christian literature is
all over the mental map on these two questions. Butterworth,
who understood the divinity of humanity as well as any
teacher of his generation, sometimes spoke in both categories.

> We live in the Presence … we live in God. It is the
> milieu of our life. We can't get out of it. There is
> nowhere to go to find God. Just "Be still, and know
> that I AM God" [Psalm 46:10]. Be still and let the
> Divine Flow manifest in you and through you. This
> is "The Omnipresence of God."[9]

When Butterworth advises stillness so the *Divine Flow* can *manifest in and through* the individual, he leaves the door open for God's *Omnipresence* to well up within, or flood to us from a loving Father-Mother beyond limited human consciousness. Not a Supreme Being, but Supreme Being-Itself, "the milieu of our life."

For a contemporary book on prayer as a "Let It Out" phenomenon, take Linda Martella-Whitsett's *How to Pray Without Talking to God.* This well-written and thoughtful work is not wary of controversy, and Martella-Whitsett presents her arguments with an intellectual rigor that engages people at multiple levels. Since we are exploring a theology of prayer in our current work, the tools of critical analysis apply to the study of this important book on how to pray without communicating.

The heart of Martella-Whitsett's argument is her doctrine of God, which shapes the way she believes people should pray. She rejects God as a Supreme Being in favor of "an understanding of the Divine as All That Is, not a person but a power."[10] In rapid succession, she declares God is not an Invisible Parent, Santa Claus, or Bodyguard. She repudiates biblical passages like Isaiah 66:13 (where God is compared with a comforting mother), and says contemporary works like James Dillet Freeman's "Prayer for Protection" and Mary Stevenson's "Footprints in the Sand" are equally meaningless, because there is no God "out there."[11]

Martella-Whitsett is not the first voice in the Judeo-Christian heritage to raise the culturally uncomfortable problem of God as a Supreme Being. In fact, her critique of ethical monotheism travels in good company. By the mid-20th century, major voices were sounding the alarm over the untenable position of supernaturalism. Thomas J. J. Altizer is perhaps the best known of the pack. His "God is Dead" theology made the cover of *Time* magazine at Easter, 1966. Altizer's sensationalism—he called his major work *The Gospel of Christian Atheism*—sold books but frightened many readers who might have considered the argument he was raising if presented less glaringly.[12]

Paul Tillich, one of the most respected theologians of the era immediately before Altizer's heyday, had said many of the same things and influenced Altizer's radical thinking. Tillich, who was better received but a little less popularly known, declared God is not a Being but *being-itself*. According to Tillich, God does not "exist" as other beings exist, but God is existence itself. Tillich contrasts the limited idea of theism's supernatural God with God as being-itself.

> The God of the theological theism is a being besides others and as such a part of the whole reality … He is seen as a self which has a world, as an ego which relates to a thought, as a cause which is separated from its effect, as having a definite space and endless time. He is a being, not being-itself.[13]

One of Tillich's foremost interpreters, Anglican Bishop John A. T. Robinson, popularized the nontheistic ideas of Tillich and Altizer, especially through the publication of Robinson's widely read book *Honest to God*. Half a century later, its clarity of thought still rings like a bell, awakening postmodern Christianity. Building on the work of pioneers like Rudolf Bultmann, Bishop Robinson pointed to the Christian heritage as a mythology constructed on the earthbound bones of Saints and prophets. Robinson observes how prescientific language of the biblical world is effortlessly translated into modern thought by spiritualizing its content.

Yahweh, the God of Israel, was a sky-god. Consequently, the writers of the Bible located heaven literally in the clouds above their heads—why else would Jesus ascend there physically? Although not yet equal to Dante's fully developed medieval vision of hell, the early Christian land of the dead borrowed heavily from the Hebrew *sheol* and the *hades* of Greco-Roman polytheism, locating it somewhere in the bowels of the earth.

This biblical mythology lingers in metaphors of contemporary language. Why is "up" better than "down"? When a spurned lover on a TV soap opera calls the cheating partner "lowest of the low," what makes *low* a bad descriptor of conduct? If a public official has a reputation for *high* morality and *lofty* character, does that indicate the superiority of *up* over *down*?

Robinson notes we have translated the physical up-and-down language of a prescientific worldview into spiritual terms. God is no longer physically "up there," but has removed Himself to a respectable distance, perhaps Plato's unseen world of the ideal forms, or an Absolute Realm beyond space and time.[14] It is difficult to imagine such a mythological deity having any power to act upon the consciousness of believers except through inspiration gained through their personal reflection. This, of course, is exactly the argument set forth by Linda Martella-Whitsett.

After sacking the concept of a supernatural Supreme Being—a critique which, as we have seen, many progressive theologians find appealing—Martella-Whitsett's next goal is deconstruction of older prayer forms. She boldly pronounces the popular practice of speaking *to* God as immature yearning for a custodial parent-figure.

> Sooner or later, every child must grow up. Everyone must become self-sufficient. Those who do not mature live out their lives handicapped by dependency. Sooner or later, I believe, everyone must

evolve in spiritual understanding and claim divine self-sufficiency. All spiritual masters have done so, even as they credit the One Power that is inclusive of their humanity as well as greater than it. Those who do not mature spiritually feel powerless and dependent upon a divine parent they must plead with and please.[15]

While making a strong point about spiritual self-sufficiency, the straw dog in the meadow of this argument is her tendency to imply all conversation with God is neurotic dependency based on pleading and pleasing, not unlike Luther's obsession with personal unworthiness due to his perception of sin. Obviously, supplication for Divine assistance does not constitute the full range of prayer as communication.

Native American communion with the Spirits of the Grandfathers is hardly motivated by fear or dependency. Neither is fear a factor when the presiding Witch opens a Wiccan ceremony by "Calling the Quarters" to invoke the guardians of the Watchtowers of the four directions. In some Christian traditions, the classical formula for prayer follows the acronym ACTS—*Adoration, Confession, Thanksgiving, and Supplication.* None of these particularly need to be motivated by fear.

Even Luther broke through his fears to a sense of divine grace and began to feel reconciled with God and neighbor through communicative prayer. Luther's movement in consciousness was a new mindfulness of the loving nature of God, and he achieved it through a combination of inner reflection upon Scripture and outer prayer to a fresh vision of God beyond himself.

Some might also find the book's effectiveness constrained by an undue emphasis on verbal hygiene. Martella-Whitsett urges people to be hypercautious about every word they say, and her list of revisions often sounds like a theological adaptation of Orwellian Newspeak. Her zeal for linguistic correctness requires rewriting the "Lord's Prayer" and other classics because of perceived dualistic language. She translates James Dillet Freeman's "Prayer for Protection" into nontheistic idiom, effectively draining the original version of its power.

In this regard, she follows a longstanding fetish in New Thought churches about adjusting traditional lyrics to eliminate doctrinal errors. Frankly, the idea that heretical images must be purged from hymns and sacred readings seems out of place in a movement like Metaphysical Christianity, which prides itself in mystical symbolism. A more consistent position might be to sing the hymns and say the prayers as written, then fit any required interpretation into the educational program. After all, we feel no hesitation about caroling, *"We Three Kings of Orient Are ..."* without ever riding a camel or wearing a crown. Personally, I have always believed that anyone who cannot sing "Jesus Loves Me" with the heart of a child has no poetry in his soul.

Although her conclusions may not work for people who still find God-language helpful, Martella-Whitsett hits the target when critiquing the problems of faith built strictly upon a monotheistic Supreme Being. She rightly describes that God as "a human personality with supernatural powers—a comic book superhero!"[16] Her summary of theism's doctrine of God is thoughtful, Tillich-like:

> God is not a person. We personally, individually, express God as we realize and embody the Divine Life, Love, Intelligence, and all the Divine Capacities. God is the One Power in all and through all, Life Itself, Love Itself, the indescribable yet recognizable Divine Force. The divine *is* the invisible Good we can choose to make visible. This understanding prompts a new *why* and a new *how* to pray.[17]

Linda Martella-Whitsett's cogent, step-by-step guide to nontheistic prayer adds a strong voice to the "Let It Out" side of the controversy and represents an important perspective in rethinking Metaphysical Christianity for the 21st century. Her work with the Five-Step Prayer Process, popular in Unity, and clear articulation of the power released by prayers of denial and affirmation, provides practical application for the theology of Altizer, Robinson, Tillich, and more recent works, such as the writings of Bishop John Shelby Spong. Nevertheless, the question remains: Is rejection of prayer to God the "One Way" to God-within? Is it possible to forge a comprehensive answer that reconciles dualistic communication with monistic reflection?

Option 3: Quantum Modalism

In the centuries following the earthly life of Jesus, Christians struggled to understand who he was and what kind of relationship to God he enjoyed. Some said he was just a good human, chosen by God to act as His son (adoptionism). Others said Jesus was totally divine, with no humanity other than a physical resemblance to our species (docetism). The viewpoint that finally prevailed at the Nicene Council of 325 C.E. proclaimed Jesus as *fully God and fully human*, an integral part of an eternal Trinity—Father, Son, Holy Spirit. All three "Persons" were considered equally divine, a singular God in three separate and distinct expressions. Saint Patrick would later use a three-leaf shamrock to explain to his Irish converts how three parts can be separate yet form an inseparable whole.[18]

Now we come to the reason for this somewhat obscure diversion into historical theology. A possible solution to the problem of prayer as *communication* or *reflection* might come from an unlikely source, the methodology—not the specific theology—of *modalism*, an early Christian heretical sect that rejected the three separate persons of the Trinity. Modalism is "the theological doctrine that the members of the Trinity are not three separate persons but modes or forms of God's self-expression."[19]

Modalists said God was indivisible and unitary, but the Divine Unity could be perceived as *Father, Son,* or *Holy Spirit* depending on how the believer looked at the singular God-head. There even is a hint of Metaphysical Christianity in the modalist viewpoint. For example, the idea that humans create their own reality is quite similar to the third of Connie Fillmore's Five Principles. "We are cocreators with God, creating reality through thoughts held in mind."[20]

As we have seen in our cross-cultural study of response to the universal urge for spiritual awareness, the cocreation principle extends to Ultimate Reality itself. An Arabic-speaking child born in Saudi Arabia (a country nearly 100 percent Muslim) will likely see the world through the lens of Islam; a Spanish-speaking child born in Bolivia (95 percent Roman Catholic) is likely to experience life through a Catholic-shaped window. We are incapable of complete objectivity because we are already partisans of the culture that taught us its language and customs. We shape our world by the way we look at it, and no two people look at their worlds exactly alike.

There is practical evidence for this principle in everyday life. Joyful people attract more joy; sad people tend to draw melancholy, or at best empathetic, acquaintances. But let's move beyond the emotional content of human life and consider the way we relate to people in our world. In my family, I am a father, grandfather, son, husband, brother, and brother-in-law. In my work world, I am all these things: writer of books and magazine articles, graduate school instructor, theologian, novelist, preacher, clergyperson, radio talk show host, retired public school teacher, and retired U.S. Army chaplain.

At any given moment, circumstances will determine which of these roles I will be playing. When my daughters approach me, I am Dad without relinquishing my role of grandfather, husband, or brother-in-law. Although all my children are now adults, I will always be Dad—on this plane of existence, at least.

This is what the modalists essentially said about the three persons of the Trinity. God is Father, Son or Spirit, depending on how we look at the Divine face. Modalism sounds oddly quantum-postmodern (i.e., light is a particle or wave depending on how the observer views it). Could the same be true for the Divine Presence encountered in prayer—divinity is encountered within us when we go within, and in the Cosmos when our attention is drawn to the heavens?

The Modalist-quantum solution reconciles what otherwise appears to be an incompatible diversity of prayer styles in Metaphysical Christianity, which could be especially helpful for those who are content to pray *from* God, *as* God, *with* God, or *to* God, with no thought of contradiction. It all depends on my intent when praying. I can center on the Divine-within during moments in the Silence; or my part of God can walk beneath the starry night sky and pray to the Divine Mystery. A reformed Modalist solution allows both "I AM" and "I-Thou" prayer. Eric Butterworth's description of divinity hidden deep within human consciousness works perfectly with the "Prayer of Faith" by Hannah More Kohaus, recorded long ago by Myrtle Fillmore and still played regularly over the public address system at Unity Village:

> God is my help in every need;
> God does my every hunger feed;
> God walks beside me, guides my way
> Through every moment of this day.
> I now am wise, I now am true,

Patient and kind, and loving too;
All things I am, can do, and be,
Through Christ the Truth, that is in me.
God is my health, I can't be sick;
God is my strength, unfailing, quick;
God is my all, I know no fear,
Since God and Love and Truth are here. [21]

If we create the world by what we think—Connie Fillmore's Unity Principle No. 3—does it not also apply to prayer? Doesn't all perception of communion with God ultimately return to the old parable about blind disciples groping the elephant? Cross-culturally, the way people see God depends on the way they look at God.

Hindus can believe in One Presence/One Power, yet are perfectly content to see monism outpicturing as thousands of deities.

Muslims proclaim God is unitary, peerless, an All-Powerful Other; they must affirm the *Shahada: "There is no God but God …"* before they can embrace Islam.

A Jewish theologian like Martin Buber discovers an *I-Thou* relationship with the divine; Jewish Kabbalists find God through a form of monism.

Some Buddhists believe in a spiritual universe without any God whatsoever; other Buddhists pray to exalted beings, which are not officially considered gods but clearly possess some of the divine characteristics.

Why not see the question in quantum terms: *Observers determine the result by what they seek?* Personally, I need a medley of ways to connect with the awesome majesty we call God. Sometimes God shows up as naturalistic theism; nature's ongoing "program" is the Divine. Sometimes God appears as the mystical vision of monistic panentheistic, which affirms we are "in" God as a dolphin dwells in the ocean, yet God is also beyond our reality as the One Presence/Power that empowers the multiverse to exist.

Truth be told, sometimes I need the plain ol' *come-to-Jesus* God of the ceiling, somebody who responds when I hit the panic button and cry *"Help, Lord!"* When my helicopter was shot down by enemy fire in Vietnam, March 1971, I was praying to Jesus, Buddha, Vishnu, the Virgin Mary—you never know who's on office duty in heaven that night. Yes, it was dualistic, anthropomorphic, and theologically untenable—and I'd do it again. If I'm cocreating the Universe with God, there are times I want an Ultimate Somebody on the other end of the 911 call, a bona fide interventionist Supreme Being, who can send in the cavalry, not just send me to Calvary. Fortunately, those feelings of supernatural urgency pass, and I am usually able to center on God as the transpersonal Presence and Power working in and through the Universe without violating the laws of physics or manipulating the free choices of sentient beings.

Sometimes, the most comforting words in the Cosmos are simple thoughts of support, such as the greeting of a telephone prayer line: *"Silent Unity, how may we pray with you …?"* Theologically, it is not inconsistent for a monistic panentheist (like me) to stroll under the night sky and give thanks to God. I like to think of it as the *I-Thou* prayer as my part of God communicating with the rest of the One Presence/One Power.

So here's Shepherd's Universal Prayer Rubric, which seems inclusive enough to accommodate all historic and contemporary practices: *Pray any way that works for you.* Every glimpse of truth is a piece of a vast mosaic. How dare anyone say you MUST believe the elephant is like a leaf, when you're not even touching the elephant but swimming with the dolphins?

Check Your Knowledge

1. Describe the "Let It In/Let It Out" Controversy.
2. Why did Martin Luther's spiritual advisor tell him to "go out and commit some real sins and come back when you have something to confess"?
3. What did Swami Vivekananda say about a personal God?
4. Summarize the main ideas in Linda Martella-Whitsett's *How to Pray Without Talking to God*.
5. What theological critique does Martella-Whitsett raise about James Dillet Freeman's "Prayer for Protection"?
6. Who were the Modalists, and how does their struggle for a meaningful Christology suggest a new way to look at interaction with God?

Discussion Starters

1. Do you pray *to* God, or concentrate on finding God-within? Can someone do both without contradiction?
2. Describe the natural prayer process you have followed when you have reached a crisis in your life. Did it work for you?
3. How careful must we be with the prayer language we use? Should we work toward a uniform style of prayer?
4. Have you had any experiences with prayer as practiced by members of a very different religious group from yours? Describe.
5. Discuss and critique "Shepherd's Universal Prayer Rubric": "Pray any way that works for you."
6. What kind of prayer do you think works best? What does "works best" mean to you?

Suggested Activity:
Write a Prayer to Open a Session of the United
Nations General Assembly

Note: This can be done as an individual or group activity, or as a meditation exercise.

- After careful reflection, write a one-page prayer (about 250-300 words) you feel is appropriate to read aloud as guest Chaplain at the opening session of the United Nations General Assembly.
- If you are in a group, share your prayers aloud.
- Respectfully ask questions and give each other feedback.
- No prayer police!
- However, do not hesitate to ask tough, clarifying, theological questions.

3

PRIMORDIAL RELIGION AND DEEP HISTORY

The Master said, "The men of former times, in the matters of ceremonies and music, were rustics, it is said, while the men of these latter times, in ceremonies and music, are accomplished gentlemen. If I have occasion to use those things, I follow the men of former times."[1]

—*Analects of Confucius*, XI.1

Whether or not individuals are aware of their embedded theology, its influence frames the dialogue about what prayer means. Taking for granted that we approach religious studies wearing whatever cultural lenses we have acquired in life, this study will attempt some degree of objectivity to examine the evolution of the God concept both historically and culturally. The term *evolution* is somewhat misleading, because there is no reason to suppose simpler forms of religion inexorably morphed into increasingly complex theological systems in a linear timeline. In fact, every type of belief system we shall study can still be found among some portion of the human family in the 21st century. I am definitely not suggesting belief in many gods is superior to ancestral worship but inferior to belief in a single Supreme Being.

The sequence basically follows a historical progression, but complex adaptations of earlier forms have moved some religious systems into multiple categories. Human religions have not developed in sterile, laboratory settings but a cross-cultural, practical world where tailoring religious ideas remains a survival strategy. Citing a few examples:

- Catholicism, with its vast array of saints reachable through prayer, has occasionally been compared to a modified polytheism like Hinduism today. This is an oversimplification, since praying to Hindu gods and communication to Christian saints are not the same theologically, but the aim of the individual believer toward a multitude of prayer targets has more in common than either faith community might want to acknowledge.

- Eastern Orthodox Christianity has long believed individual souls will become progressively exalted in this life and the next as God draws the faithful into closer relationship, a divinization process called *theosis*. This view is similar to, but not the same as, recognizing a divine nature in humanity, which is held in New Thought Christianity. For Eastern Orthodoxy, theosis begins with sinful individuals who by faith in Jesus Christ are gradually absorbed into the Divine. The emphasis here is about *what God does*, not about *awakening humans to what they already are*, as New Thought communities tend to believe.

- Although most Buddhists reject the concept of a Supreme Being, some forms of Buddhism pray to the Buddha-nature in themselves while others pray directly to Buddha.[2]

- Some tribal societies, such as the Zuni of New Mexico, exist inside a circle of gentle relationships, peaceful supernatural forces, and benevolent magic. Others, like the Doubans of Melanesia, inhabit a hostile world where they fear poisoning by the hands of their neighbors, struggle to avoid baleful spirits hostile to human life, and practice black magic.[3]

Obviously, we live on a planet where religious thought has evolved to fit a variety of niches. Yet there are common factors shared by all religions, for example, the concept of spirit-force in the world. People throughout the ages have recognized places that possess special power. Who has not reacted to a majestic scene in nature, like our chimpanzee cousins at the waterfall? Humans can find spirit-power in situations far less grand. One person's muddy stream is another person's Jordan River or sacred Ganges. Acts of worship for a tribe in the hill country are acts of sacrilege for the clan living in the adjacent valleys. The Hebrews were stoning people to death for doing what their Canaanite neighbors were doing in church, that is, visiting male and female "sacred prostitutes" to enhance personal and community fertility.[4] Even today, playing Bingo is commended as a fundraiser in one Christian congregation and condemned the sin of gambling in the church across the street. What we take into any encounter with the holy will powerfully shape the experience. Muslims seldom see visions of the Virgin Mary; Catholics are unlikely to discover Vishnu or Shiva in deep meditation. As the old sociological maxim goes: *There are no tiger gods where there are no tigers.*

Working Definition of Religion

Welcome to a new look at prayer, meditation, ritual, and a wide variety of spiritual practices. Our approach will be critical but respectful study from a historical, cultural, and theological perspective. Since we shall be discussing religious activities past, present, and future, let's start by clarifying a controversial term, *religion*. The trendy debate about whether one should self-identify as "spiritual, not religious" requires a sidebar before proceeding.

When people in Western traditions respond positively to the statement "spiritual, not religious," it is probably because the word *religious,* and its noun form *religion,* has become associated with institutional authority over the centuries, as in the expression *organized religion.* By this definition, religious people are those who regularly attend church, mosque, temple, or synagogue and subscribe to the official doctrines of the faith. They belong to a club with specific rules about who gets to join and how all members must think, act, feel. Religious people, by this definition, divide humanity into the saved and unsaved, or some variation on exclusory classification. This may have worked in a culturally divided, vast, and mysterious world, when humans needed to postulate a miraculous universe ruled by an unseen divine King-Judge. But today's science has resolved much of the mystery and shrunk the world. Now we can easily look over the fence and see neighbors from other cultures, faiths, races, and worldviews. No wonder more and more people identify as spiritual rather than religious.

However, the word *religion* deserves to be taken in a much broader context than the bogeyman of progressive spirituality. Barbara J. King, professor of anthropology at the College of William and Mary, writes:

> In modern America, religion is sometimes assumed to represent an opposite pole from genuine engagement with the spiritual or sacred, because religion is equated with institutionalized, organized religion … An anthropological inquiry into the prehistory of religion, however, is a very different thing because it aims to search out the very first stirrings of any sort of spiritual imagination. Relatively indifferent to patterns in or developments of modern institutionalized religions, it has far more to do with the experience of encountering the sacred in everyday life.[5]

This book uses the term *religion* the way it is applied by students of world faiths, social scientists, historians, archeologists, and other professionals. Our working definition of *religion* will be *an established system of beliefs and practices that addresses ultimate concerns, such as an appreciation of life's value and the mystery of existence; provides tools like individual and communal ritual, prayer, and celebration for understanding and responding to events in the natural world; and sets standards to encourage and support healthy human relationships and develop a flourishing community life.*

This is not an exhaustive definition, nor does it address the genuine concerns of those who want something mystical without a load of institutional baggage. However, such a definition provides a tradition-friendly, inclusive, comprehensive way to understand the whole range of human spiritual experience, and therefore, describes what the word *religion,* or its adjectival form *religious,* means in these pages.

Let Us Prey ...

Nobody knows when our biological ancestors experienced their first moment of prayer. It may have been when hunter-gatherers saw prey for the taking, and high hopes for success in the hunt stirred their large brains to express gratitude. Most likely, the event came before language itself, experienced non-verbally in feelings of exultation and apprehension for the majestic beauty and terrible dangers of the natural world. Perhaps mystical communion even predates the evolution of Homo sapiens. In her Lyceum 2008 paper, theologian Nancy Howell suggested other primates might share the human sense of the sacred.

> [Primatologist] Jane Goodall has written that chimpanzees in Gombe appear to display in a distinct way in the presence of a particularly magnificent water-

fall. She conjectures that the apes exhibit something akin to awe, which is a component of experience that later is expressed and interpreted as religion when language develops in humans.[6]

What prompted our species to pray, create ritual, and contemplate the numinous? Some traditions among the major world religions—notably a majority of believers in monotheistic Judaism, Christianity, and Islam—claim the drive for spiritual awareness came to humanity by special revelation from on high, in moments of contact with Something beyond ourselves. Other faiths—for example, Theravada Buddhism—tend to believe primordial reverence came from within, either as intuitions from an evolving, indwelling spiritual consciousness, or side effects of the survival instincts humans today might call curiosity and imagination.

Either way, individual spirituality and community-based religion appears to be universal. Anthropologists have noted that cultures without religion have never existed. Every tribe, clan, kingdom, and cultural block has practiced some kind of interaction with the cosmos that involves some of the elements in our working definition of *religion*. The ubiquitous presence of spiritual activity suggests a deeply important function in human consciousness that cannot be ignored. And there is growing evidence to suggest human religious impulses gave rise to civilization itself.[7]

For example, why did people build the first towns? Seems like an easy question: They found places where economic factors made it possible to produce and store more food, safely raise their children, and carry on the shared, diversified responsibilities of village life. As rural communities grew from villages to towns, the inhabitants needed walls to shelter them from human marauders and wild beasts, especially in the night.

For additional protection, they invoked gods and magical spirits to guarantee fertility, enhance the harvest, and shield their proto-cities from natural and man-made calamities. The ancients seem to have believed the balance between heaven and earth must be maintained by human actions that demonstrated fidelity with the divine forces. So altars of sacrifice blossomed, and religious semi-professionals (shamans) of the hunter-gatherer lifestyle became priests and priestesses in the new urban centers, which led to the construction of permanent shrines and temples in support of clergy-driven rituals.

This is a rough outline of what many archaeologists and cultural anthropologists have believed about the sequence of civilization. The movement toward urbanization was driven by economics and security, for example, the need to share resources for the common good. Humans abandoned hunting and gathering after they learned how to plant and harvest grain. They settled down near a source of water because fields cannot travel with nomads. These small settlements grew into villages and towns, which required common defense and a division of labor. More complex art and pottery flourished as people had time to spare for the finer pursuits. Religious institutions and the structures to house them—shrines and temples—came later in support of the spiritual and ritualistic needs of an established community.

If you have taken a course in the history of civilization, you are probably nodding … *Yes, yes. And your point is?* Here's the point: All of the above is most likely *wrong*. Not just wrong, but seriously *backwards*-wrong. To explain the growing shift in the cultural development paradigm requires a road trip to ancient Turkey. (Warning: Fasten your cultural seat belts.)

Göbekli Tepe: World's First Temple?

German-born archeologist Klaus Schmidt has discovered a vast and artistically delightful temple complex in southeastern Turkey near the Syrian border. According to a growing number of scholars, Göbekli Tepe is older than the pyramids.

No, that doesn't say it strongly enough. The complex is *7,000 years older than the Great Pyramid and 6,000 years senior to Stonehenge.*

The ruins are so ancient they predate villages, pottery, domesticated animals, and agriculture. Furthermore, Schmidt has cataloged more than 50 sites buried safely beneath the soil of Turkey, where people built them about 11,500 years ago. What's more amazing is the nature of the ruins. There is no water source, no trash heaps, none of the telltale signs of human habitation. Whoever built the temples carved animal symbols on stone monoliths six millennia before the invention of writing. And like all prehistoric builders, they did it without beasts of burden, metal tools, or the wheel.

The symbols prominently included dangerous creatures such as lions, scorpions, snakes, and spiders. The sites were not lived in; they were ceremonial centers—temples. That means humans raised temple buildings first, then figured out how to service their religious complexes by domesticating grain, raising herd animals, and constructing permanent family dwellings in the area.

> Schmidt's thesis is simple and bold: it was the urge to worship that brought mankind together in the very first urban conglomerations. The need to build and maintain this temple, he says, drove the builders to seek stable food sources, like grains and animals that could be domesticated, and then to settle down to guard their new way of life. The temple begat the city.[8]

Prehistoric hunters and gatherers most likely assembled at ceremonial sites, probably for seasonal celebration and fertility rites, long before they decided to formalize the location worship with stone structures. If Schmidt is correct about the development of material culture, it means human temples—permanent structures for communal worship—rose before any other hut, house, or hogan. The need to worship drove people to abandon nomadic life and find stable food sources. This eventually led them to develop agriculture and create nontemporary settlements to protect their crops. Writing in *Newsweek*, Patrick Symmes observes:

> Religion now appears so early in civilized life—earlier than civilized life, if Schmidt is correct—that some think it may be less a product of culture than a cause of it, less a revelation than a genetic inheritance. The archaeologist Jacques Cauvin once posited that "the beginning of the gods was the beginning of agriculture," and Göbekli may prove his case.[9]

People have been predicting the downfall of organized religion since writing was invented. But the temples at Göbekli Tepe predate writing by thousands of years. There appears to be something hardwired into humanity that requires us to give thanks, to offer gifts to the divine—first fruits of field and flocks, devotions of our minds and hands, acts of service in support of something immeasurably greater than ourselves. When our ancestors cried unto their gods for deliverance, it was not simply the whimpering of frightened people in a thunderstorm; it was the first stirrings of faith that a moral order undergirds in the cosmos, faith that something like justice must eventually prevail. Klaus Schmidt is under no illusions that humanity has gotten religion right through time, but he does seem to believe in the evolution of collective consciousness when he asserts that new ways demand new practices.

When the people who managed the Göbekli Tepe complex abandoned their temple, they decided to bury the stones with dirt, which makes it one of the best preserved Neolithic sites. "When you have new gods," Schmidt says, "you have to get rid of the old ones."[10]

Apparently, religious reflection is at least as old as civilization itself. Without written language, the Göbekli Tepe builders left no book of worship or rationale behind their building efforts. "Schmidt speculates that nomadic bands from hundreds of miles in every direction were already gathering here for rituals, feasting, and initiation rites before the first stones were cut," writes Symmes. "The religious purpose of the site is implicit in its size and location."[11]

"You don't move 10-ton stones for no reason," Schmidt said. "Temples like to be on high sites. Sanctuaries like to be away from the mundane world."[12]

Yet this seems like an overstatement. If the religious impulse dwells within all humans, the manner in which it outpictures is far from uniform. Places where individuals have celebrated ritual and gathered as communities of faith have been vastly diverse. Mountain and valley, cave and seacoast, desert and jungle—wherever humans walked, holy ground appeared. One truth I have learned from a lifetime of ministry in multifaith communities is spiritual preferences have nothing to do with correctness and everything to do with comfort zone. Problems among religious communities almost always spring from an inability to allow "the benefit of the doubt" to someone with a radically different point of view. Theological reflection about the cultural, psychological, and metaphysical nature of interfacing with the divine can clarify the varieties of spirituality in the world and open doors to better under-standing of humanity's ongoing controversies.

Common Ground

Although we have no idea what specific rituals or prayers our ancestors offered at the first temples, the organization at these prehistoric worship centers suggests some common goals. For example, their massive stones frequently line up with key dates in the solar year. Builders of Göbekli Tepe and Stonehenge apparently oriented their megalithic temple complexes on constellations and the seasonal shifts.[13]

Isolated from their daily struggle for food and safe lodging, it is difficult for 21st-century city dwellers and suburbanites to understand how vital the regular progression of the seasons was to our nomadic ancestors. The oldest profession is not the one involving sale of illicit services; it is the hunter-gatherer. Everyone reading these words has hunter-gatherers in the family tree, because stalking game and scavenging wild edibles was the sole occupation of Homo sapiens from the time our hominoid ancestors evolved in Africa a few million years ago until about 8000 BCE, when humanity developed agriculture. Until relatively recently in the history of this planet, the job description of our species has required us to move with the rhythms of the earth.

Seasonal changes—predicted by spring and autumnal equinoxes, winter and summer solstices—marked the four corners of the year. Hunter-gatherers had to know where and when to hunt and gather, because most plants and many animals were only seasonally available. The quest for a reliable calendar was the world's first search for the Holy Grail. Even our multi-great-great-grandparents in the hot zones of ancient Africa needed to know when to expect rainy and dry seasons, and when the herds migrated to greener pastures.

The young world was a beautiful yet frightening place. Success at setting the major dates—summer and winter solstice, spring and autumnal equinox—must have been a major breakthrough for hunter-gatherers. They had no supermarket to visit when the food stores grew short. Our ancestors needed to calculate when cold seasons began and ended, when nuts and edible plants appeared, and when migratory herds passed their way. Following the regular progression of seasons was likely the central event in their lives. And maintaining a sense of balance with the unseen forces of nature meant more than a feeling of emotional well-being; it was the very stuff of survival.

Mother Nature can be a fickle lady. Winters linger, suppressing the food supply. If the pockets of hunter-gatherer cultures that persist today are typical of human tribal life after the Ice Ages, more of the daily food calories were probably obtained by gathering rather than hunting. When rivers swelled and flooded, more food was lost as migratory patterns shifted. Drought hit the human population hard. The earth rocked with tremors. The sky blackened, torrential storms struck and spit fire on the trees, sometimes setting the whole world ablaze. Neolithic people fell to disease, injuries, animal predators, and the hard labor of Stone Age life. They did not live in Bedrock next to Barney and Betty Rubble.

And there was death itself, the ultimate mystery. Loved ones suddenly gone, sometimes the very young, who along with the elderly, suffered the most in troubled times. New babies came to replace the losses, and the renewal of the earth every spring brought green edibles and young game. Fertility was the other side of death. Those who do not reproduce will have no one to continue the species. Homo sapiens did not consciously know it, but that is apparently what happened to its cousin, *Homo neanderthalensis*.

The harmonious passage of seasons and the regular flow of life were likely the most important concepts in early human consciousness. Maintaining the balance between the life of the people and the awesome power of Nature was arguably the motivating first force in communal religion. Stone carvings abound in images of fertility and beasts of their world, not pretty trees or majestic mountaintops, although if chimpanzees display a sense of awe at the beauty of nature, it was likely present in early Homo sapiens.

Maintaining harmony with the flow of life seems a logical purpose for religion in a society of hunter-gatherers, but a natural question arises from that behavioral observation: When the goals of protection from harm and provision of food are either met or thwarted, what emotions surface? Gratitude and frustration come to mind, and when interfacing with Power that appears to be beyond conscious control—in the baseline case of humanity versus nature—both success and failure demand some sort of response.

People learn reciprocity and cooperation through community living. Trade and sharing increase everyone's chances for survival. If I kill a bison or antelope today and you don't, I will share my food with you. Why? Because next week you'll succeed in the hunt when I fail. If we eat only the food we take, the result is a cycle of starving and gorging. Reciprocity allows all players to work together for the greater good. The same is true of trade. I give you something of value I can spare; you give me something back in the same way. We both benefit. Harmony is established. Trust grows.

When the hunt is grandly successful, we gather to frolic and feast. We dance around the fire and boast of our bravery and cunning, which entertains the community while educating and motivating the youth. If a tragedy occurs or the hunt is an abysmal failure, we gather to grieve for the loss and support one another in our pain.

Did these gatherings in the primeval mist begin the practice of gathering to celebrate and mourn? Did the sense of awe at the majesty of nature and the grand sweep of life's seasons awaken in humanity a primordial sense of transcendence, an intuition of Power beyond ourselves to which we are inextricably bound as children of the earth?

Did the ancients begin to look up at the night sky and give thanks or ask for relief? Did their sense of disharmony and imbalance at life's frequent challenges prompt them to gather and renew organic ties to the Great Mother Earth, by dance, song, and reciprocity offerings? Could this energy—for celebration and renewal—be an outpicturing of the passion for balance and wholeness, the key motivating factor in much of the religious history of humanity? Eight thousand years after Göbekli Tepe, the Hebrew psalmists will say it this way:

> Out of the depths I cry to you, O LORD.
> LORD, hear my voice!
> Let your ears be attentive
>   to the voice of my supplications![14]

> When the LORD restored the fortunes of Zion,
> we were like those who dream.
> Then our mouth was filled with laughter,
> and our tongue with shouts of joy;
> then it was said among the nations,
> "The LORD has done great things for them."
> The LORD has done great things for us,
> and we rejoiced.[15]

These two songs from the Jerusalem Temple prayer book, known today as the Book of Psalms, represent supplication and thanksgiving to a personal, theistic God, which the builders of Göbekli Tepe would likely have found as incomprehensible as quantum physics. But the fact that worshippers gathered before recorded history discloses a continuity of spiritual practice that continues to this day. Nor does a person have to be formally "religious" or even "spiritual" to feel the tug of greater purpose. Even atheists celebrate Earth Day.

What provokes men and women to participate in acts of religion? Throughout history, gratitude and fear about a beautiful and dangerous world have brought the twin motivators of thanksgiving and supplication to bear in human consciousness. For who could doubt the power of Thor's Hammer, or the desperate need for Mother Earth to return with full-breasted, swollen-belly fertility, as the goddess is often depicted in prehistoric art? Field, flocks, and family depended on the natural turn of seasons, the stability of weather above and earth below. In our Internet world, old mythologies have fled to video games, but the hunger for prosperity and wholeness lingers today. Who can receive a diagnosis of terminal illness without feeling tremors like the earth has been struck by the hand of a god?

It is the same energy that drives the human spiritual-religious quest in the 21st century and will continue to do so into the distant future. How ancient are the impulses? Community bonfires warded off animal predators for countless ages; nighttime fires were the original *"Light That Shines for You."* Today, Silent Unity's around-the-clock prayer line receives requests for prayer from around the world, often praying with those whose world is out of balance, people who need to feel the harmonic flow of good restored to their lives.

Languages have changed, but the impetus to find and maintain a positive relationship between the human and the divine seems to be universal. Even those religious traditions that hold the human is divine, or has a divine component, have nevertheless provided techniques to restore the balance to the individual whose consciousness drifts out of harmony with its divine-human likeness.

Humanity needs its religions, because life will always exceed expectations. Discovery of new possibilities in this vast universe will continue to mystify the human mind, and there comes a point when mystification requires mysticism. We stood in awe of the thunderstorm; our descendants will stand in awe of wonders yet undreamed as they venture forth into Carl Sagan's Cosmic Ocean to explore the endless galaxies of deep space. If history is any indicator of what is to come, the human response to the majesty of life will continue to resemble our chimpanzee cousins at a towering waterfall, to drink in the experience as if standing upon holy ground.

If sacred structures teach us anything—from Turkey's Göbekli Tepe to British Stonehenge, Jerusalem Temple to Cambodian Angkor Wat, Parisian Notre Dame to Salt Lake City Mormon Tabernacle to the Baha'i House of Worship in suburban Chicago—they document how religion empowers people to celebrate joyful, awe-filled moments and to endure calamity with tenacious faith in life's abounding possibilities. Humans find in their gods the strength to adapt and survive. Church historian Martin Marty says postmodern humanity has learned how to manufacture a matrix of everyday and sacred to meet those needs today:

> The old debates revolved around binary categories: societies were *either* secular *or* religious; worldly *or* otherworldly; materialist *or* spiritual; favoring immanence *or* transcendence, etc. The use of such polarizing concepts is valid in some contexts, but it does not adequately express the ways that individuals, groups, and societies actually behave; most people blur, mesh, meld, and muddle together elements of

> both the secular and the religious, the worldly and
> the other-worldly, etc. In adjusting to the complex
> world around them, people confound the categories
> of the social scientists, theologians, and philosophers:
> they simply 'make do' with a syncretic and charac-
> teristically modern blend of attitudes—call it religio-
> secular.[16]

Are we back to the question discarded at the beginning—
spiritual versus religious? Or is Martin Marty describing the
religion-building drive at work in every human culture, the
power that brought our ancestors to seek freedom of religious
expression in the New World, and before that Stonehenge,
and before that Göbekli Tepe? Is the need to congregate, give
thanks, and celebrate written into the DNA of our species?
If so, the "church" will never stop gathering for worship
because humans will demand it.

When I attended seminary in the early 1970s, everyone
was predicting the demise of the local church, meaning the
big stone building at First and Main. Some professors and
students joked about congregations saddled with upkeep on
their large physical plants, which we laughingly called an
"edifice complex." The hip new idea was the house church—
private homes where small cells of believers met to pray
and study together. We saw these as a more authentic form
of first-century Christianity. If congregations persisted at all,
they would meet in shared public centers, partnering with
groups like A.A. or secular counseling services. Full-time professional clergy was a dying occupation. Leadership of the
church in the future would come from people in tent-making
ministries, where clergy worked at full-time jobs and served
their dwindling, specialized congregations on a part-time,
voluntary basis. Rites of passage like weddings and funerals
could easily be handled through this arrangement, and minis-

ters could learn their craft through extension courses and private study or intensive, short seminars hosted by the remaining schools of religion.

Of course, history has shown the future-forecasters of the end of the local church got it all wrong. Churches are alive and well, albeit more conservative and less aware of the options within Christianity. However, this study is not about whether the fundamentalists raising their cathedrals in the cornfields of North America, or ancient people at Göbekli Tepe, or the Celts at Stonehenge got it right theologically. What social scientists have done is to force religious thinkers to address the irrepressible hunger within humanity for communities to gather in celebration, ritual, and prayer. Since people have celebrated and prayed together since ancient times, it is reasonable to conclude that something that fulfills this need for community worship will continue into the future. All other specifics are negotiable, which is the ongoing task of theology in each generation. The church of the future may not resemble Göbekli Tepe, or Stonehenge, or Westminster Cathedral, but it will continue the functions of religious community that appear to be hardwired into human consciousness.

This book studies some of those functions, especially those surrounding individual and communal prayer, ritual, meditation, celebration, and the creation of sacred space. Since all of the above require some kind of overview about the nature of the divine, we shall begin by looking at the evolution of the God concept.

Check Your Knowledge

1. Describe Jane Goodall's observations about chimpanzees at a waterfall.
2. Summarize the author's working definition of *religion*. Do you agree?
3. What is the oldest profession? Do you have any of these "professionals" in your family tree? Explain.
4. How many cultures have evolved without some form of religion? Why does the author think that's significant?
5. How might Klaus Schmidt's discoveries at Göbekli Tepe upset the paradigm for the development of civilization?
6. Why was it so important for our ancestors to know when the seasons would change?

Discussion Starters

1. Do you believe nonhuman species (whales or dolphins, not aliens) can pray? What might be encoded in their whale songs?
2. What might have prompted ancient people to build Göbekli Tepe, a project that must have taken several lifetimes? Remember, they did it "without beasts of burden, metal tools, or the wheel."
3. How did the ancients look at the world? Do you ever find yourself feeling the power of nature the way they must have? What is it like?
4. Community gatherings around the fire are often an opportunity for social and spiritual activities. Have you had any experiences like that?
5. How will the church of the future find holy ground? Will humans discard buildings and go back to nature, or does establishing a sacred sanctuary fill some deep need?

6. What do you think people are saying when they call themselves "spiritual, not religious"? Is this an important issue for you?

Suggested Activity:
Communion With Great Mother Earth

Note: This can be done as an individual or group activity, or as a meditation exercise.

Begin by moving outdoors to a place with very few markers of civilization. The more primitive the better, but if you live in a city, then a public park will do. Assume a comfortable body position—stand, sit, or kneel. Your choice.

Imagine yourself outdoors in the youth of the human race. Think yourself back to the earth as it was in primordial times. Before cities sprawled over hills. Before roads scarred the land. The earth is a maiden, fresh and clean, and our species gropes in the mist to find our way. In this natural setting, give thanks to the four directions. Bless the changing seasons—winter, spring, summer, fall—and the animals and plants Mother Earth sends our way as the year rolls by. Raise your arms to the sky and sway with the Rhythm of Great Mother Earth. Chant whatever sound or word comes to mind …

Move as your body feels its need to turn and change positions. You belong here. You are One with your Mother, the Earth. Give thanks, feel the joy of life through the movement of your feet.

Stay as long as you need to renew your hunter-gatherer energies. There will be more work to do. But you can always return here, and receive power from the Great Mother.

PART
TWO

EVOLUTION OF THE GOD CONCEPT

Praying Into the Mystery

You must travel the back roads of silence,
weave your way through riddles
too tall to scale, wander with your soul
open as a barn door with a broken hinge.
Let the winds of wonder carry you as easily
as the thermal drafts like a dry leaf
into the swillways of high-flying angels
and migrating waterfowl. You must find
a way to cage certain urges, especially
those that tell you to run in the opposite
directions of experiences that nest next
to the holy, next to those sacred things
that wait like windows and doorways
and passages into the mystery. Enter
reciting your own name and the color
of your favorite stone. Don't be afraid
to look in your own backyard. The secret
waits in ordinary things, in yellow roses,
the sweet fragrance of your morning tea.

—Fredrick Zydek[1]

4

ROOTS OF THE GOD CONCEPT
Animatism, Animism, Polytheism

You are a child of the universe,
no less than the trees and the stars;
you have a right to be here.
And whether or not it is clear to you,
no doubt the universe is unfolding as it should.[2]

With so many ideas gushing to the surface of consciousness—like a tapped well of pure, cool water, alternated by occasional jets of fire and steam—a few questions come to mind before we plunge into the depths of the God concept. The most obvious difficulty is that not everyone sees the value in studying prayer and spirituality through the lenses of history, theology, and the social sciences. Some folks, who prefer practice without critical reflection, might reasonably ask:

1) Why are we wasting time discussing these ideas? Prayer is action.
2) Do I really need information about god-types from comparative religions?
3) Can't I just talk to God and forget the anthropological-theological nonsense?
4) What if I just want to be alone with God?
5) Suppose my goal isn't communication with a Supreme Being at all, but communion with the divine within me?

6) What if I want to find the Silence, beyond words, the quiet
sense of Oneness beneath, behind, and beyond all things?

Thoughts in Response

All these are excellent points. Of course, anyone can pray
without deep study of prayer. Spirituality is like a walk in the
forest—multisensual, engaging mind and senses at multiple
levels. A walk in the woods requires no special knowledge to
enjoy its beauty, but how much more could a person experience after even a brief course in nature studies and forest ecology? Deeper knowledge deepens the experience.

The great prophets and teachers of humanity learned the
lessons of their religious heritage and took time to reflect
on that background before formulating their new spiritual
insights. Moses in the desert of Sinai, Buddha under the
Bodhi tree, Jesus in his frequent treks to lonely and desolate
places, Muhammad at his cave of revelation. Each of them
came to their realizations as part of a culture that educated
its children through wisdom teachings, which provided them
with the basic tools they needed to reject the strictures of religious thought of their day and expand their consciousness to
a higher level. Exploring a belief system increases its worth to
the believer, as Stoic philosopher and Roman Emperor Marcus Aurelius explained in his *Meditations:*

> To live with the gods is to show them at all times a
> soul contented with their awards, and wholly fulfill-
> ing the will of that inward divinity, that particle of
> himself, which Zeus has given to every man for ruler
> and guide—the mind and the reason.[3]

To think critically about the unspoken assumptions people
bring to prayer does not denigrate any method for reaching spiritual awareness. In fact, deep analysis can deepen

respect for religious diversity and introduce new forms of spiritual expression. We shall see more evidence of this richness in human religious systems as our journey continues. Just as globalization of trade has brought flowers and fruit that evolved in faraway lands to our gardens and kitchen tables, intercultural understanding of religious practices has the potential to enrich the spiritual diet of humanity. And the East-West supplements flow both ways. Meditation is no longer the sole province of Asian masters but practiced in suburban churches; Hindu and Buddhist youth sing spiritual songs borrowed from American and European folk music and study the writings of Henry David Thoreau and Martin Luther King Jr. as spiritual guides. When it comes to the possibility for sharing ideas and practices, we've only just begun.

Animatism: The Mountain Has Spirit-Power

Looking at the evolution of God-thought, one can reasonably infer that less complex forms came first, so we shall proceed under the assumption that simpler systems existing today generally reflect the most ancient solutions to the mystery of life. This will become apparent as we progress in our study. Let's begin with what may be the simplest human religious expression, *animatism.*

Late 19th-century anthropologist Robert R. Marett observed that members of some nontechnological societies perceive energetic spiritual activity within natural phenomena. They look to majestic peaks and feel the mountains have spiritual power, but they do not personify the mountain as a spirit or a god. To describe this belief system, Marett coined a new term, *animatism.* Dennis O'Neil of Palomar College offered this definition:

> A belief in a supernatural power not part of supernatural beings is referred to as **animatism**. For those

who hold this belief, the power is usually impersonal, unseen, and potentially everywhere. It is neither good nor evil, but it is powerful and dangerous if
misused. It is something like electricity or "the force"
in the *Star Wars* movies.[4]

To the animatist, certain objects in nature have special
power. One can almost hear Darth Vader murmuring about
Luke Skywalker's ability to dodge his laser lock: *"The force
is strong with this one."*[5] Anthropologists have coined another
term for this special spirit-power, *mana*.[6] The concept of localized spirit-power is widespread in simpler societies. Professor O'Neil explains an adaptation found among Pacific Island
Polynesian cultures:

> For them it is a force that is inherent in all objects,
> plants, and animals (including people) to different
> degrees. Some things or people have more of it than
> others and are, therefore, potentially dangerous. For
> instance, a chief may have so much of it that he must
> be carried around all of the time. If he were to walk
> on the ground, sufficient residual amounts of his
> *mana* might remain in his footprints to harm ordinary
> people if they later stepped on them. Volcanoes and
> some other places were thought to have concentrated
> *mana* and were, therefore, very dangerous.[7]

Much later in the evolution of human thought, sophisticated belief systems will find positive/good in events that at
face value appear negative/evil, such as Buddhism's insis-
tence on right mindfulness in the face of tragedy and Christianity's belief that God can bring good results from even hor-
rific loss. For the traditional Buddhist, suffering is overcome
by detachment from desire; for the traditional Christian, suffering is part of life and can be transcended by faith in the

Christ. However, the animatist view of the cosmos is so basic that it usually contains no distinction between positive and negative experiences.

Think of *spirit* in animatism as *power without consciousness*, impersonal energy, like a lightning strike or blazing fire. The power behind *mana* avoids thorny questions of good and evil by operating within a spiritual order that is totally amoral, value-neutral, and indifferent to human experience. It is simply spirit-power, raw energy that must be handled with extreme care. Fire can light the night to warm the community and ward off predators, or cook food to make it safer and more appealing to eat, or burn down the forest and inflict terrible pain on scorched flesh. *Mana* has neither will nor intelligence. It offers the brilliance of a sunrise, majesty of a mountaintop, rushing wetness of a flowing stream. In this belief system, humans learn to manage *mana* by ritual, magic, or simple avoidance, or suffer the consequences.

Belief in spirit-power in the physical world is the path leading to science and religion. Capuchin friar Keith Clark wrote hauntingly about his spiritual experience with spirit-power personified in the forests around his friary in rural Indiana during the early 1970s.

> I got to know the trees quite personally. They all seemed to pray—each in its own way. Some were nervous and quivering in their prayer. Some looked depressed. There were a few young trees whose prayer was fledgling prayer ... but they prayed. The pine trees prayed together in their rows. The oak trees seemed uninspired, but they continued to pray. One tree on the property was taller than all the rest. It was a cottonwood tree ... Its prayer was dignified. It prayed in a way I knew I never could ... Even on what seemed like a perfectly still summer night, the

cottonwood still murmured its prayer. It was faithful to prayer.[8]

The next step along the evolutionary journey takes humanity into deeper relationship with a spiritual universe.

Animism: The Mountain Is a Spirit

Animism begins the process of seeing the spiritual power(s) of the world as personal, caring, and responsive to human activity. Because of their obvious sound-alike qualities, animism and animatism are sometimes confused. However, they are anthropologically as different as water vapor and ice. *Animatism* is an impersonal force, outcroppings of spirit-power in a specific location, representing consciousness without focused soul-power. *Animism* on the other hand takes the divine-human encounter to a new level; the animist discovers the power of a particular spirit in nature and communes with it. The mountain does not merely *possess* enhanced, impersonal spirit-power (animatism); the mountain *is a spirit* (animism). Not yet a god with a history and distinct personality, the mountain nevertheless is a personal, spiritual entity who can be contacted by prayer and ritual, and whose taboos must be respected. To complicate matters—as humans are inclined to do about things of the spirit—contemporary studies often reveal overlapping layers in the population of the spirit world in extant indigenous cultures. Some supernatural powers are animatist, others animistic, and they coexist with little difficulty to the believer.

> In most animistic societies, however, there is no clear differentiation between personal spiritual beings and impersonal forces. More commonly, people perceive these powers existing side by side and interacting with each other. Spirits frequently possess practitio-

ners of animistic beliefs or these practitioners receive information from spirits that indicate which spiritual powers are causing sickness or catastrophe.[9]

As we shall see later in this study, an easygoing tolerance for unformed spirit-power will not be true of monotheism, which tends to absorb or obliterate more rudimentary forms of religion. Animism today frequently appears among indigenous people, but identifying localized spirit-beings is such a basic response that it occurs among more sophisticated societies as well.

> Animism can be found in many tribal or primal religions. Primal religions are those which are ancient, in existence before the advent of world religions such as Christianity, Buddhism, Hinduism. There are many such religions in East Asia, particularly in rural or undeveloped areas, island communities and among tribal groups or minority nationalities. Animism is also found within most of the world religions in East Asia, in the form of folk religion.[10]

Some local spirits need to be placated, because they tend toward capricious or hostile behavior. Animistic prayer is often simple and direct, employing "prayer, sacrifice, or offering as a means to communicate with the spiritual world." Some animists establish formal "shrines, temples, or sacred places."[11]

If modern studies are indicative of the past, animistic practices can emerge from historical incidents that grow into folk tales. An event early in 20th-century Japan provides a good example. A giant tropical snake, which lived in the Suma Garden of Kobe, died due to long-term exposure to a temperate climate. The *Japan Times* newspaper reported:

> Someone made the discovery on looking at an alma-
> nac that the day on which the reptile died was a Day
> of the Snake, and remembered an old superstition
> that toothache may be cured by worshipping a snake.
> The grave of the Suma snake consequently began to
> be visited by the superstitious, who proclaimed to the
> world the supernatural means of healing toothache
> by worshipping there ... Some of the people whose
> toothache has been cured by the spirit of the snake
> have decided to build a shrine on the ground where
> the reptile was buried. The place has already been
> fenced in and a sign erected preparatory to the com-
> mencement of work.[12]

This is the classic pattern of animism. In death, the snake
became a supernatural being, but not yet a god with a detailed
history and personality. The snake's gravesite possesses
mana, but only because the spirit of a specific, deceased rep-
tile dwells therein. To use a modern analogy, animistic spirits
come from central casting. They are the red shirts of *Star Trek*,
locally important but shallow, nameless creatures who serve
a vital yet limited function. If their part in the script grows,
taking a bigger role in the wider narrative, they will acquire
a backstory (myths) and become not just extras but named
characters, gods, and goddesses. With that movement in the
drama of human consciousness, the production shifts from
animism to polytheism.

Polytheism: The Mountain Is a God (or Goddess)

With passage of time, the spirit force of the mountain (animatism) evolves into a specific mountain spirit (animism),
which later acquires personhood as one of many gods or goddesses (polytheism). Either the mountain itself is a local god,
or a god presides from his sanctuary in the mountain. Polytheism is not an extinct belief system that fell with the Roman

Empire; belief in multiple deities remains quite popular. Neo-paganism has made converts throughout the Western world, and indigenous polytheistic cultures abound in the 21st century. The *polytheism.net* website reports:

> Polytheism still represents much of the world today. Except for the monotheistic (belief in one God) religions of Christianity, Judaism, and Islam, most of the world's religions are overwhelmingly polytheistic. Polytheism characterizes the beliefs of Hinduism, Mahayana Buddhism, Confucianism, Taoism, and Shintoism in the East, and also contemporary tribal religions in Africa and the Americas. These religions are widely practiced throughout the world and remain very popular in their ancestral areas.[13]

Buddhist scholars might take issue with putting Mahayana on the polytheistic list, but as we have already noted, there are followers of the historic Buddha, Gautama Siddhartha, who honor the Buddha-nature in many expressions. Buddhism's take on the divine is so unique that we will look at their theology later in this study.

The presence of paganism in the contemporary world often surprises Westerners. To understand its resilience in a science-driven age, we must return to basics again. Polytheism was born in a prescientific world of localized, concrete experiences. Our ancestors who survived likely did so because they noticed natural patterns all around them. Migratory waterfowl stopped at *this* lake every fall and spring. Predators roamed *those* hills in the distance. With all the phenomena of the natural world present in the immediate sensory neighborhood, complete with repetitious patterns suggesting well-conceived planning, why not surmise an invisible intelligence standing behind the natural order—supernatural gods and goddesses, supervising forest and field, sending rain from those clouds overhead? When villages grew into city-states, protective gods became even more important.

> The most prominent Roman gods were what might be termed the Olympian gods. This set of deities, derived from the Greek gods said to live on Mount Olympus, included Jupiter, Juno, Mars, Venus, Neptune, Apollo, Diana, Ceres, Bacchus, Mercury, Minerva, Vesta, and Vulcan. The most important of these for the Romans were Jupiter, the king of the gods, and Mars, the god of war, both of whom were thought to be especially interested in the success of Rome.[14]

Polytheistic deities came with assorted spheres of influence, and the more popular a god became, the more diversified were his investments in human life. For example, Apollo was the god of prophecy, but he was also called the sun god, the god of truth, music, poetry, archery, and the protector of children. He had some influence over healing, and his protection was invoked in time of plague. Apollo was so popular that among the Olympian deities of Greece and Rome, he alone was called by the same name in both languages. Greek Zeus became Roman Jupiter; the god of war changed from Ares to Mars; even Apollo's twin sister was Artemis in Athens but Diana to Rome.

Not all polytheism is Olympian, meaning a small band of high-powered deities loosely related by interconnected histories. Shinto, which means "way of the gods," has multiple deities, called *kami*, based on the powers of nature, personal family ancestors, and souls of heroic figures who have died. Believers often behold the world as a divine sphere and kami is the divine essence everywhere present. The chief supernatural being in Shinto is *Amaterasu*, the Sun Goddess. Her symbol of a red sun became identified with the island complex of *Nippon*, the Land of the Rising Sun, which lies east of the Asian mainland; hence it is the source of the sun every morning.

> The mythologies in Shinto describe her as the divine ancestor of the Emperor of Japan's lineage. They say she sent her grandson, Ninigi, from heaven to rule Japan. Ninigi's great grandson, Jimmu, is a quasi-historical figure who is described in the Shinto tradition as being the first emperor of Japan in the 7th century C.E. So, Amaterasu is both a nature kami as well as a highly auspicious ancestor kami. The Ise Shrine in Japan is the site of her veneration.[15]

Notice how Shinto has grown into a complex, universal system from what appears to be animatist-animist roots. It is ironic a nation that produced the militaristic *Code of Bushido* and was ruled for centuries by professional soldiers, the samurai, looks to a female deity as its chief ancestor and spiritual guide. As typical with polytheism, Shinto practice is ritual-heavy, with ceremonies for every turn of the calendar and many lesser events: New Year, changing seasons, blooming time of chrysanthemum and cherry blossoms; celebration days from mythological events, Japanese history, and agricultural markers. Add to these national observances the rites of passages for families and individuals—births, funerals, marriages, achievements in the life of a child—and visits to shrines of family or ancestral departed, which require "ritual washing, making offerings, clapping hands, and bowing."[16]

> These rituals do for the Shinto community what other rituals do for the people of every other religion: provide a means of worshipping and encountering

whatever is considered divine or "ultimate" in a way
that is meaningful and brings order to life in a world
that often feels chaotic.[17]

Audible prayer provides continuity, especially in polytheistic religions like Shinto. Gods above, gods below. Comfort at
the rituals of changing seasons, the regular flow of life from
birth to ancestral worship. All linked by ritual and spoken
words that bind the community together.

Polytheism is an organic, musty, earth-brown, dew damp-
ened, smoke-scented, hands-on religious experience, which
calls worshipers to concrete, localized experiences of a spiritual universe through animal and grain offerings. It brings
the cave fire of the animatist hunter-gatherer to the altar of
a marble temple and reminds the community, like Caesar's
slave riding in the triumphant chariot beside him amid
Rome's adulation, to remember they are mortal. No denigration of humanity's station is required, other than maintaining
a level head in the face of great achievement or abysmal failure. Hints of Buddhist detachment can be found in Western
polytheistic philosophies, such as Stoicism, which said a person in right consciousness "is utterly immune to misfortune
and that virtue is sufficient for happiness."[18]

Polytheism is characteristically inclusive and toler-
ant of other beliefs. If multiple deities populate the cosmos,
there was always the chance one might offend a divine being
unaware. Romans wanted the favor of the gods and goddesses so badly they attempted to list all the known titles of
whatever deity they addressed, adding a safeguard line: "...
or whatever name you care to be called."[19] This polytheistic tendency surfaces in the Book of Acts, when the apostle Paul discovers the people of Athens have built an altar to an unknown
god, just in case they missed one.

Roman polytheism was opportunistic and expansion-ist, and imperial politics turned theological inclusivism into a strategy for war. When Caesar's legions conquered new lands, they eagerly seized new gods and goddesses from the conquered people, adding the foreign deities to their own, ever-expanding pantheon. This militant heterodoxy actually became a routine military tactic for the ever-practical troops of the Senate and People of Rome. Roman priests shamelessly attempted to woo the local gods away from a hostile force before battle.

> This attitude is vividly illustrated by a ritual called *evocatio*. This occurred when the Romans were about to attack and possibly destroy an enemy city. Before launching the assault, the Roman priests would for-mally invite the gods of the city to abandon it and take up residence and be worshipped at Rome.[20]

Romans were less like modern religious fanatics than pru-dent pragmatists who dreaded thought of offending unseen powers. Even with an inclination toward superstition, philo-sophical skepticism also played a part of Roman polytheism. A good illustration comes from a historic scandal involving Admiral Appius Claudius Pulcher.

While he was preparing for sea battle against a Carthag-inian fleet, the Admiral's augers informed him the sacred chickens kept aboard his flagship were skittish and refused to eat, an extremely bad omen in Roman religion. The behavior of birds and signs in the skies were thought to be communi-cations from the gods. If Pulcher had behaved as expected of a Roman commander, he would have canceled the attack immediately. Instead, the glory-hungry Admiral said, "If they won't eat, then let them drink." He threw the sacred chickens overboard, where they promptly drowned.

The Roman fleet was defeated, and Claudius Pulcher became a scorned man in Rome for disobeying the powerful omen. Had he won the battle, the people likely would have laughed off the fowl incident. If the sacred chickens had gobbled their food and Rome lost anyway, the public outcry probably would have centered on Pulcher's poor leadership. Nevertheless, stories often reinforce ritual practices.[21]

Religious ritual in polytheism is often complex and demanding, and sometimes separate cultures will merge through community practices. The exacting requirements in the Japanese Tea Ceremony have their origins in polytheistic Shinto and monistic Zen. Some ritual observances of the monotheistic Roman Catholic Church have their roots in Etruscan and Roman polytheism.

The expansion of trade and widening spheres of influence brought Rome into contact with a new way of thinking about the divine. When Romans first encountered Judaism, they were at once impressed and befuddled. Inclusive polytheism of Rome opened its arms to accept yet another series of divine images into its pantheon. However, Jews had only one god, and they vehemently refused to provide an image of Yahweh—graven images? To the Children of Israel, all graven images were an abomination.

Roman culture made a distinction between *religio*—which are spiritual traditions with a long history, deeply embedded in a community, that binds people together—and *superstitio,* new practices incorporating magic and personal power, meant for the select few, and therefore, a divisive force in community life. By Roman values, Judaism was a true *religio,* an ancient faith centered in the home and bound the people together. However, the Italian legions had encountered nothing comparable to exclusive monotheism. *Only one God, theirs alone?* Begrudgingly, the Emperor granted Judaism an exemption from the obligation to worship his image, normally required as a loyalty oath to Rome. The antiquity and community-stabilizing function of the Jewish *religio* had earned them acceptance.

When Christianity began its ascendency, its followers at first were covered by the Jewish clause. However, late in the first century Christianity started distinguishing itself as a non-Jewish movement, perhaps because Palestinian Jews had risen in rebellion against Rome. The faith of Moses was starting to look like today's Taliban. Besides, most Christians came from gentile backgrounds and had no emotional ties to Israel or the recently destroyed Temple. Ironically, when the new faith of Jesus decided it was no longer a sect of Judaism, Romans began to reclassify Christianity from *religio* to *superstitio* and to see Christians as immoral disturbers of the peace.

All of the Roman arguments against early Christianity were grounded in the polytheistic notion of inclusivism and community unity, which Christians violated by refusing to participate in public ritual. For an imperfect modern analogy, think of someone at an outdoor sporting event who refuses to stand for the national anthem and displays proterrorist bumper stickers on his vehicle. Polytheists simply could not understand why the followers of Jesus would not honor their civic ceremonies in honor of the historic gods with the same cordiality Romans accorded the religions of all people. Since Christians were now recognized as non-Jews and practitioners of a new *superstitio*, the Jesus people must be treasonous, seditious, and anti-Roman. Politically, they were none of those, but Christians definitely wanted to upset the Hellenistic social order by replacing ancient, affable polytheisms with an uncompromising, exclusive alternative: *monotheism*, belief in One God. We now turn to this stage in the development of the human ideas about the divine.

Check Your Knowledge

1. What does the text identify as the key question that must be addressed in studying prayer?
2. Compare and contrast *animatism* and *animism*.
3. What is *mana*? What sorts of objects can possess it?
4. How did a snake become the center of animist spiritual practice in Kobe, Japan?
5. When a mountain spirit acquires personality, history, and a name, what has it become?
6. Describe Roman polytheism's characteristic attitude toward other people's religious practices. How did this impact early Christianity?

Discussion Starters

1. Did animatism grow into animism, and then polytheism? Why are there still practitioners of all three in the contemporary world?
2. Have you felt the power of nature and momentarily regarded it as an intelligent force? Describe your experience.
3. Do dogs and cats, whales and dolphins have spirit-power? What about horseflies and earthworms?
4. What causes people to offer sacrifice to supernatural powers? Have you put out cookies and milk for Santa, who has the essential characteristics of a holiday god?
5. How important is ritual in your world? Why?
6. What celebrations or rituals could you create based on the worldviews of animatism, animism, or polytheism? What would prayer look like from each perspective?

Suggested Activity:
Ritual of Sacrifice

Notes: As with all activities in this book, you can participate physically, take it as a meditation exercise, go there in consciousness, or skip the suggestion entirely. Sacrifice is about communion with the deep Presence and Power within and outpictures as the universe, the God-energy sometimes called *substance*. The following is an easy, One-Person Ritual to offer thanks for the flow of good in our lives.

Establish an Altar to the Divine Presence and Power

It can be indoors on a small table covered with a cloth of your choosing. Place upon the altar symbols that are spiritually meaningful to you, leaving a space in the middle for your sacred vessel. Find a small platter, dish, or something that can hold your offering. Next, decide what you want to "offer" and the objective of the offering.

Choose Your Offering

Want to give thanks for the fowl of the air, who delight your yard throughout the year? Need to release fears or celebrate joys by burning slips of paper or origami figures? Your altar needs to accommodate the type of sacrifice you want to offer. Birdseed usually requires a different vessel than one set aside as a fiery bowl. (And don't burn anything indoors!) You can move the birdseed or flame-offering outside if necessary, or carefully set up the altar in some external, safe location. Other offerings might include dried fruit, bits of cooked food, fresh flowers, shiny buttons, old shoes—not to be burned, to be released, and disposed of appropriately after your offering period has run its course.

You can also write beyond-the-tithe monetary gifts to non-profit organizations or special church offerings, to be mailed after prayerful display on your altar. I know some people who place ALL their outgoing bills in a spiritually designated location for a special blessing, a tradition that goes back at least as far as the old Silent Unity practice of praying over the mail.

Dedicate Your Gifts

Write a prayer to the Divine Presence and Power that is the object of your offering. Don't worry about getting the words right. Getting the feelings right is far more important in rites of faith. Remember, the greatest treasures you bring to any altar are the gifts of awareness, consciousness, and love. Keep your altar as long as you need, knowing your offering has been joyously acknowledged. You are the best gift the Divine Presence and Power has given to the universe. Trust your gifts.

5

EVOLUTION OF THE GOD CONCEPT

Henotheism, Classical Theism, Pantheism, Panentheism

Henotheism: *"No other gods before me ..."*

The first known ruler to implore his people to worship a single god was Pharaoh Amenhotep IV (1364–1347 BCE). He developed a system based on the ancient sun god, Ra, whom Egyptians worshipped as *Aten*, the solar disk who enlightened the land of the living and the dead. Since the sun was the singular source of light and life, Amenhotep IV decided Aten was the highest god and should be served exclusively. The Pharaoh took the name *Akhenaten* to honor his god, and decreed Aten alone would be worshipped in Egypt.

> Akhenaten made Aten the supreme state god, symbolized as a rayed disk with each sunbeam ending in a ministering hand. Other gods were abolished, their images smashed, their names excised, their temples abandoned, and their revenues impounded. The plural word for god was suppressed ... His wife, Queen Nefertiti, shared his beliefs.[1]

Akhenaten's theology did not outlive the visionary pharaoh. His successor took the name *Tutankhamen*, restored the old gods and purged the Egyptian life of solar monotheism. Although the new ruler died young, we know more about

Tutankhamen than most Pharaohs, because he was the "King Tut" whose undisturbed tomb was discovered in 1922. Exhibits drawn from its treasures have toured the world.

Few prayer fragments have survived from the Akhenaten era, apparently missed by King Tut's demolition squads. The following is a selection from a tablet found near Akhenaten's abandoned capital city; it may be the oldest prayer to an exclusively worshipped high god:

> How manifold it is, what thou hast made!
> They are hidden from the face (of man).
> O sole god, like whom there is no other!
> Thou didst create the world according to thy desire,
>
> Whilst thou wert alone: All men, cattle, and wild beasts,
> Whatever is on earth, going upon (its) feet,
> And what is on high, flying with its wings.
> The lord of every land, rising for them,
> The Aton of the day, great of majesty.[2]

Notice the concrete link to the physical universe? Aten is not an abstraction, but an observable, unitary deity who rises each morning and warms the day. We begin to hear something of the psalmist's language in this far older work. Yahweh, the God of Israel, is also a sky-god, but if his throne begins in the heavens, its foundation is clearly planted on Jerusalem's Mount Zion:

> 'Let us go to his dwelling-place;
> let us worship at his footstool.'
> Rise up, O LORD, and go to your resting-place,
>   you and the ark of your might.
> Let your priests be clothed with righteousness,
>   and let your faithful shout for joy.
>
> For the LORD has chosen Zion;

he has desired it for his habitation:
'This is my resting-place for ever;
  here I will reside, for I have desired it.'³

There is a "however" attached both to the theology of Akhenaten and ancient Israel, which most readers of the Bible fail to notice. Early Hebrew faith did not claim there were no gods. Like Akhenaten, the Torah merely insisted the people of Israel must worship none but their chosen god, the inscrutable YHWH of Sinai. Look carefully at the opening words of the Decalogue (Ten Commandments) given to Moses:

> Then God spoke all these words: I am the Lord your God, who brought you out of the land of Egypt, out of the house of slavery; you shall have no other gods before me.⁴

Nowhere in the Decalogue does Yahweh declare Himself the *only* divine being. He claims the right of *first allegiance*. The concept of a solitary Supreme Being will arise centuries later in Jewish thought. At this stage in history, the God of Israel seems content with insisting His chosen people serve Him first. Not yet a monotheistic statement, the Decalogue marks a halfway point between polytheism and monotheism, a metaphysical worldview that has been called *henotheism*. This idea may sound disquieting to traditional Christians, who grew up with Sunday School lessons and sermons from the Old Testament. Didn't Hebrew prophets constantly warn Israel against sacrificing to other gods?

That is exactly the point. Jeremiah and his professional associates railed against honoring other gods, which indicated the practice was going strong. In fact, according to the scriptural account, some of the more brazen Hebrews were in-your-face henotheists. Listen to the rebuff they delivered to Jeremiah when the prophet demanded fidelity to Yahweh alone:

> "As for the word that you have spoken to us in the name of the LORD, we are not going to listen to you. Instead, we will do everything that we have vowed, make offerings to the queen of heaven and pour out libations to her, just as we and our ancestors, our kings and our officials, used to do in the towns of Judah and in the streets of Jerusalem."[5]

Evidence for henotheism as a metaphysical worldview among Israelites appears in multiple passages of the Hebrew Bible. The most obvious occurs when Yahweh presides over the assembly of gods (and presumably goddesses), sometimes translated as the *divine council*. The Council was believed to be a heavenly senate, and like most governing bodies in an absolute monarchy, the God of Israel considered their input to be suggestions rather than legislation. Sometimes, Yahweh read them the riot act. Here is perhaps the most vivid portrait, from Psalm 82.

> God has taken his place in the divine council; in the midst of the gods he holds judgment: "How long will you judge unjustly and show partiality to the wicked? (Selah) Give justice to the weak and the orphan; maintain the right of the lowly and the destitute. Rescue the weak and the needy; deliver them from the hand of the wicked." They have neither knowledge nor understanding, they walk around in darkness; all the foundations of the earth are shaken. I say, "You are gods, children of the Most High, all of you; nevertheless, you shall die like mortals, and fall like any prince."[6]

Some biblical interpreters have attempted to spin *"You are gods ..."* into a statement about the indwelling divinity of humans. Even the author of John's Gospel attempts to dredge up this proof-text to establish the divinity of Jesus:

> Jesus answered, "Is it not written in your law, 'I said, you are gods'? If those to whom the word of God came were called 'gods'—and the scripture cannot be annulled—can you say that the one whom the Father has sanctified and sent into the world is blaspheming because I said, 'I am God's Son'?"[7]

It is very tempting to make this connection, especially since metaphysical Christianity agrees with the underlying concept of an indwelling divinity. However, even a cursory reading of Psalm 82 shows the author is clearly referring to a henotheistic god of Israel presiding over a celestial council that contains no human representatives. The same motif of henotheism can be found in the opening chapter of Job, where Satan is a member of the Council, not a pitchforked Devil, hot from Hades. Henotheism probably expresses itself in the Creation myth of Genesis 1, where the divine name is plural (Hebrew, *Elohim*) and God appears to be addressing his crew: "Then God said, 'Let us make humankind in our image, according to our likeness.'"[8] Even Adam's eviction notice sounds like a decree published before the divine council:

> Then the Lord God said, "See, the man has become like one of us, knowing good and evil; and now, he might reach out his hand and take also from the tree of life, and eat, and live forever"—therefore the Lord God sent him forth from the garden of Eden, to till the ground from which he was taken.[9]

The concept of henotheism is also helpful in understanding the otherwise bizarre remnant of pre-Hebraic thinking preserved in Genesis 6.

> When people began to multiply on the face of the ground, and daughters were born to them, the sons of God saw that they were fair; and they took wives for themselves of all that they chose. Then the Lord said, "My spirit shall not abide in mortals forever, for they are flesh; their days shall be one hundred twenty years." The Nephilim were on the earth in those days—and also afterward—when the sons of God went in to the daughters of humans, who bore children to them. These were the heroes that were of old, warriors of renown.[10]

What's going on here? Perhaps this represents a clarifying little data-dump by early Hebrew editors. Whoever wrote the previous chapter (Genesis 5) went merrily through the list of humans who had lived hundreds of years, a streak of longevity capped by Methuselah's 969th birthday. The editorial board found the glitch and fixed it with Genesis 6, which explains why multicentury longevity isn't happening anymore. The Genesis editors converted a polytheistic legend into the more acceptable henotheistic framework. Since the "sons of God" no longer impregnated human females, humans could forget about living for centuries; we get no more than 120 years. That extraordinary length was necessary to explain the three phases (40 years each) in the lifespan of the Hebrew Bible's greatest hero, Moses. Adopted prince in Egypt, vibrant adult shepherding the flocks of Midian, and wizened old prophet leading Israel out of Egypt into the wilderness.

One is at first struck with the economy of henotheism when compared with polytheism. Meeting the ritual needs required to keep a multitude of gods and goddesses happy could be a daunting task. Who knew if some action (or lack of action) might offend a god you never even heard of? Henotheism was one-stop shopping for believers, who could go to one Source for all their religious obligations. Weather, fertility, good health, prosperity, love, and career success—worshipping a henotheistic god was like opening a spiritual Wal-Mart in the ancient world. There was little risk of offending other divinities, since the henotheistic high god was their boss.

Eventually, the emphasis on *serve one god first* evolved into *serve one God only*, and finally morphed into the great cry of absolute monotheism: *"There is no god but God."* However, rejecting all other expressions of divinity was only one of two major routes to a unitary concept of the One Presence/One Power, as we shall see next.

Two Routes to Monotheism?

Polytheism identifies the divine as a complex of supernatural beings, distributed across nature. Henotheism, as we have seen, does not require people to abandon belief in multiple deities, but demands they prioritize their acts of loyalty. Serve the high god first, or exclusively. To become a solitary Supreme Being, the God of Israel had to contend with powerful, regional deities: *Baal,* the god of fertility, lightning, and thunder; *Astarte,* lovely goddess of the evening star, fertility, sexuality, and war; *Molech,* who demanded fiery sacrifices of live children; and a host of sky and earth deities springing from cultures as diverse as Egypt, Babylon, and Assyria.

Even among his admirers, the Hebrew Lord had another name, mentioned earlier in this chapter—*Elohim,* a plural form that could be translated *the gods.* Some scholars have suggested a female deity served as the consort of Yahweh, perhaps Asherah, the Semitic mother goddess who appears in Akkadian, Hittite, and Ugaritic writings as wife of the chief deity. In the

English Bible, *Yahweh* is usually rendered "the Lord" and *Elohim* as "God." Slowly but steadily, the god of Israel consolidated his power, merged with his alter ego as Yahweh-Elohim (the Lord God), and eventually moved his demands beyond henotheism to establish Judaism as the world's first true *monotheistic* religion. Not only shall you worship no other god; there is no other god available.

> O sing to the LORD a new song; sing to the LORD, all the earth. Sing to the LORD, bless his name; tell of his salvation from day to day. Declare his glory among the nations, his marvelous works among all the peoples. For great is the LORD, and greatly to be praised; he is to be revered above all gods. For all the gods of the peoples are idols, but the LORD made the heavens.[11]

Polytheism-henotheism-monotheism is one of several routes to a belief in the unitary nature of the divine power. While henotheism denigrates the importance of other gods, another path to monotheism oddly leads through a maximized polytheism that embraces and consolidates all gods and goddesses in a Cosmic One Power.

Sometimes people worshipped a localized deity—for example, *Father Tiber*, the river god who nourishes the city of Rome—while simultaneously honoring universal gods, like *Jupiter Optima Maximus* (Latin, Jupiter, the Best and the Greatest). A fairly common tactic in polytheistic worship to this day is to heap superlatives on whatever god is worshipped. God No. 1 is called All-Powerful, Almighty, All-Knowing, All-Wise, All-Compassionate. When the worshiper turns to god No. 2, similar titles apply: All-Powerful, Almighty, All-Knowing, All-Wise, All-Compassionate. Who would be so foolhardy to come before the god of thunder and say: *"You are very impres-*

sive, but the goddess of the ocean is greater, since she drinks every drop you throw at her."

From multiple deities invoked contradictorily as *all-powerful*, pioneers in religious thought began moving toward a new concept. Could the divine be *one* rather than many? What if the gods and goddesses were merely aspects of One Universal, All-Powerful, Supreme Being? This realization was one of the Hindu gifts along humanity's pilgrimage to monotheism.

> Hindus all believe in one Supreme God who created the universe. He is all-pervasive. He created many Gods, highly advanced spiritual beings, to be His helpers ... some Hindus believe only in the formless Absolute Reality as God; others believe in God as personal Lord and Creator. This freedom makes the understanding of God in Hinduism, the oldest living religion, the richest in all of Earth's existing faiths.[12]

In the West, the same movement from many to one can be detected in the Dialogues of Plato, the writings of Roman philosopher Seneca, and the work of other pagan thinkers, like philosopher-emperor Marcus Aurelius. It is fascinating to speculate: Would Hellenistic polytheism have grown into a Hindu-style, One-God-in-many-forms theology, if Christianity had not interrupted its evolution with a monotheism of its own?

Monotheism—sometimes called *classical theism* or just *theism*—brings new possibilities for spiritual practice. Believers can connect with the divine, a bond that is intimate, personal, and uplifting, the kind of loving mutuality that Jewish theologian Martin Buber described as an *I-Thou* relationship. Monotheism can also evoke a sense of infinite transcendence, when the believer encounters God as *Wholly Other* and numinous. "It is a mysterious sense of dread, awe, majesty, and wrath as well as love, pity, mercy, joy, peace, and a blessedness. (Rudolph) Otto used the Latin phrase *mysterium tremendum* to summarize the main components of the experience of sacred power."[13]

Islam insists on the absolute solitary nature of God and requires the faithful to pray five times daily. The Baha'i Faith, which grew from Islamic soil as Christianity did from Hebraic, raises the worship of a monotheistic God to a new height of human superlative expression:

> All praise, O my God, be to Thee Who art the Source of all glory and majesty, of greatness and honor, of sovereignty and dominion, of loftiness and grace, of awe and power. Whomsoever Thou willest Thou causest to draw nigh unto the Most Great Ocean, and on whomsoever Thou desirest Thou conferrest the honor of recognizing Thy Most Ancient Name. Of all who are in heaven and on earth, none can withstand the operation of Thy sovereign Will. From all eternity Thou didst rule the entire creation, and Thou wilt continue for evermore to exercise Thy dominion over all created things. There is none other God but Thee, the Almighty, The Most Exalted, the All-Powerful, the All-Wise.[14]

Some monotheistic religions teach eternal life, perhaps unending bliss, is accessible to the faithful. However, proclaiming a single Creator-God can also create problems for the faith.

Omnipotence and Ethical Monotheism: A Serious Glitch?

Even while providing individuals with direct access to their Creator, monotheism creates unique problems for itself. For example, *theodicy,* the contradiction of an omnipotent divine power, who presumably has the ability to prevent suffering, and a world in which the innocent often suffer terribly.

This predicament, which is unique to monotheism, was masterfully described by Rabbi Harold Kushner's 1978 book *When Bad Things Happen to Good People.*

Other complications created by monotheism come from its moral inflexibility. For example, the Supreme Being often makes nonnegotiable ethical demands and sets strict accountability for misbehavior, so His adherents can quickly find themselves facing divine judgment and exclusion from a satisfying existence in eternity. Prayer and ritual in such a context often involves language of confession, acts of penance and contrition, and assurances of pardon. Like their polytheistic ancestors, followers of ethical monotheism must worry about offending the divine, but an Olympian assortment of temperamental deities has been replaced by the Omnipotent King of Heaven ruling alone from His throne.

An all-holy God must have high standards, and anyone who has lived long enough to reach adulthood realizes how fallible even the best of us can be. It is the ancient dilemma of the Edenic myth, and most monotheistic religions have created complex solutions to overcome what they consider an estrangement between God and humanity. Prayer and ritual in those traditions expends much effort in bridging this perceived gap. Monotheism's transcendent view of the majestic, unitary nature of God has moved human consciousness to a new level, but other views of Ultimate Reality resolve the divine-human dichotomy differently, as we shall see.

Quick Summary

We have traveled a long way on this journey in consciousness. First, we looked at *animatism*, which finds individual locations and natural phenomena that seemed to possess *mana*, supernatural spirit power. Next came *animism*, which identifies the power of the mountain as a spiritual being. When the mountain spirit acquires a distinct name, personality, and mythology—one among many such supernatural beings populating the world—it has become *polytheism*. In some cases, a god or goddess stakes a powerful claim upon a group of people, demanding they prioritize all religious duties to put him/her first; we call that kind of religion *henotheism*. In the best-known historic example, the henotheistic Hebrew faith of the Ten Commandments grew into an exclusive system of worship that not only demanded primacy for Yahweh but denied the other gods had any reality beyond the imagination of artisans who carved their idols. This ultimate exclusivism is known as *monotheism*, also called *theism*, which is the dominant viewpoint of the two largest religions on earth, Christianity and Islam.

Unfortunately, monotheism tends to be judgmental and aggressive. If there is only one God who rewards righteousness and punishes sin, then logically people who do not subscribe to the One True Faith are not just exercising their right to be wrong, they are actively promoting evil. No compromise is possible. How can a person of faith compromise with evil? Many of the conflicts dividing the human family have resulted from the passionate desire of true believers to bring humanity into harmony with their vision of the Will of God.

Pantheism: The Cosmos Is God

One solution to the problem of human limitations and divine holiness is to raise the possibility that everything in the cosmos is divine. The idea of the universe as God is called *pantheism*, from the Greek words *pan* (all) and *theos* (god). Pantheism comprehends existence as the divine experiencing itself. In pantheism, the divine and the cosmos are a coextensive whole; its unitary form proclaims *God is the universe*. The lengthy list of people who have leaned toward some kind of pantheism includes important figures in Western civilization: Plato, Lao Tzu, Plotinus, John Scotus Erigena, Spinoza, Schelling, Beethoven, Hegel, Ralph Waldo Emerson, Walt Whitman, and D.H. Lawrence, to name a few whose ideas have been called pantheistic.[15]

Although pantheists see evidence of spirit in everything, contemplation of a pantheistic cosmos does not require everything and everyone to be pure, holy, and perfect. That would merely raise the judgmental aspects of ethical monotheism to universal dimensions. Variations of pantheism can accommodate multiple subordinate spirits, good and evil powers, even an optional side trip through various levels of heavens and hells, as long as the cosmos and the divine are one and the same. God is All; All is God. Nothing exists outside God, not even God. Pantheism, like nature herself, can be viewed as imbued with value or ethically neutral. Whatever exists is an expression of the divine; the totality of existence equals divinity itself. Neither the lion nor its prey has a moral advantage. Values come from human experience; we create them by interaction with a free cosmos. We make our world by what we think.

There is one more God concept in the evolution of God, which arguably links the best qualities of all the foregoing systems. It harkens back to the Book of Acts, and to the New Testament's best-known quote from Greek philosophy.

Panentheism: We Exist "in God" Like a Dolphin in the Sea

Then Paul stood in front of the Areopagus and said, "Athenians, I see how extremely religious you are in every way. For as I went through the city and looked carefully at the objects of your worship, I found among them an altar with the inscription, 'To an unknown god.' What therefore you worship as unknown, this I proclaim to you … indeed he is not far from each

one of us. For 'In him we live and move and have our
being'; as even some of your own poets have said."[16]

In this remarkable passage, the author of Luke-Acts, a two-
volume work on the life of Jesus and the rise of the Church,
gives the apostle Paul a great speech to deliver on Mars Hill in
Athens. During his sermon, Paul quotes a line from an anonymous Greek poet, usually identified as Epimenides of Crete,
who lived during the sixth century BCE: *"In him (God) we live
and move and have our being."* This thought catches the essence
of *panentheism*, a God concept popularized by the work of
church historian Matthew Fox, who finds elements of panentheism in the writings of medieval mystic Meister Eckhart. To
explain the idea, New Thought theologians C. Alan Anderson
and Deb Whitehouse cite a common analogy. "Panentheism
says that all is *in* God, somewhat as if God were the ocean and
we were fish."[17] Some of us mammal-centric observers prefer
to substitute "dolphin" for fish, but the analogy works either
way.

Stanford Encyclopedia of Philosophy adds:

> It offers an increasingly popular alternative to tradi-
> tional theism and pantheism. Panentheism seeks to
> avoid both isolating God from the world as traditional
> theism often does and identifying God with the world
> as pantheism does.[18]

Two Types of Panentheism: Traditional and Monistic

Panentheism overcomes theism's difficulties with a
Supreme Being standing outside creation, and pantheism's
problem with *God is the world*, by asserting everything is *in*
God, but the totality of God surpasses the physical universe.
The panentheistic God concept comes in at least two forms.

1) *Traditional panentheism* stresses the Omnipotence of God; although we exist in God, humans are creatures of the cosmos, created subordinate beings, who exist in a parent-child relationship with God.

2) *Monistic panentheism* raises human existence to the level of the divine—One Presence/One Power, with many localized, finite expressions of an Infinite Consciousness.

Prayer in a panentheistic worldview can be communication or deep reflection. One could pray to God "out there" as Creator-Sustainer, the divine power of the cosmos in which we live, move, have our being. Prayer could also reflect upon the indwelling divinity while visualizing the oneness of all things "in God."

A panentheistic interpretation of a well-known Hindu greeting is an example of these two movements in consciousness—inner and outer. If I say to a friend, *"Namaste,"* which literally means, *"I bow to you,"* I might be expressing our equality as creations of God, or our unity as expressions of the One Presence/One Power. Arguably, no other God-concept better accommodates both communication *with* God and reflection *as* God than panentheism.

Clearly, what this brief survey of God-concepts has already demonstrated is the versatility of human efforts to find authentic spiritual experience. However universal the urge to find a workable spirituality may be, not everyone seeking higher consciousness begins with a search for God. The next chapter examines how some people have pushed their "God concept" beyond any form of the Divine into nontheistic options, to include naturalistic theism, agnosticism, atheism, and religious humanism.

Check Your Knowledge

1. How is henotheism different from monotheism? Were Akhenaten and Moses monotheists?
2. Describe the two routes to monotheism discussed in this chapter.
3. What are some of the problems with ethical monotheism?
4. Explain the relationship between God and the cosmos in pantheism.
5. Compare and contrast pantheism and panentheism.
6. What is the difference between traditional panentheism and monistic panentheism?

Discussion Starters

1. If the Ten Commandments are a henotheistic declaration, how do they affect your view of the Bible?
2. How different would the world be today if Christian monotheism had not supplanted Roman polytheism?
3. Discuss the problem of *theodicy*: If God is an All-Powerful Supreme Being, why do bad things happen to good people?
4. Do you agree that the universe is God, as pantheists believe?
5. Discuss the quote from Acts, *"In him (God) we live and move and have our being."* Does panentheism work for you?
6. What celebrations or rituals could you create based on the worldviews of henotheism, theism, pantheism, and panentheism? What kind of prayer might each of these offer?

Suggested Activity:
Temple of the Mind

Prepare for meditation by selecting contemplative music. The only musical rule is your background sounds must be strictly instrumental or rhythmic chanting in a language you do not speak. Beethoven, Buddhist monks, or the Beatles, play whatever best expresses your sense of the sacred structure you are about to build.

Find a comfortable place and assume any body position that works for you. When you have become reasonably still, let your imagination take you to a sacred building—a temple of the mind.

First, place your temple on the perfect site. A mountain meadow, rock ledge by the sea, thick green rain forest, or bustling metropolis. Any place you want. And don't feel like you need to limit your temple to 21st-century Earth. Sacred space can appear at any time or place—past, present, or future, this planet or a ringed world with five moons.

After you have located your site, take a good look at the temple. Does it have steeples, belfries, or soaring arches? Have you raised minarets to call the faithful to prayer? Is it white marble or brick or gleaming metal? Make it a thing of beauty, dedicated to the divine mystery at large in the cosmos.

Visit your temple and inspect the grounds. What do you see as you approach? Gardens, trees, animals, people? What does the building look like, and what kind of light illuminates it? Are there special smells, textures, sounds of bells or chimes in the air? Is the day hot, warm, cool, or cold? When you are ready, enter your basilica and explore it leisurely on a multisensual level. Are there candles or sacred fires, chanting in the distance or silence? Can you smell paraffin or incense or flowers? Sit or kneel or stand. Feel the floor and seat beneath you. What kind of imagery do you find—statues, frescoes, stained glass windows, or mosaics on the floor? Are there prayer alcoves, altars, vaulted ceilings—or is your house of worship unadorned, austere? It's your temple. Decorate it any way you want. This is your perfect place to honor the highest ideals you cherish. Let your mind bring you surprises. Be still and know.

Once you have the place well established in your consciousness, find somewhere in your temple and go to prayer. Or sit quietly and listen. It's your temple ...

The beauty of this exercise is its flexibility. Not only can you return to your temple any time you want, the structure and location bends itself to your creative needs. Change it, expand it, or reduce its size. Attach smaller prayer chapels; add prayer towers and flower gardens. Move it to desert, tropical island, or snow-swept tundra.

After all, it's your temple ...

6

NONTHEISTIC OPTIONS

Prayer involves shedding the delusion that we are the center of the universe or that our lives are so important to some external deity that this deity will intervene to protect us. Prayer is a call out of childish dependency into spiritual mastery. So praying and living deeply, richly, and fully have become for me almost indistinguishable.[1]

—John Shelby Spong

So far, all the religious models we have evaluated were heavily slanted toward personal relationships between the individual and some kind of metaphysical Presence and Power. From the hunter-gatherer animatist standing in awe at the supernatural power of the thunderstorm, to polytheism's multiple points of human-divine contact, to Martin Buber's *I-Thou* and panentheism's claim that we exist "in" God, some kind of inner-outer transaction occurs between human consciousness and Something beyond ourselves. Now we take the evolution of the God concept beyond God, into the fascinating but controversial territory of humanistic spirituality that excludes all forms of the *super*-natural and *meta*-physical at the entry point—naturalistic theism, agnosticism, atheism, and religious humanism.

As we enter these new lands, it will be important to remember that *describing* a point of view as accurately and objectively as possible is not the same as *endorsing* it. As I tell my students in graduate theological education, *"Describe before you prescribe."* In that spirit, let's step over the boundary marker into uncharted territory, where no spiritual Presence or Power exists beyond the imagination of the individual seeker. Some people and concepts we shall encounter out there might even prove to be angels in disguise.

Naturalistic Theism

In his book *God and Religion in the Postmodern World: Essays in Postmodern Theology*, David Ray Griffin says:

> God need not be thought of as a supernatural being; theism need not be supernaturalism; *naturalistic theism* is not a contradiction in terms … God is not the external creator of a wholly contingent world; God is essentially the soul of the universe.[2]

Naturalistic theism is another way of saying *God is the impersonal force of nature.* Unitarian Universalist author George N. Marshall points to conclusions drawn by those who hold this God concept:

> The world that the sciences are discovering is marked by evolutionary processes, only in part controlled by people. Our highest good lies in discovering and serving this creativity. The God of creativity operates within nature under specifiable conditions and, thus, is not marred by the mysteriousness of a supernatural God. Preserving and destructive forces are also recognized as involved in the creative process.[3]

Nature seems to know what it is doing without requiring "the mysteriousness of a supernatural God." In fact, there is no apparent grand plan. Nature seeks balance rather than distant goals. A prairie is not trying to evolve into a rain forest. Kangaroos have no long-range strategy to develop big brains and start graduate schools in Australia. Evolution is not about intentional ascension of the phylogenetic scale as much as it is incremental shifts to compensate for environmental pressures. Life seeks balance within a stable ecosystem. Too little success and the species starves; too much success and the food supply is decimated with the same results.

Nothing in nature suggests evolutionary forces are shuffling individual species and whole ecosystems along some developmental assembly line. Rather than an orthogenetic, onward-and-upward, progressive march from the primordial soup to Homo sapiens, the process of biological evolution is better understood today as a *response mechanism* by which living organisms attempt to cope creatively with their world. Successes and failures are measured by mutated improvements which, in the environment where the organism lives, add survival traits that can be passed to successive generations.

If we are part of the grand symphony of life, humanity's goal must be to seek balance as well. Sometimes humans achieved this goal through dominance, sometimes cooperation, but the drive was always to protect the food supply and shelter its young in a balanced environment. Smarter parents can often do the job better, and when massive climactic shifts occur, natural selection favors the more adaptive species.

Sometime in the distant past, our ancestors learned how to find shelter and make warmer clothes during the long winters and ice ages. However, they also began to suspect any adjustment in technology, while vital to survival, was merely riding the cold winds of chance. Even better clothes and improved hunting skills could not always compensate for natural disasters. So why not stabilize nature itself? Why not commune with the awesome force that moves the seasons, the mysterious process behind the periods of change and stability? The ancients saw that power as supernatural and thought it could be cajoled into a supportive relationship with humanity.

Today's naturalistic theists find nothing metaphysical standing behind the wind and storm, but they appreciate nature's awesome power nonetheless. At times, astronomer Carl Sagan seemed to approach naturalistic theism. For example, when he defined humanity as the cosmos getting to know itself.[4]

Naturalistic theism differs from pantheism because it does not see the universe as a spiritual entity, and parts company with pure atheism because it finds the mysterious force of nature to be worthy of religious devotion. It differs sharply from the mystical view that *everything is holy*, because naturalistic theism holds the universe is at once profane, frequently violent, and sometimes pointless, yet worthy of contemplative reverence.

Prayer from this perspective might include elements of earth-based spirituality, ecological rites like public and private observances of Earth Day, meditation exercises in a natural setting, or simple communion with nature as the Source of one's being. Gardening, nature walks, even surfing or swimming could be understood as ceremonial participation in the natural world. Religious symbols of naturalistic theism might include images of mountains, valleys, flocks of animals, or Earth viewed from space. Perhaps the most iconic photograph for naturalistic theism was provided by Voyager 1 when it rotated toward our home world and took a photograph from 4 billion miles away. Sagan described the spiritual implications of the image, which has come to be known as the pale blue dot:

Our planet is a lonely speck in the great enveloping cosmic dark. In our obscurity—in all this vastness—there is no hint that help will come from elsewhere to save us from ourselves. It is up to us. It's been said that astronomy is a humbling, and I might add, a character-building experience. To my mind, there is perhaps no better demonstration of the folly of human conceits than this distant image of our tiny world. To me, it underscores our responsibility to deal more kindly and compassionately with one another and to preserve and cherish that pale blue dot, the only home we've ever known.[5]

Since hunter-gatherer days, the motivating drive of spiritual quest has often reappeared in various forms of naturalistic theism. Facing a world it did not create, our species struggled to make sense of the cosmos while living the most satisfying life possible. Religious impulses from deep within humanity have produced countless ways of tackling the same question: *What's it all about?* But the quest for a satisfying answer is so daunting that some people have concluded there is none available.

Agnosticism

If science is the study of verifiable facts "gained through observation and experimentation,"[6] then the most "scientific" God concept is to suspend judgment on the existence or nonexistence of any spiritual Presence and Power in the cosmos until all the facts are available. That is the very definition of *agnosticism*, an "intellectual doctrine or attitude affirming the uncertainty of all claims to ultimate knowledge."[7] Agnostics say we lack empirical evidence to conclude scientifically whether or not God exists. Carl Sagan, as mentioned above, approached the cosmos with a sense of reverence that sometimes sounds like naturalistic theism. Others have called the well-known author and space scientist an atheist. Sagan, however, rejected both belief and disbelief as unscientific. *"An agnostic is somebody who doesn't believe in something until there is evidence for it, so I'm agnostic."*[8]

An atheist is someone who is certain that God does not exist, someone who has compelling evidence against the existence of God. I know of no such compelling evidence. Because God can be relegated to remote times and places and to ultimate causes, we would have to know a great deal more about the universe than we do now to be sure that no such God exists. To be certain of the existence of God and to be certain of the nonexistence of God seem to me to be the confident extremes in a subject so riddled with doubt and uncertainty as to inspire very little confidence indeed.[9]

As good scientist, Sagan refused to rule out future discoveries about the existence of some sort of metaphysical process at work in the universe, although he felt the available evidence pointed to a natural order working without divine assistance. This perspective describes the essence of the Greek root words *a-gnosis*, "without knowledge." Agnostics conclude we have no tools to make a reliable determination, and lacking such knowledge, the question of God or no-God must remain open.

Although agnosticism sounds postmodern, skeptical voices are not new in the discussion of metaphysics and spirituality. The *Nasadiya Sukta* is a Hindu creation hymn from the *Rig Veda*, which was composed around the same time YHWH allegedly communicated with Moses (1400 BCE). Its unknown author candidly expressed doubts about a spiritual universe standing behind observable reality.

Who really knows?
Who will here proclaim it?

Whence was it produced?
Whence is this creation?
The gods came afterwards, with the creation of the
universe.
Who then knows whence it has arisen?
Whence this creation has arisen—perhaps it formed
itself,
     Or perhaps it did not.
The one who looks down on it, in the highest
heaven,
Only He knows.
Or perhaps He does not know.[10]

Moving westward, Greek philosopher Protagoras (490–420 BCE) had similar misgivings. "Concerning the gods," he wrote, "I have no means of knowing whether they exist or not or of what sort they may be, because of the obscurity of the subject, and the brevity of human life."[11] Even the Bible has its dark night of the soul when an author or two finds belief a difficult burden. This is especially true for the Book of Ecclesiastes, which was controversial from antiquity. Its place in the canon was hotly contested by rabbinical scholars, because many believed the work was fatalistic and agnostic. For example, this gloomy passage:

For the fate of humans and the fate of animals is the same; as one dies, so dies the other. They all have the same breath, and humans have no advantage over the animals; for all is vanity. All go to one place; all are from the dust, and all turn to dust again. Who knows whether the human spirit goes upward and the spirit of animals goes downward to the earth? So I saw that there is nothing better than that all should enjoy their work, for that is their lot; who can bring them to see what will be after them?[12]

Some scholars today doubt Ecclesiastes would have made the Hebrew Bible without the old tradition—incorrect, according to modern studies—that King Solomon himself wrote the work.[13] Bible-blogger David Plotz writes:

> I now understand why Ecclesiastes is the favorite Bible book of people who don't much believe in God. It offers the only viable competition to the Bible's main theme of heaven, redemption, and judgment. If you believe in God, you can explain injustice and wickedness on earth with an afterlife or judgment day, where the good get their just desserts. (Pecan pie for me, please!) But what if death is just death? What if there is no afterlife, no second chance? How do we live then?[14]

More recent, Rev. Leslie Weatherhead (1893–1976), popular British author and preacher, confronted the 20th-century church with his best-selling book *The Christian Agnostic*. Weatherhead actually stops short of genuine agnosticism about God and the existence of a spiritual reality, but he throws down a challenge for all Christians to be skeptical about church teachings, especially those based in mythology and running contrary to known science. "I am an angry old man," he wrote, "and I feel I must get the fire out of my bones, as John Wesley would say, before I die."[15]

What kind of "spirituality" would dovetail with an agnostic perspective on life? Meditation might well be a universal technique, applicable for all God-concepts we have studied so far, even providing applications for nontheistic communion with the cosmos. Meditators of various traditions report feeling empowered by inner resources to reach a state of transcendent calm amid the outer turbulence of life. Agnostic spirituality might also include elements of naturalistic theism, earth-based reverence for life, and exploration of various forms of conventional ritual to commemorate worthwhile concepts from historic religions.

Whether someone has decided not to rule God in or out, attending public events that celebrate the deeper meanings of life could inspire in that person an appreciation for the human struggle to live at peace with neighbors and enemies. Spiritual agnosticism need not be haughty or dismissive; in fact, it probably requires the individual to rise to the highest level of objectivity possible. Agnosticism calls people to become followers of the purest form of skepticism, the kind of benign curiosity identified in the Rig Veda. *"Who really knows?"*

Atheism

Some people, after exposure to the claims of religion, decide to ground their belief system in a frank statement of disbelief. They are *a-theists*, which comes from Greek root words meaning "without god(s)." Passing beyond uncertainty about God, atheists have made a faith-based decision: God does not exist. In fact, not only God, but the whole concept of a spiritual dimension to the universe is a figment of human imagination.

The literature of atheism has a long history, going back at least to Hellenistic times. The Roman poet Lucretius was one of the chief exponents of *materialism*, which has atheistic implications. Lucretius objected to all human belief systems. "So powerful is religion at persuading to evil," he wrote. "All life is a struggle in the dark."[16]

Until recently, atheism was often considered a pariah in monotheistic Western culture. Many people who were raised in the Cold War remember politicians railing against Godless Communism. More recent, atheist writers have tossed their barbs at the religious establishment to the naughty delight of millions. Some people are frankly delighted Richard Dawkins, Sam Harris, Christopher Hitchens, and a battery of lesser known advocates of atheism have actually begun to popularize disbelief in God. For example, take this quote by Mark Thomas at his *Atheists of Silicon Valley Godless Geeks* website:

> Just about everyone is an atheist when it comes to other gods—the gods that other people believe in or that nobody believes in anymore. I'm an atheist about all gods because there's no reliable evidence for any god …[17]

If atheism is about disbelief in a god, then everyone can claim to be an atheist about some deities. Muslims, Jews, and Christians acknowledge the Supreme Being who first revealed Himself (gender intentional) to Abraham and Moses. They are unanimously atheists about the Hindu elephant-headed god Ganesh, son of Shiva and Parvati, two other deities that generate an atheistic response in monotheistic cultures.

As already noted, ancient Romans were far from evangelical about their paganism and frankly couldn't care less what people believed. However, in the arena of public and private religious behavior, what people did, or failed to do, mattered enormously. Offending the gods by ignoring public rituals could bring disaster upon everyone. To the pragmatic Roman, ritual observance was simply hedging one's bets, a lesson Admiral Claudius had learned after the destruction of his Roman fleet. The Roman populace branded Jews, and later Christians, as atheists because as monotheists the two groups refused to honor the gods.

One such remembrance in the form of a story related in a letter from one Christian group to others is the *Martyrdom of Polycarp* (written in the decades following

Polycarp's death in the 160s CE). It is here that we find the explicit charge of atheism. The angry crowds shout out "away with the atheists!" in reference to the Christians.[18]

Mark Thomas says life's uncertainties motivate people to believe in powerful forces working for us invisibly:

> The idea of an all-controlling, caring supernatural god is a very attractive one. It can make our mortal lives seem less frightening, more comforting. Somebody's in control and won't let bad things happen to us.[19]

Atheists refuse to hedge their bets; they reject all external supernatural powers, and not just because they feel such claims are unfounded and irrational. *New York Times* bestselling author Sam Harris, writing in his book *Letter to a Christian Nation,* says the temptation to seek external solace must be resisted because our attention belongs on our own resources—not an external, divine power. He calls faith a "pickpocket who loans the victim his own money on generous terms," then adds:

> Your own consciousness is the cause and substance of any experience you might want to deem "spiritual" or "mystical." Realizing this, what possible need is there to pretend to be certain about ancient miracles?[20]

While atheism is tempting, especially when it rejects the same gods who fail to work for me, it also comes short of the "mystical" experience Harris mentions, because the utter rejection of any spiritual energy empowering the cosmos can lead quickly to a fragmented, disconnected view of life rather than the grand symphony of existence which even nontheistic people have encountered, for example, in naturalistic theism.

Can there be a form of spirituality for atheists? Some think not. Political critic and humorist Bill Maher, an outspoken advocate of atheism, derides the whole notion of prayer. In a published account of an interview by Piers Morgan of Cable News Network, Maher equates prayer with human self-delusion.

> MORGAN: Do you still do any of that? Do you ever pray? MAHER: Pray? No. Praying is trying to telepathically communicate with an imaginary friend. I wouldn't do that. Of course not. Atheists don't pray. So for the past 15 or 20 years, that's been my view. [21]

Surprisingly, other atheists say there definitely is a kind of spirituality for self-described nonbelievers. Sam Harris is in the "yea" column on this point. He even insists on the right to invoke religious language in his writings.

> I will have to confront the animosity that many people feel for the term "spiritual." Whenever I use the word—as in referring to meditation as a "spiritual practice"—I inevitably hear from fellow skeptics and atheists who think that I have committed a grievous error ... there seems to be no other term (apart from the even more problematic "mystical" or the more restrictive "contemplative") with which to discuss the deliberate efforts some people make to overcome their feeling of separateness—through meditation, psychedelics, or other means of inducing non-ordinary states of consciousness. And I find neologisms pretentious and annoying. Hence, I appear to have no choice: "Spiritual" it is.[22]

By claiming the language of spirituality, Sam Harris acknowledges an irrepressible longing within the species Homo sapiens to "overcome their feeling of separateness" and celebrate life. The cross-cultural yearning for meaning and connectedness transcends the content of any belief system. We stand at the door of the cave, peer into the thunderstorm, and know instinctively we are participating in Something Greater than ourselves.

What life means to the individual—the content of specific belief systems—will vary due to sociocultural and geographic factors. The only choices for a spiritual outlook need not be Pollyanna or Jean-Paul Sartre. There are plenty of options between affirming a solitary Supreme Being and rejecting all forms of connectivity. For example, the cosmic monism of pantheism and panentheism offers alternatives that allow an expansive view of reality that is nevertheless grounded in a scientific model.

The *Atheist Revolution* blog site raises questions along similar line of thought:

> Do atheists need spirituality? I think this question needs to be reframed in order to be meaningful. Think of it this way: atheists (like everyone else) vary in terms of their need for spirituality. Spirituality is vital to some atheists, and we could appropriately label such persons as needing spirituality. For others, the need for spirituality may be low enough that it would be hard to recognize it as such.[23]

The article, titled "Atheist Spirituality," notes the obvious truth that reverence for life and the majesty of the universe can be encountered by anyone, believer or not. This declaration, written by someone who rejects all things supernatural, tracks with everything this work has discovered since we began studying the primordial hunger for religious rites at Göbekli Tepe. It is not the *object* of prayer and ritual that matters most; the motivator of spirituality is an onboard program running in the human species that generates a *persistent urge* to find connections, meaning, and stability in our complex, terrifying, magnificent cosmos.

> One can be deeply spiritual while simultaneously rejecting anything recognizable as religious belief of religious practices ... One of the most commonly described experiences of spirituality involves a sense of one's interconnectedness to others and a dissolving of self-other boundaries ... Practically, we might see a spiritual atheist as highly empathic, aware of his or her connection to others, concerned with equality and social justice, regularly awed by the beauty of nature, etc. Such descriptors apply in varying degrees to all persons, theist and atheist alike.[24]

Although the human family has never agreed on specifics about the various iterations of the God concept, we share the need to reach within and beyond ourselves for solace and celebration.

Religious Humanism

Another form of nontheistic "faith" that generated a lot of energy in the 20th century is Religious Humanism. George N. Marshall sketched its basic outline:

> Humanity will find the resources and enough additional support within the natural universe to create a better life in a better society. This will be achieved if people turn from concentration on a future life and God to this life. In the social and natural sciences, together with the arts and the humanities, are to be

found our most helpful guides in living wisely and creatively and in the realization of a sense of at-home-ness in the universe.[25]

We should note the American Humanist Association takes issue with the expression *Religious Humanism* and its frater-nal twin, *Secular Humanism*, instead pushing to defragment all forms of the movement under the catchall term *Humanism.* They observe the term "secular-humanism" has been demon-ized by the religious right.[26] However, there is a profound dif-ference between those who celebrate humanity in gatherings and rituals and those who feel no need to congregate with like-minded Humanists.

Probably the church with the highest density of religious humanists is the Unitarian Universalist Association. My pro-fessional career began as an ordained Unitarian Universalist minister and military chaplain, and while my primary fellow-ship today is with Unity, I still hold ministerial standing in the church of Ralph Waldo Emerson and so many pioneers of modern thought.[27] Some of my UU friends jokingly call themselves, "Atheists who can't kick the habit of going to church."[28] But the truth is, UU's hold divergent theologies, as their denominational website proclaims:

> In addition to holding different beliefs on spiritual topics, individual Unitarian Universalists may also identify with and draw inspiration from Atheism and Agnosticism, Buddhism, Christianity, Human-ism, Judaism, Paganism, and other religious or philo-sophical traditions.[29]

Religious Humanism differs from straightforward athe-ism because of humanism's emphasis on human-centered social action, involvement in the political process, and "faith" in the ability of humanity to extricate itself from its troubles. Not unlike classical prophets, great humanist thinkers have held that people could fix their problems, even while doubting whether the better choices will be made. The centrality of humanity informs Humanist spirituality, which holds that no energy should be spent on adoration or communion with a nonexistent deity. The Humanist Manifesto of 1933 declared, "We are convinced that the time has passed for theism, deism, modernism, and the several varieties of 'new thought'."[30] Humanity must thrive or perish without benefit of any *deus ex machina*.

Economic justice, equal rights, education unfettered by superstition, and personal freedom are central tenants of humanism. When it comes to ethics, one might argue that the Humanist is the best Christian of all, believing in the golden rule and affirming a world at peace where no one dominates anyone else.

Religious Humanism can arguably be called a *religion* because it wrestles with questions of ultimate concerns; raises issues such as ethics and social justice; gathers people to celebrate life; addresses ultimate concerns, such as an appreciation of life's value and the mystery of existence; provides tools like individual and communal ritual and celebration for understanding and responding to events in the natural world; and discusses ways to encourage and support healthy human relationships while building a better world for all.

Humanist spirituality, designed by those who embrace this religious perspective, often resembles practices from other traditions in form. The website *Spiritual Humanist* finds such imitation necessary.

> Spirituality is certainly possible without religion, but we do not have thousands of years of practice, tradi-

tion, and ritual to accomplish it so naturally. Instead we have to work at it by proactively providing various aspects of spirituality that religion naturally provides.[31]

Some of the recommended Humanist practices include social gathering with like-minded families, various forms of meditation, discussion about historical figures of the past and family histories; rites of passage, marriage ceremonies, funerals, community traditions, music and singing; and various forms of counseling. These are "areas that a Humanist must pay special attention to since they are not naturally present."[32]

It is worth noting the lines between traditional theistic thought and Religious Humanism are often blurred by a common desire to improve the quality of life in this world. Perhaps the blue ribbon for this fuzzy congeniality goes to the popular song "Imagine" by John Lennon. All sorts of churches and religious organizations sing Lennon's haunting song, even though the lyrics present a straightforward, humanist worldview. In fact, the song so perfectly summarizes the basic concepts of communism—no property, no nations, no afterlife, no religion—that it has been called a Marxist hymn. Imagine that.[33]

Nontheistic Spiritual Religion

Our study now moves to Buddhism, a world faith that in many ways defies classification. Buddhist spirituality represents a distinctly different theology among the faiths of humanity. Clearly a religion rather than a philosophy of life, Buddhism shares some of the traits found in Naturalistic Theism, Religious Humanism, and Panentheism. Its ethical norms are compatible with the some forms of Jewish, Christian, and Islamic thought, yet its belief in a spiritual universe operating without a Supreme Being sets it apart from monotheism.

By accepting reincarnation, Buddhism aligns itself with Hinduism, Shinto, and Sikhism. Its commitment to inclusivity, peaceful living, and vegetarianism has made Buddhist teachings highly attractive to many Western thinkers, especially Quakers and Transcendentalists. The next chapter will take a quick look at Buddhist prayer and meditation.

Check Your Knowledge

1. What does *"Describe before you prescribe"* mean?
2. How does Naturalistic Theism differ from pantheism?
3. This chapter asked whether evolution is intentionally going someplace. Explain the problem.
4. Carl Sagan called himself an agnostic based on what scientific principle?
5. What is atheism? Why did the Romans call early Christians atheists?
6. Why does the text call Humanism a religious faith?

Discussion Starters

1. Which of the nontheistic options mentioned in this chapter is most appealing to you? Least?
2. Does Naturalistic Theism provide a satisfying alternative to supernatural theism?
3. Discuss the ideas introduced from Leslie Weatherhead's book, *The Christian Agnostic.* Can a person be an agnostic and still be a Christian?
4. Have you read any of the new books on atheism? Why do you think atheism has become a popular topic in literature today?
5. Humanists say we must place human needs and aspirations at the center of any religious system, not faith in God or some other form of spiritual delusion. How do you respond?
6. Discuss some ways to respond to someone who says, "I don't believe in God." How might your reply change if the skeptic is a friend, family member, colleague, or casual acquaintance?

Suggested Activity:
"Imagine" a Humanistic Spiritual Service

What kind of ritual or spiritual practices might work for the nontheistic options mentioned in this chapter? This exercise invites you to release all preconceived notions and design a deeply spiritual service for naturalistic theists, agnostics, atheists, and religious humanists.

- Begin by listening to a recording of "Imagine" performed by John Lennon. Listen carefully, making notes.
- Imagine this hymn as part of a spiritual service that does not include any reference to the Divine.
- What would such a spiritual experience feature?
- Design the order of service, to include readings, music, etc.
- If you are working in a group, you can decide whether to share the task or work separately and match notes when ready.

7

THE NONTHEISTIC
RELIGION OF BUDDHISM

*He who experiences the unity of life sees his own Self in all
beings, and all beings in his own Self, and looks on everything with an impartial eye.*
*In the sky, there is no distinction of east and west; people
create distinctions out of their own minds and then believe
them to be true.*
Peace comes from within. Do not seek it without.[1]

—Gautama Siddhartha, the Buddha

Buddhism is unique among the faiths of humanity. Consequently, prayer and spirituality in Buddhism are uniquely
difficult to categorize. Like naturalistic theism and religious
humanism, most Buddhists object to any vision of supernatural intervention in time and space. The Buddhist cosmos
operates by natural principles, not the whims of divine will.
However, like monotheists, many Buddhists go beyond nontheistic religions and find a complex metaphysical system at
work within the physical universe.

Reincarnation is a prime example. In harmony with other
East Asian religions, Buddhists believe humans experience
a series of births-deaths-rebirths, which offer the individual
soul plenty of opportunities to learn its lessons and attain
enlightenment—another metaphysical concept.[2] Although
Buddhism shares many values of religions that reject a per-

sonal god—notably an interest in individual progress and cooperation with others—it parts company with naturalistic theism and religious humanism by finding a moral and ethical order embedded in the operating system of the universe.

For example, according to the *Noble Eightfold Path,* the path to enlightenment requires Right Speech, Right Action, and Right Livelihood, which implies there can be *wrong* speech, actions, and occupations. Paradoxically, most Buddhists hold that no supernatural power exists to establish or maintain the moral order of life. Nor is any explanation required. To the Buddhist, that would be like asking, "What is a mountain by the sea?" *It is what it is.*

Buddhists often push further, professing disinterest in *why* a particular discipline works; if movement toward enlightenment occurs, the practice is self-validating. Western theologians want to discuss metaphysical subjects such as the nature of consciousness, ontology, and eschatology; Buddhist thinkers want to work in mindfulness of the connectivity among all living beings. This does not mean Buddhism has no doctrine. In fact, Buddhists seemed to enjoy making lists of principles and practices: *The Triple Gems, Four Noble Truths, Six Perfections,* and the *Noble Eightfold Path.* Even with an up-and-running theological system to examine, the typical Buddhist scholar is more concerned with spiritual practice than analysis of ideas.

Take prayer to *bodhisattvas,* for example. While some forms of Buddhism disdain supplication to any supernatural being, Tibetan Buddhists pray to ascended humans (*bodhisattvas*) who have dedicated themselves to bringing enlightenment to all. When observed by Westerners, those prayers begin to sound like reverence for saints in the Roman Catholic or Orthodox tradition.

Unity theologian Dr. Jesse Tanner says, "When I asked Buddhist scholars about this contradiction, they were puzzled by the question. 'It's a technique for enlightenment,' they said. Praying to the bodhisattvas is a spiritual technology, a means to an end."[3] Tanner says the goal is to cultivate the mind. Prayer to something outside is a perfectly acceptable starting point for a Buddhist, even one who rejects all divine powers.

As with any large religious tradition, there are plenty of variations that seem to contradict the basic tenets of other Buddhist traditions. Pure Land Buddhists pray to an actual spiritual entity, *Amitabha Buddha* (*Amida* in Japanese), who they believe will grant immortality to the faithful after one final rebirth in the "Pure Land" to the west. This is not a meditation exercise; there really is a place of joy and peace where the faithful will be reborn. Pure Land Buddhism sees the goal as attainable but only through faith in Amitabha, who is a female version of the Buddha. Salvation by faith is a theme monotheisms tend to employ, yet here is an adaptation of the redemptive plan flowing from an essentially nontheistic tradition.

As the worldwide Christianity community stumbles with its burden—to transform the world into a Kingdom of God after wasting two millennia fighting among the family—some people in Europe and the Americas have found Buddhist practices increasingly more uplifting. Before discussing its potential to inform new concepts in prayer and spirituality today, a brief historical review of Buddhist origins and a look at its basic doctrines seems necessary.

The Awakened One

Gautama Siddhartha was born in India in the fifth or sixth century BCE. He was of noble lineage, but probably not a *prince* (i.e., not the son of a king, as the term is used today). Gautama's father was more likely a local ruler, the equivalent of feudal lord in medieval Europe. As the story goes, sometime in his early childhood, a fortune teller predicted two great destinies awaited young Gautama: great warrior or great saint. For Gautama's father, it was a no-brainer: Should his son become a great warrior—perhaps Emperor of all India—or wander around homeless, begging for bowls of rice? You have to admit, the old man had a point.

Gautama's father decided the key to his son's future was to ensure that the boy never saw or experienced anything unpleasant. If pain or suffering crossed his son's path, he feared Gautama might turn aside from worldly power and become an ascetic.

So he surrounded Gautama with young healthy people. So whenever the boy left the palace for a ride, his father sent mounted soldiers ahead to clear the roads of the old, the poor, and the sick. Finally, Gautama's father arranged a marriage for his son to a princess named Yasodhara. She was beautiful, cheerful, modest, and faithful. They had a son. Life was perfect.

Even so, the young noble suspected something wasn't right.

One day, Gautama encountered a sick man whom his father's advance patrols had missed. Later, he saw an old man, a corpse, and a wandering holy man. He realized the world was filled with suffering, and he wondered what caused human misery and whether it could be avoided. Gautama asked one of his servants about the holy man he had seen. Why did this bent old man seem so serene? The servant replied that he had probably seen a saint, someone who already achieved enlightenment. Gautama decided to take the same path. He left his beloved wife and son, renounced wealth and power, and assumed the role of an itinerant monk. His father's nightmare had come true.

At first, he attempted what Luther would try 2,000 years later. He punished himself with harsh ascetic disciplines. Fasting to the brink of starvation and other extreme measures, he tried to seize his salvation by force of will. The young seeker continued his efforts for six years. He became thin as a dry stick, but enlightenment still evaded him. Neither the path to worldly power nor ascetic excesses had brought him peace. So Gautama sat down under a Bodhi tree and vowed not to stir until achieving enlightenment.

After seven days, he realized neither wealth and power nor mortification of the flesh brought inner peace. He decided a Middle Path was best. Gautama recognized life was fraught with suffering, and the cause of suffering was *unfulfilled desire*. Therefore, to overcome suffering one must overcome desire itself. At the moment of his realization, Gautama Siddhartha became the *Buddha*, the *Awakened* or *Enlightened One*. A collection of sayings attributed to him, *The Dhammapada*, describes the fundamental need of all sentient beings to release and let go:

> Take no delight
> Even for heavenly sensual pleasures.
> One who delights in ending the craving
> Is a disciple of the Fully Enlightened One.[4]

Buddha taught a simple creed with deep implications, clarified by the *Four Noble Truths*, the fourth of which requires following an *Eightfold Path*. The teachings in this set of guidelines are typically Buddhist, concerned more about practice than theory. While sitting under the Bodhi tree, Buddha had arrived at a solution to the ancient challenge of how to respond to a world we cannot always control.

Four Noble Truths

Gautama Siddhartha laid out the problem and codified his solution in basic points known as the Four Noble Truths:

1) **Life is suffering.** Human life is inherently painful. It cannot be avoided. People we love will age and die. Nothing on earth is eternal.

2) **Suffering is caused by desire and attachment.** Even pursuit of good material goals or happiness in relationships eventually results in suffering, whether the desires are thwarted or satisfied, because nothing lasts.

3) **Desire and attachment can be overcome.** Eliminating desire will result in mastery over suffering and an open path to Nirvana. This is a state of high consciousness sometimes described as enlightenment, although the word itself means *extinguishing*.

> Attaining nirvana—reaching enlightenment—means extinguishing the three fires of greed, delusion, and hatred. Someone who reaches nirvana does not immediately disappear to a heavenly realm. Nirvana is better understood as a state of mind that humans can reach. It is a state of profound spiritual joy, without negative emotions and fears. Someone who has attained enlightenment is filled with compassion for all living things.[5]

4) **The way to enlightenment is an Eightfold Path.** This is the Middle Way of Buddhism, between self-indulgence and severe asceticism. Buddha had found neither extreme worked in his quest for enlightenment. He outlined the process in eight principles.

Journalist Prerna Malik makes an important point about the centerpiece of Buddhist thought: "The Eightfold Path is not sequential but interconnected. Every single path supports the other and in order to practice one path properly, you need to practice the other seven properly as well."[6] Buddhism is a practice-based religion that teaches that spiritual merit can be earned by always doing and saying the right things. The Eightfold Path outlines basic practices to release the true Buddha nature within every person.

The important concept to grasp is that Buddhists believe actions and attitude coincide to move the individual further along the path to enlightenment. Many Christians believe they cannot earn their salvation because it is a free gift from God, attainable only through faith, not works. Buddhists disagree; acts flowing from spiritual awareness (mindfulness) move the soul along its path to Buddha consciousness. Buddhists seem to agree with the New Testament Letter of James:

> If a brother or sister is naked and lacks daily food, and one of you says to them, 'Go in peace; keep warm and eat your fill,' and yet you do not supply their bodily needs, what is the good of that? So faith by itself, if it has no works, is dead.[7]

This idea is echoed in the Baha'i Faith: "Work done in the spirit of service is the highest form of worship."[8] Buddhism is an action and consciousness religion, and the two are inseparable. When a Buddhist does an act of kindness, the *action* is a spiritual practice with actual consequences in the development of the soul.

Noble Eightfold Path

To expound properly on the concepts of the Noble Eightfold Path would require a multivolume set of books; literary economy in a comprehensive work about prayer allows for only a brief description of each principle. We'll take a quick look.

- **Right Understanding**, "… begins with the intuitive insight that all beings are subject to suffering and it ends with complete understanding of the true nature of all things. Since our view of the world forms our thoughts and our actions, right view yields right thoughts and right actions."[9]
- **Right Purpose** is a commitment to self-improvement, which includes: renunciation of desire, the intention to do good works, resistance to anger and animosity, and "the intention of harmlessness, meaning not to think or act cruelly, violently, or aggressively, and to develop compassion."[10]

In fact, compassion is one of the key concepts in Buddhist theology. It flows through all parts of the Noble Eightfold Path, and is a rough equivalent to the New Testament of agape, *selfless love*. Compassion emphasizes the important mental discipline good pastoral counselors, like Jesus, have always practiced—to *care* without becoming *ensnared* in the problem or circumstance.

The Venerable Bhante Yatirawana Wimala, traveling Buddhist monk and Chief Sangha Nayaka (Head Monk) to the United States from Sri Lanka, spends his energies providing relief supplies and doing ministry among disaster victims around the globe. Bhante literally goes places where even United Nations peacekeepers fear to tread. In an email to his friends and supporters, Bhante reported he was taking some time off, because the suffering was so intense he could not focus on showing compassion for others. After endless days of sifting through rubble for bodies, he found himself crying alone at his quarters night after night. Here is the kindest person I have ever met—a Theravada Buddhist monk trained in Eastern spiritual disciplines, who meditates hours daily and exudes peace like a refreshing breeze when he enters a room—yet he found the pain of an endless flood of disaster victims finally "got to him," as we say in the West.

To serve others, compassionate persons must not *feel* what others feel. Although compassion knows what others feel, it must remain centered and enable helping persons to be available to others in their pain. Like the parable of Jesus, people need to take the log from their own eyes before removing the speck from the eye of a neighbor. This principle applies to a wide variety of circumstances. If an emergency room doctor can't focus on helping the injured, it's a good time to consider a long vacation or a career change. Compassion in action is a good example of Right Purpose.

- **Right Speech.** Buddhists are enjoined to abstain from deliberate lies and deceitful conversations; also to avoid slander, malicious talk, or any kind of harsh language that might offend others. Idle chatter is also on the prohibited list. They attempt to express their Buddha consciousness by gentle, friendly, and positive talk, and to practice economy of words.

- **Right Action** means to act kindly and compassionately, to be honest, to respect other people's property, and "to keep sexual relationships harmless."[11] *Right Action* is not simply about things you do; attitudes are action too. Bhante Wimala believes negative thoughts always bring discomfort. "When you are angry or fearful, look at your mind and body—it will be tense, anxious, and stressful." Having a good reason to be angry or hateful doesn't exempt you from the consequences of it. Holding onto negative emotions causes you to suffer. "It hurts to be angry," Bhante said. "It hurts to hate people. It even hurts to dislike people."[12]

- **Right Livelihood** means earn a living legally, harmlessly, and peacefully. Buddhists must avoid certain professions: peddling weapons of any kind; trafficking in living beings, including raising animals for slaughter, working in meat production industries, selling humans as slaves, and engaging in the sex industry; also selling intoxicants, poisons, and illegal drugs.[13]
- **Right Effort** could be considered an essential precondition for all the steps along the Eightfold Path. Nothing will happen unless the individual is motivated to take action. Any sort of desire, wholesome or not, might stimulate behavior. "The same type of energy that fuels desire, envy, aggression, and violence can on the other side fuel self-discipline, honesty, benevolence, and kindness."[14] But the objective is *right* action, which avoids doing harm to self or other beings, and seeks wholesome, life-affirming activity.
- **Right Mindfulness** gathers many themes under one heading. Buddhists speak of "mindfulness" with a special tone of reverence, and in some ways the word summarizes the whole of Buddhism. To be *mindful* is to be aware of something at deep levels.

> Virtuous conduct casts out lust. The calm of true concentration and mental culture conquers hatred. Wisdom or right understanding, also called direct knowledge resulting from meditation, dispels all delusion. All these three types of training are possible only through the cultivation of constant mindfulness (sati), which forms the seventh link of the Noble Eightfold Path.[15]

Internationally acclaimed scholar and Zen master Thich Nhat Hanh says mindfulness is "the energy to be here and to witness deeply everything that happens in the present moment, aware of what is going on within and without."[16] Walking through the forest with senses alert to the oneness of all things, like Thoreau at Walden, is only a shadow of what the Buddhists mean by mindfulness. Thich Nhat Hanh writes:

> People usually consider walking on water or in thin air a miracle. But I think the real miracle is not to walk either on water or in thin air, but to walk on earth. Every day we are engaged in a miracle which we don't even recognize: a blue sky, white clouds, green leaves, the black, curious eyes of a child—our own two eyes. All is a miracle.[17]

Thoreau in the woods is practicing what B. Alan Wallace calls "bare attention" rather than mindfulness. Wallace says the Eightfold Path goes beyond intensified perception in the Western sense of consciousness, because mindfulness requires focused concentration rather than heightened awareness in general, and the concentration of mindfulness has an ethical dimension.[18] Theravada Buddhism, for example, teaches its practitioners to concentrate on a specific point, like breathing, to become mindful of singular happenings, but it also asks people to regard all beings with respect, which flows from an ethical commitment to practice harmlessness.

- **Right Concentration**—"means *wholesome concentration* (*i.e.*, concentration on wholesome thoughts and actions)."[19] Properly understood, the steps of the Noble Eightfold Path are neither sequential nor isolated; they are an interactive mechanism, not unlike the Jewish Law, which forms an operating system for everyday life. At the entranceway to the Vishva Niketan Buddhist Retreat Center in Colombo, Sri Lanka, a large yellow sign with black letters in the Sinhala, Tamil, and English languages reminds incoming guests of their need to practice right concentration in this sacred space:

While You Are in Vishva Niketan

Observe Noble Silence
Keep Every Step With Mindfulness
Speak Every Word With Awareness
Learn to Look at Every Thought With Mindfulness
Keep the Premises Clean
Keep the Environment Clean
Look After Plants as Living Beings[20]

Notice how the ethical dimension interweaves with the spiritual, typical in many schools of Buddhist thought. The sentences are imperatives, but they lack the *Thou Shalt Not* tone of Judeo-Christianity. Whoever compiled the list at Vishva Niketan phrased it so gently that visitors may not notice they are reading a series of directives. By inserting the first person singular pronoun before each line, the seven commandments become affirmative prayer:

I Observe Noble Silence
I Keep Every Step With Mindfulness
I Speak Every Word With Awareness
I Learn to Look at Every Thought With Mindfulness
I Keep the Premises Clean
I Keep the Environment Clean
I Look After Plants as Living Beings

Silent Meditation or Solar-Powered DVD Prayer Wheels?

The question of Buddhist prayer is complicated because, like Christianity, in Buddhism a wide diversity of "denominations" takes different forks in the road of spiritual practice. Some Buddhist traditions pray to Buddha; others meditate before the image of Gautama Siddhartha with almost no thought to prayer as communication. Some Buddhists spin prayer wheels, and not just one revolution equals one prayer ... *billions*. High-tech models holding eight DVD's full of prayers, empowered by solar panels, strive for enlightenment through green energy sources. The Tibet Tech website describes the new equipment:

> Buddhist texts teach that mindfully turning a prayer wheel produces the same merit and benefits as having recited the number of prayers (mantras) inside the prayer wheel multiplied by how many times the prayer wheel spins around. Each revolution of a Tibet Tech prayer wheel releases over 84 billion prayers.[21]

There are far too many Buddhist prayer forms to survey adequately in a single chapter. For example, as mentioned before, Tibetan Buddhists pray to ascended humans (*bodhisattvas*), and Pure Land Buddhists pray to *Amitabha Buddha*, sometimes seen as a female form of the Buddha. Zen Buddhists contemplate parables called *kōans*, which are frequently nonsensical to the Western mind. This is not meant as criticism, since that nonsense is precisely what the Zen master wants to accomplish, to free the mind from subject-object illusions and grasp the natural flow of all things. Dr. John B. Noss, pioneer in the study of world religions, told his classes about the classical Zen Buddhist attitude: *"He who asks is wrong; he who answers is wrong."* Noss explained that *to ask* or *to answer* affirms the false belief in separation, which Zen masters attempt to exorcise from their disciples.[22]

Is there a common thread, something non-Buddhists can adapt to their spiritual practices? One unifying factor in Buddhist spirituality seems to be the list we just discussed, the Noble Eightfold Path, interpreted through the lens of *compas-*

sion. Whether meditating or praying, the Eightfold Path can provide concepts around which to build almost any kind of spiritual practice. Imagine a minister, priest, or rabbi going about the daily tasks of a clergyperson while contemplating *Right Action* or *Right Mindfulness*. Muslim or Mormon, Baptist or Baha'i, would thoughts about *Right Speech* or *Right Concentration* set a positive tone for confident living?

Not just theists, but agnostics, atheists, and religious humanists might find ethical-spiritual themes for improving life in the concrete world by contemplation of *Right Livelihood* or *Right Effort*. All of the above could develop rituals, celebrations, holidays, and "spiritual" exercises around the steps of the Noble Eightfold path.

The ancient, nontheistic religion of Buddhism brings to postmodern humanity the gift of awareness, centered in compassion for the earth and all living beings. It is a starting place where most of us can find common ground, even without shaving our heads and donning a monk's robe. As Bhante Wimala writes in his book *Lessons of the Lotus:*

> When I travel, in my heart, I see no Buddhists, Christians, Jews, Janis, or spiritualists; no Germans, Swedes, Thais, or Israelis. I see no colors, genders, or ages. I see eager, caring, conscious people who are both struggling and playing with the same issues as everybody else. When I have that realization, I cannot help but try to extend only smiles, laughter, and understanding to all … When your heart blossoms like the lotus and you see the world through the eyes of such a pure heart, you will see all human beings with respect, caring, and love.[23]

Check Your Knowledge

1. In regard to its God-concept, how is Buddhism unique among the world religions?
2. Describe Buddha's childhood and youth. What were foretold as his two possible destinies?
3. How did Buddha reach enlightenment under the Bodhi Tree? Describe the Four Noble Truths, his concept about how to end suffering.
4. Explain briefly the elements in the Noble Eightfold Path. Is the path sequential?
5. What did the Venerable Bhante Y. Wimala say about anger and hatred?
6. Clarify what *compassion* means for Buddhists.

Discussion Starters

1. Do you feel Gautama Siddhartha was correct in his assessment about the nature of suffering and how to overcome it?
2. Discuss the "Middle path" of Buddhism.
3. Not every enlightened soul elects to become a *bodhisattva.* Are you more interested in personal growth or in helping others attain it? (Be honest.)
4. Which step(s) of the Eightfold Path most appeals to you, and why?
5. The author suggests Buddha's ideas might assist all religionists in their quest for spirituality. What common ground does Buddhism offer?
6. What do you think of high-tech prayer wheels?

Suggested Activity:
You Are the Buddha

Find a comfortable place to sit. Meditate for 10 minutes upon ONE of the steps in the Noble Eightfold Path:

Right Understanding

Right Purpose

Right Speech

Right Action

Right Livelihood

Right Effort

Right Mindfulness

Right Concentration

Notes: Some people find it helpful to relax in silence for a minute; ring a soft bell one time to announce the beginning and ending of the meditation period, and rest in silence another minute after concluding.

If you are in a study group, share your insights when ready.

PART
THREE

FINDING SACRED SPACE

Praying Into the Living Center

Nothing in your vocabulary
will get you to this place.
You must pray with what the body
knows but cannot put into words.

Search through your instincts.
Let them lead the way. They
lived in the language of light
long before you could even grunt.

Remember that evening on the plains when
the sun spilled its jar
of oils as far as the eye could see?
Let your spirit slide to the center

the same way. Let it wander just beyond the
reach of your doubts
and slightly above the logical explanations
you leave in their wake.

Trust what the lungs have learned about
breathing and what the eyes have discovered about light.
They know the way better than you.

Follow their lead the way musicians pursue
a good tune. Pray the way you think God
listens, then wait to hear that mystery call
your name.

—Fredrick Zydek[1]

8

CROSS-CULTURAL SAMPLER, PART 1

Prayer in Islam and Pentecostalism

You get more churches burned down in the United States in the last two years than in the last hundred, because of the lack of understanding of culture and diversity and the beauty of it.

—Edward James Olmos[2]

The study of religious history shows people have crafted a wide range of practices to satisfy the universal hunger for meaning, balance, and harmony in their world. As noted previously, all religious truth has a local component; there are no tiger gods where there are no tigers. New insights frequently appear after stepping outside one's cultural box, so Chapters 8 and 9 continue the "many paths" approach by sampling various prayer techniques, primarily among three radically different communities of faith today: Muslim, Pentecostal, and Neo-pagan.

Comparative religion provides some tools to understand selected examples, but once again it is important to remember we approach this study with a set of values in place. Sometimes browsing another faith will feel relatively comfortable, because the tradition we are visiting shares common ground with our own belief system. For example, it is much easier for me to find a comfort zone when discussing the role of women in society with Reformed Jews, Quakers, or Lutherans than to have the same conversation with traditional Muslims, many of whom follow Shariah law. By the liberal standards of Western civilization today, women in conservative Islamic countries are clearly second-class citizens. Of course, advocates of Shariah see the situation differently. For them the Western system of values objectifies women and degrades them into sexual objects while maintaining a double standard in employment and economic advancement. At a lecture given at Montreal's McGill University titled "Islam—Elevation of Women's Status," Sheikh Ali Al-Timimi said:

> The Western view is that women are elevated only in the West and that they are getting more and more rights with the passage of time, while their sisters— they say—in the Islamic world are still being suppressed. The Muslims who they encounter say that in actuality it is the Islamic system that provides the true freedoms for men and women alike, and women in the West as well as men, are deceived into an idea of freedom which really doesn't exist.[3]

This is an important issue, but we will not attempt to sort out all the cultural differences among the world's religions in a single volume about prayer. The above values conflict between Shariah and Western traditions provides another example of how the lenses we wear affect the way we see the world. Our task when encountering diversity in spiritual practice is to recognize that some ideas that raise the hairs on the back of our neck may be sacred principles to members of another group. Some traditions condemn as blasphemous what others celebrate as blessed; one tribe's taboo may be a sacramental meal to a neighboring clan; one theologian's anathemas may be another's algorithms. *Understanding* does not mean *endorsing*, or even approving. Any theology that welcomes "many paths" needs to honor the implications of those words.

Muslim Rosary?—Comparing Islamic and Roman Catholic Prayer

Since we have already noted Islam's disagreement with Western culture about the status of women, let's look at a few similarities between Muslim prayer and comparable behavior in the world's largest Christian denomination, the Roman Catholic Church. Both religions are starkly dualistic; Muslims and Catholics worship God as the Supreme Being. Conversation with God is creature-to-Creator, like a servant before the King. In fact, subservient body positions, such as kneeling, are an important part of both Islamic and Catholic prayer conduct. These acts of subservience further accentuate the distance between the individual and the Almighty. Whether derived from Sultan or Caesar, the human-Divine relationship arguably mirrors the imperial power structures of the world in which the two faiths were born. Rather than feeling oppressed, Muslims glory in recalling the awesome, Unknowable Nature of God. The Quran declares:

> He is God, the One other than Whom there is no god, the knower of the hidden and the manifest, the Compassionate, the Merciful. He is God, the One other than Whom there is no god, the Commander, the All-powerful, Pure and Without Defect, the Bestower of Safety, the Protector, the Precious, the Mighty, the Sublime, the Most Elevated. Exempt and purified be He from the partners which they ascribe to Him.[4]

Islam has "Five Pillars" and the requirements for all Muslims begin with prayer. The first Pillar obliges affirmation of the *Shahada,* declaration of faith: "There is no god but God, and Mohammed is the messenger of God." The second Pillar commands prayer in a highly disciplined pattern: five times a day, in the direction of Mecca, following a precise series of spoken words from specific bodily positions. "Prayers are performed at dawn, noon, midafternoon, sunset, and night. A Muslim may pray almost anywhere, such as in fields, offices, factories, or universities."[5]

While researching this chapter, I discovered a Muslim website that assists believers worldwide in setting the time for obligatory prayer.[6] According to this source, on Thursday, July 4, 2019, the prayer times for observant Muslims in Kansas City, Missouri, are listed as 3:59 a.m.; 1:23, 5:19, 8:48 and 10:46 p.m. However, prayer times shift with the rising and setting of the sun, and there are complex tables for computing the precise moment it must begin.

Another online source, the *Prayer Times Calculation* website, attempts to explain the science behind the process, but the math is beyond my intellectual pay grade, a cultural reminder that Muslims invented *algebra*, an Arabic word. The site lists seven different calculating bodies—the Muslim World League, Islamic Society of North America, plus national agencies in several countries—none of whom agree on the procedure for setting the exact moment when prayer begins.[7]

Chaos in date-and-time selection beleaguers many large families of faith. Chinese, Vietnamese, and Tibetan communities often celebrate different New Year's Days. Christian traditions offer a wide assortment of dates to observe Easter and the holidays commemorating the birth of Jesus. Some commentators have remarked that Hinduism solved the problem by creating a holiday for every day in the year.

Roman Catholic monastic orders follow a pattern of daily prayer times similar to the Islamic regimen. When I have taken self-directed retreats at the Cistercian (Trappist) Monastery of the Holy Spirit near Conyers, Georgia, one of the options was to attend community prayer. Monks assemble in the Chapel seven times a day. The prayer routine begins in the predawn dark at 4 a.m. for *Vigils,* and ends with *Compline* shortly before 8 p.m. Technically, all members of the priesthood, plus nuns and members of monastic orders, are required to perform routines of prayer published by the Church. All Catholics are encouraged to do likewise, but only the professionals and laity who work at Catholic institutions have the duty of saying the *Daily Offices.*[8]

However, Islamic prayer periods are not just required for those with religious vocations but five times daily for all observant Muslims. Before dawn breaks, loudspeakers on minarets awake the population with the musical cry, *"Prayer is better than sleep!"* Throughout the day in some Muslim countries, traffic halts in the street and the commercial activities of the whole nation pause whenever the faithful turn to God in prayer. Shops and stores often have special rooms set aside for pedestrians to dash in and kneel on prayer rugs oriented toward Mecca.

> A day is not here set apart for prayer, and in this sense no Sabbath is known to Islam. Islam requires that a Muslim should be able to disengage himself from all worldly occupations and resort to his prayers, even when he is most busy.[9]

Encountering Islamic daily prayer as a non-Muslim is not unlike a non-Catholic attending the Latin Mass for the first time. Prayer is generally in Arabic, which contributes to the atmosphere of sacredness but makes it initially difficult for Westerners to follow. The ritual itself is repetitious and involves multiple positions. When engaging in movement, the whole body is at prayer, not just mind and mouth.

Besides the kneeling on prayer rugs, the best known Islamic example of using the whole body at prayer are the practices of *whirling dervishes*, Sufi dancers who lose themselves in physical praise of God beyond words. Sufism itself is Muslim mysticism, through reflection, poetry, and motion. Sufis aspire to bring believers into blameless perfection before God in this life rather than awaiting the rewards of paradise.[10]

Islam and Catholicism share another point of contact—*prayer beads*. And the similarity is not just between those two highly dissimilar traditions. Sometimes beginning students of world religions are surprised to learn that something akin to prayer beads or the Rosary are employed to keep track of prayer repetitions among groups as divergent as Orthodox Christians, Jews, Buddhists, Hindus, Sikhs, and Bahá'ís. In some instances, prayer beads afford one of the few common practices shared by otherwise alien religious traditions.

Takeaways. Our quick look at Islam has shown Muslim prayer is …

- **Regular.** It frames the daily schedule. Life in Islamic countries shapes itself around prayer times.
- **Other-directed.** The direction of movement is toward an appreciation of God as Creator and Sustainer of the Universe.
- **Deeply respectful.** Rugs and mats shield the worshipper from contact with the ground during prayer. Body positions indicate submission to God's Will.
- **Multisensual.** Prayer requires sounds, movement, and shifting body positions, which engages the sense of touch and kinesthetic sense. Musical vocal sounds from lofty minarets call the faithful to prayer; most prayers are chanted.

- **Individual and corporate.** Prayer can be alone or in groups; home, shop, school, or mosque.
- **Obligatory.** Prayer is required to fulfill the Muslim's commitment to the Divine-human covenant.
- **Ritualistic.** Recitation of published prayer may seem like mindless repetition to traditions that emphasize creating new prayers for each occasion, but the structure of ritual can actually set believers free to experience prayer without the need to make it up as they go along.

This last point has sometimes been the complaint of old guard Catholics, many of whom continually objected to the elimination of the Latin Mass after Vatican II. The sentiment finally prevailed, and in 2011 Pope Benedict XVI issued instructions about how to reinstate Latin in those congregations who desired the older form. Ritual need not be cognitive to provide meaning.[11] Not creative input, but participatory involvement, like driving along a rocky seacoast and drinking in the beauty. How many listeners are uplifted by Beethoven without reading a note of music?

As Jesus says in the Sermon on the Mount, mindless repetition avails nothing. But anyone who has walked a labyrinth or chanted a mantra understands the power of *mindful* repetition to move the Divine-human conversation beyond words. This brings us to the second example of prayer.

Pentecostalism

Movement and body position play a key role in religious families with little else in common (e.g., Hindus, Native Americans, and Orthodox Christians). An expression of conservative Protestantism known as *Pentecostalism* prays with a unique combination of sound and motion. Pentecostals draw their name from the Book of Acts. According to the biblical author, the Holy Spirit descended upon the apostles at the

Jewish Feast of Pentecost and they received a second baptism in spiritual fire. After tongues of flame appeared over the disciples' heads, they preached to crowds of people who understood their message regardless of what languages the visitors spoke. The bodily reenactment of that experience identifies Pentecostalism today.

> One of the greatest privileges of the born again and cleansed believer is to receive the gift of the Baptism of the Holy Spirit or Holy Ghost by faith. The Holy Spirit was sent by the Father and the Son to the church on the Day of Pentecost ... We believe the initial evidence of receiving the gift of the Holy Spirit is by speaking in tongues as the Spirit gives utterance ... While speaking in tongues is the initial evidence, the gifts of the Spirit and the fruit of the Spirit must be evident in the life of the spirit filled believer.[12]

This experience is part of a greater phenomenon called the Charismatic Movement, after the Greek word *charisma*, (χάρισμα, gift). It is sometimes called the "Full Gospel" movement by some adherents, who believe all the gifts of the Apostolic Age are available today.[13] Other conservative Christians—notably, large Baptist denominations—have vigorously attacked the "Full Gospel" approach.[14] (For a crisp exchange between the two sides, see notes on the above.)

The practice of ecstatic utterance, speaking or praying in unknown tongues, also presents in non-Christian groups. The following Old Testament passage strongly implies something very similar happened to King Saul, the first ruler of Israel:

> When they were going from there to Gibeah, a band of prophets met him; and the spirit of God possessed him, and he fell into a prophetic frenzy along with them. When all who knew him before saw how he

prophesied with the prophets, the people said to one another, "What has come over the son of Kish? Is Saul also among the prophets?" A man of the place answered, "And who is their father?" Therefore it became a proverb, "Is Saul also among the prophets?" When his prophetic frenzy had ended, he went home.[15]

Scholars of religion and social scientists call the phenomenon *glossolalia*, and it is wildly cross-cultural. Instances of ecstatic utterances have been noted among Haida Indians of the Pacific Northwest, Shamans in the Sudan, the Voodoo cult of Haiti, Aborigines in Australia, Tibetan monks, and Eskimos in circumpolar subarctic regions.[16] Studies show glossolalia is neither language nor communication but *nonlinguistic prayer* in which participants detach the cognitive functions of speech from the act of making verbal sounds. Chanting mysterious sounds in Transcendental Meditation provides a comparable experience, except charismatic prayer spills forth as long streams of nonsense syllables rather than a single mantra provided to the practitioner, which is based on an unknown Sanskrit word. Since the charismatic experience is so widespread, it is logical to conclude nonlinguistic prayer addresses needs that reach beyond fundamentalist Christianity.

Although Charismatic practices have been part of Christian culture since New Testament times, the modern expression seems to originate with conservative Protestant groups. Since the mid-1960s, the hunger for an experience of God has propelled the practice beyond its roots into mainstream Protestant and Catholic congregations, sometimes including pastors, priests, and nuns. The wide-ranging Charismatic Movement is too complex to consider in a few pages, so we shall limit our field of investigation by focusing on Pentecostalism, aware that the result will be a glimpse rather than a panoramic overview.

A key element in understanding Pentecostalism is that it is thoroughly *revivalistic*, that is, designed to incite varying degrees of emotions. Participants in revivalistic traditions can move from serenity to frenzy during the experience, all leading inexorably to stages of greater commitment, which range from initial conversion of the unsaved soul to high levels of heavenly bliss.

Revivalism began as a populist movement in 19th-century Protestantism, partly as a reaction against the staid intellectualism of Calvinism. In its most vigorous expression, revivalist meetings are characterized by "an unrelenting series of intense spiritual exercises, punctuated with cries of religious agony and ecstasy, all designed to promote religious fervor and conversions."[17]

Hollywood has found that much raw emotion too hard to resist. Several movies have featured revivalism, for example, *Leap of Faith* (1992) starring Steve Martin. A generation earlier, Burt Lancaster and Jean Simmons headlined the motion picture *Elmer Gantry* (1960), based on the 1926 picaresque novel by Sinclair Lewis. *Elmer Gantry* was inspired by the work of Aimee Semple McPherson, the Canadian-born revivalist preacher who moved to Los Angeles in the 1920s and founded the Foursquare Gospel Church. McPherson was young and attractive, a truly *charismatic* figure in both the popular and theological sense of the word. She packed the house with revivalist preaching, hands-on healing, and demonstrations of glossolalia. Although highly controversial and given to personal indiscretions, McPherson did much to popularize Pentecostalism and is often cited as one of the movement's founders.[18]

The revivalist-charismatic pattern continues in Pentecostal services today. Worshippers will spontaneously display the "gift of tongues" by uttering what sounds like a string of words in a foreign language. Sometimes the speaker, or an interpreter from the congregation, "translates" what has been said; other times, translation is not possible because multiple expressions of tongues are happening simultaneously as members of the congregation pray in unknown languages.

Another key component in Pentecostalism and all revivalist worship is *praise.* Standing amid a congregation that is engaging in praise to God through joyful words and inspirational music can be exhilarating, even for someone who may not share Pentecostalism's typically conservative belief system. The Hebrew and Christian Scriptures contain dozens of passages about *praise.* Three words in Koine Greek, the language in which the New Testament was written, convey nuanced variations of this idea—*psallo, aineo,* and *doxazo.* In his First Letter to the Corinthians, the apostle Paul uses *psallo.* You need not read Greek to recognize its connection to psalmody, the musical prayers chanted at the Temple in Jerusalem. Paul picks up a cadence not unlike Pentecostal revivalism when he writes:

> I will pray with the spirit, but I will pray with the mind also; I will sing praise (*psallo*) with the spirit, but I will sing praise with the mind also.[19]

The Gospels use *aineo* (to extol, promise or vow) and *doxazo* (to glorify, praise). We get the term *doxology* from the latter word.

> The crowd was amazed when they saw the mute speaking, the maimed whole, the lame walking, and the blind seeing. And they praised (*doxazo*) the God of Israel.[20]

Although glossolalia is not everyone's gift, "praise" seems universally available to all who want to give thanks. Personally, I like to "praise" God because the Universe is pretty, warm bread from the oven that tastes good, the smile of a friend makes me feel loved, and the sound of the sea crashing on the beach reminds me of the depths out there, unfathomable, secure, steadfast, trustworthy. To me, that's the essence of what Jesus was saying when he began his great prayer, *"Our Father, who art in heaven hallowed be thy name ..."*

Takeaways. For the practitioner, charismatic prayer is:

- **Intimate**. Offers emotional *experience*, not intellectual reflection.
- **Self-validating.** Verifies faith by the gift of tongues. Confirms belief in a way that transcends theology.
- **Incontrovertible.** Demonstrates the actual Presence of God to the worshipper. No one can refute a personal experience.
- **Mystical.** Brings the individual and the Holy Spirit together in a sacramental encounter.
- **Energizing.** Electrifies other congregants and bolsters their faith.
- **Immediate.** Creates an intensely now-centered worship experience. People await the phenomenon of glossolalia like Moses on Mount Sinai, expecting God to show up.
- **Multisensual.** Provides whole-body contact between the believer and the God of the New Testament.
- **Transcends language.** Vocalizes without attachment to words, like chanting a polysyllabic mantra. Expresses vocally that which cannot be expressed verbally.

A possible metaphysical Christian application for the gift of tongues today might be to try the practice as vocalized, nonverbal meditation. Paradoxically, glossolalia might also be seen as moving beyond words, a vibratory variation on what mystics call entering the Silence, related to the sacred *Om* of Hindu practice.

> Before the beginning, the Brahman (absolute reality) was one and non-dual. It thought, "I am only one—may I become many." This caused a vibration which eventually became sound, and this sound was Om. Creation itself was set in motion by the vibration of Om. The closest approach to Brahman is that first sound, Om. Thus, this sacred symbol has become emblematic of Brahman just as images are emblematic of material objects.[21]

The late Marcus Bach was one of the finest world religions scholars of the 20th century and a much-published author. He and I share some history, although we've never met. Dr. Bach was a member of the United Church of Christ, the denomination of my youth, and he wrote the Q&A column in *Unity Magazine®* for many years before I took over after his retirement in 1993. The liberal-intellectual UCC is hardly noted for charismatic worship, but in 1980 my hometown newspaper, the *Reading Eagle*, published an interview with Dr. Bach, which touched on his encounter with glossolalia.

> Describing a personal experience with the phenomenon, he said, "It's an overpowering, highly emotional, deeply physical, and ecstatic spiritual experience in which you suddenly feel overpowered by a spirit. Although it sounds like gibberish—it's the unknown tongue."[22]

Dr. Bach's response was typical of his inclusive mind. He moved so easily among faith groups that people from supposedly incompatible religious factions thought he was one of them, and they were right.

Check Your Knowledge

1. List some points of similarity between Roman Catholicism and Islam. What takeaways does Islam offer non-Muslims?
2. What is the *Shahada*? Give its English meaning and tell what role it serves in conversion to Islam.
3. How often are Muslims required to pray, facing what geographic reference point?
4. Explain the Pentecostal experience of *glossolalia*.
5. Give other examples of charismatic utterance in history and today.
6. What takeaways does charismatic prayer offer for non-Pentecostals?

Discussion Starters

1. Muslims are sometimes unfairly portrayed as universally fanatical in Western media. What is the boundary line between fervent belief and fanaticism?
2. What do you think of the Islamic requirement to pray multiple times daily?
3. The chapter states that in Islam, "The direction of movement is toward an appreciation of God as Creator and Sustainer of the Universe." Compare and contrast that position with your personal doctrine of God.
4. Have you ever spoken in tongues? Do you have any family or friends who practice the charismatic gifts in prayer?
5. How is speaking in tongues different from chanting a mantra in an unknown language, like Pali or Sanskrit?
6. What elements in Pentecostalism, if any, would you like to see incorporated in worship services at your church?

Suggested Activity:
Islamic or Charismatic Prayer

Note: These activities cannot be done in a group, but you could try them at home and discuss the experience at the next class session.

Option No. 1—Islamic Prayer Circle

Set your goal to pray five times a day for a week. We are not presuming to re-create actual Islamic prayer but merely following their daily regimen, so feel free to pray in any manner comfortable to you. The directions are quite generic. Here is the schedule, quoted verbatim from "Islamic Prayer Timings" by Hulda, at the *About.com* Guide website.[23]

Fajr (predawn): This prayer starts off the day with the remembrance of God; it is performed before sunrise.

Dhuhr (noon): After the day's work has begun, one breaks shortly after noon to again remember God and seek His guidance.

'Asr (afternoon): In the late afternoon, people are usually busy wrapping up the day's work, getting kids home from school, etc. It is an important time to take a few minutes to remember God and the greater meaning of our lives.

Maghrib (sunset): Just after the sun goes down, Muslims remember God again as the day begins to come to a close.

'Isha (evening): Before retiring for the night, Muslims again take time to remember God's presence, guidance, mercy, and forgiveness.

Option No. 2—Praying in Tongues

This is an active meditation exercise. Give yourself permission to experiment a little.

After becoming still, try expressing your prayer by non-verbal sounds. Detach your thought mechanism from speech apparatus and babble away. Don't worry if you sound strange; nobody but God is listening. Let the holy gibberish flow … Be not afraid. You cannot get it wrong.

9

CROSS-CULTURAL SAMPLER, PART 2
Neo-Paganism/Wicca

Diana, queen of night,
In all your beauty bright,
Shine on us here,
And with your silver beam
Unlock the gate of dream;
Rise bright and clear.
On earth and sky and sea,
Your magic mystery
Its spell shall cast,
Wherever leaf may grow,
Wherever tide may flow,
Till all be past.
O secret queen of power,
At this enchanted hour
We ask your boon.
May fortune's favor fall
Upon true witches all,
O Lady Moon![1]

Our final delicacy in this three-part sampler of world prayer comes from a source that is at once geographically close to home for Western religionists, yet far afield from the God-concept of monotheistic faiths. Pentecostalism worships one God, although Christians generally allow their God to display as a Trinity—Father, Son, and Holy Spirit. Islam is even more adamantly monotheistic, requiring the uncompromising declaration *"There is no God but God ..."* at the entry point to the Muslim religion.

Neo-paganism disagrees. It is *polytheistic*, honoring many gods and goddesses. According to the *Religion Facts* website, "Neopaganism (or Neo-Paganism or Paganism) is a broad designation that refers to any nature-based or earth-based religion, most of which pattern themselves on ancient western pagan religions."[2] The best-known form of Neo-paganism is probably *Wicca*. Some people assume the two terms are interchangeable, but they are not. Anyone who worships a combination of gods and goddesses can be called a pagan (polytheist) but they are not all Wiccans.

> Wicca is one form of Neopaganism. Thus all Wiccans are Neopagans (or Pagans), but not all Pagans are Wiccans. The main difference between Pagans who refer to themselves as such and Wiccans is that Wiccans practice magic and witchcraft.[3]

To further complicate matters, not all witches are Wiccans, and even Wicca has many Traditions (they use capital "T"). For example, some call themselves Alexandrian, British Traditional, Celtic, Covenant of the Goddess, Dianic, Eclectic, Sacred Wheel. Others practice privately; Solitary Wiccans sometimes sardonically referred to themselves as "Craft Singles." By definition, all these fit the broader field of magical observance, all of which falls under the generic category of Neo-paganism (i.e., new versions of ancient polytheistic worship and ritual). Someone who observes a renewed Olympian worship of Greek or Roman gods may have no interest in spells, incantations, and other magical recreations. Classical paganism was complex and modular; its modern recreation seems even less structured.

For simplicity sake, my references generally come from the Wiccan tradition, since I have enjoyed personal and professional contacts with followers of Wicca. Yet the multiple side roads along the pagan path are not considered weaknesses but strengths. Author Patti Wigington celebrates modern polytheism's amazing diversity:

> You can pray to anyone you like. You can pray to a god, a goddess, or the Grand High Poobah of the Toaster Oven. Pray to whoever—or whatever—is most likely to take an interest in your dilemma. If you're working on protection of your home, for example, you may wish to call upon Vesta or Brighid, both guardians of the hearth. If you're about to enter into a nasty conflict, perhaps Mars, the god of war, would be willing to step in for a bit of fun.[4]

Do they take their religion seriously, or is Neo-paganism a middle class spiritual hobby, not unlike role-playing medieval life at a Renaissance fair? Do adherents really believe they are communicating with Greek, Roman, and Egyptian deities that have not been worshipped in centuries? I asked a group of Wiccans that very question at a Neo-pagan gathering in South Carolina a few years ago. Some of my friends—who call me a "friendly cowan," their term for nonpagan—said they performed rituals to various gods but really believed in a single Reality behind all existence. As they described the concept, it sounded like something akin to the One Presence/One Power of Metaphysical Christianity, or the cosmic monism of Vedic Hinduism. They said the names applied to various deities are just ways of looking at the many faces of God. Apparently, switching gears from One Presence/One Power is not necessarily required; the pagan path is by definition pluralistic. Popular workshop leader Myth Woodling writes:

> Any person can practice a Neo-Pagan path in which s/he worships a deity which is viewed as a multiplicity of deities who are all facets or aspects of Divinity … This is monism. Sometimes, it involves the worship of "All-That-Is" a gender-less or androgynous being. It can be expressed in the old misquote: "All the gods are one God and all the goddesses are one Goddess, and there is one Divine Source."[5]

However, other Neo-pagans I spoke with professed their belief in multiple spiritual entities, divine beings, which could be contacted by humans and had the ability to intervene in the physical world—gods and goddesses, for lack of a better term. They were adamant that the visible diversity of the Universe makes sense in a spiritual context as well. Pagan author and website host Ravenna Angelline says the consciousness of the worshipping community can actually create a god or goddess:

> Depending on the person you are speaking with, they believe they are communing with the essence of the deity they pray to, the idea that the deity they pray to is an egregore—a thoughtform that has had so much attention that it becomes an entity of its own. On the other hand a person may believe they are literally praying to that deity.[6]

Woodling urges deeper participation in the mysteries of life by creation of new ritual. "If you feel some deity, gender, or aspect of the Divine is neglected, go forth and make thine own offerings of love and worship."[7] Wigington describes paganism today as a moveable feast, amazingly flexible in celebration and worship.

> Ultimately, prayer is a very personal thing. You can do it out loud or silently, in a church or backyard or forest or at a kitchen table. Pray when you need to, and say what you wish to say. Chances are good that someone is listening.[8]

Pagan Holy Days

Neo-pagan holidays are also called *Sabbats*, a term borrowed from Judaism. Eight Sabbats form the Neo-pagan Wheel of the Year: Samhain (October 31–November 1); Yule—circa December 21 (Winter Solstice); Imbolic—February 2; Ostara—circa March 21 (Vernal Equinox); Beltane—May 1 (May Day); Litha—circa June 21 (Summer Solstice); Lughnasadh—August 1; and Mabon—circa September 21 (Autumnal Equinox).[9] Let's look at prayer and ritual for three Sabbats.

Samhain (pronounced *sow*-en). Followers of the pagan path often begin their liturgical year at Samhain on the evening of October 31, the night before All Saint's Day, which is celebrated by nonpagans today as Halloween. Some believe "the veil between the worlds is thinnest on this night …," making Samhain "an excellent time for divinations. Feasts are made in remembrance of dead ancestors and as an affirmation of continuing life—a time for settling problems, throwing out old ideas and influences."[10] Samhain prayer often incorporates positive images of life and the death, as in the prayer sequence below by author Galen Gillotte. The tag *"Blessed Be,"* which closes the first and final portions, is the Wiccan equivalent to *Praise God* or *Hallelujah*, or more directly, *May you be blessed*.

Samhain Night Prayer to the Goddess[11]

Opening:

Hail Dark Lady of the Crossroads,
of wisdom hard-won,
grant me Thy blessing, purify my heart,
and teach me the truth of my soul;
show me that death is but the gateway to life.
Blessed Be.

Main prayer:

Lady,
You offer me a lambent grail
of softly glowing moonlight,
as between one heartbeat and the next
souls flit from life to life
with death a well-worn pathway
of the Wise—
a place of respite and release.
Deeply I drink—
a willing sacrifice to eternal motion—
a moment of spirit upon the wind
and another life experience to embrace.

Closing Prayer:

I bow to Thee Hecate, Diana, Mari and thank
Thee for Thy blessing—the Cauldron of Night
full of life, and death, and life again;
Thy magic gives me wings.
Blessed Be.

The universal theme of this prayer is expressed in the opening portion: "… show me that death is but the gateway to life." The human race has looked Death in the face and declared, *You are not the end but the gateway to life.* Samhain celebrates that long-ago decision to have faith in the worst moments of existence.

Yule is observed as the Winter Solstice, which falls around December 21. Neo-paganism's celebration of Yule is not to be confused with Christmas, even though expressions like the *yule log* and *yuletide greetings* have found their way into Christian lore. In fact, the traditional Church year owes much to the old pagan festivals. From the spring fertility rites of the mother-goddess *Ostare,* to the gift-giving galas of Roman Saturnalia in December, Christians co-opted popular pagan holidays and refurbished them as Holy Days of the Church. For Neo-pagans, the Winter Solstice remains a jubilee of renewal.

> This is the time of death and rebirth of the Sun God. The days are shortest, the Sun at its lowest point. The Full Moon after Yule is considered the most powerful of the whole year. This ritual is a light festival, with as many candles as possible on or near the altar in welcome of the Sun Child.[12]

The following "Yule Prayer Song" by Colombe invokes a ceremonial reverence for the return of the light in the darkness of winter.[13]

Yule Prayer Song

Mother Earth
I offer to you this song
For I am earth
and to the Earth, I belong
Mother Earth
help me grow as you need me to
Mother Earth
show me what I am here to do

'Cause I am growing, I am changing
on this darkest day
I am growing, I am changing
in my darkest place
I am growing, I am changing
on this darkest day
I am growing, I am changing
in my darkest place
Blessed Be! [14]

Beltane is the old term for May Day. A festival of light, Beltane commemorates the sun's full release from winter bondage, bringing spring and summer once more. In ancient practice, bonfires on hilltops announced gatherings for ritual. "The fires further celebrate the return of life, fruitfulness to the earth and the burning away of winter. The ashes of the Beltane fires were smudged on faces and scattered in the fields. Household fires would be extinguished and relit with fresh fire from the Bel Fires." Merriments included "frolicking throughout the countryside, maypole dancing, leaping over fires to ensure fertility, circling the fire three times (sun-wise) for good luck in the coming year, athletic tournaments, feasting, music, drinking" and children gathering May flowers.[15]

Beltane was a festival of prosperity. To sustain life required annual increase—crops, livestock, wild game, and humans. In an agrarian society, everything depended on fertility in harvests, domestic animals, and children to tend the fields. Hardscrabble living made healthy human reproductive capacity an absolute necessity, because only a few infants would survive the cold winters and perpetual outbreaks of disease long enough to reach adulthood. Beltane celebrated fertility because it was a life-and-death issue for whole populations. One killing frost, episode of the plague, or prolonged drought and the community could literally cease to exist.

Beltane was celebration of "… unashamed human sexuality and fertility." Such associations include the obvious phallic symbolism of the Maypole and riding the hobby horse. Even a seemingly innocent children's nursery rhyme, "Ride a cock horse to Banbury Cross …" retains such memories. And the next line "… to see a fine Lady on a white horse" is a reference to the annual ride of "Lady Godiva" through Coventry. Every year for nearly three centuries, a sky-clad village maiden (elected Queen of the May) enacted this Pagan rite, until the Puritans put an end to the custom.[16]

Sky-clad is an anthropological euphemism for totally nude. The sky-clad lifestyle is practiced full-time as a spiritual discipline by Digambara monks of the Jain religion in India. A few Wiccan groups today perform their rituals sky-clad, but Neo-pagans have told me privately they were horrified at the thought of bearing their souls and bodies to the elements, not to mention casual observers. "Most of us are way too self-conscious," a slightly portly female friend said. "When we want to get medieval, we go with a coarse robe, not the Lady Godiva look."

Since we have been exploring Wiccan Neo-paganism, it seems appropriate to include at least one example of a "spell" in our look at the spirituality of witchcraft, which requires a brief discussion about the distinction between magic and prayer. Arguably, the difference between conventional prayer and casting spells has to do with the *intent* of the practitioner. Prayer usually aims to bring the worshipper in line with some Higher Power or enlightened consciousness within. Communion with God focuses on opening the practitioner to Divine resources, often by getting one's ego out of the way—the cliché for which is "Let Go and Let God."

Magic, on the other hand, often attempts to call upon powers beyond the individual and direct it to do as the practitioner desires. This is a wildly oversimplified generalization, but nevertheless, it charts the boundaries between tradition ideas of magic and prayer. Magic is self-consciously manipulative, like clicking a switch; prayer yields to the higher wisdom of something deep within or far beyond oneself, depending on the gracious nature of God. The above is intended as descriptive analysis, not approval or disapproval of magic or prayer. With that caveat in mind, let's look at an example of a healing spell.

Beltane Anti-Disease Spell

Beltane is an appropriate time to perform spells to ward off disease, as the ancient Celts once drove their livestock through the smoke of their sacred Beltane bonfires to keep disease at bay.

To perform this spell you will need a piece of white chalk and a white candle that has never before been burned. With the chalk, draw a pentagram on the floor about three feet wide. Light the white candle and hold it in your right hand. Step into the pentagram, face the direction of East, and thrice recite the following incantation:

> Beltane fire of enchantment,
> Burn without and burn within.
> Give this Sabbat spell enchantment,
> Let its power now begin!
> Ofano, oblamo, ospergo,
> Hola noa, massa lux beff,
> Clemati, adonai, cleona, florit,
> Pax sax sarax, afa afaca nostra,
> Cerum heaium, lada frium.
> So mote it be!"[17]

Takeaways. The modern reinvention of ancient polytheism offers a remarkable variety of options for people on a pagan path, some of which can be helpful to cowans as well. A brief look at Neo-paganism shows it to be …

- **Nonjudgmental.** Like classical polytheists, Neo-pagans are open to any practice or the worship of any deity that helps the individual grow spiritually.
- **Experimental.** People can pray to whatever combination of gods or goddesses they choose, or invent new ones.
- **Appreciative of diversity.** Prayer is personal, so the way each person prays is an individual choice. The respect for diversity frequently extends to political and ethical dimensions. For example, earth-based religionists are usually strong advocates of ecology and international cooperation.
- **Ritualistic.** Even though individualism is celebrated, there are acts of communal worship that follow specific ritual patterns.
- **Nonevangelical.** Pagans don't believe anyone is lost, so they feel no compulsion to save the world.
- **Joyful**. Neo-pagans display an unapologetic zest for life, reflected in the May Day celebrations of Beltane.
- **Positive.** No sense of human sin or unworthiness casts its shadow over Neo-pagan consciousness, who recall the classical polytheistic sense of life's natural goodness.
- **Holistic.** Neo-pagan ritual brings with it a sense of mind-body-Universe connection. It celebrates healing and fertility, love and peace, the physical and spiritual.
- **Heretical.** Neo-paganism is delightfully aware of itself as a modern counterculture, summarized in the following rhyme from a Beltane circle celebration:

O do not tell the priests of our Art,
For they would call it sin;

But we will be in the woods all night,
A-conjuring summer in.
And we bring you good news by word of mouth,
For woman, cattle and corn,
For the sun is coming up from the south
With oak and ash and thorn.[18]

Wiccans still recall the *Burning Times* of 16th- and 17th-century Europe, a holocaust visited by Christians upon anyone suspected of practicing witchcraft. During the Burning Times, witches were executed en masse for practicing the Craft—often by burning alive—and along with them probably thousands of nonpractitioners of magic who fell to the malevolent rumors spread by fearmongers and rivals. Church and State teamed up to destroy those who were falsely believed to be in league with the Devil.[19] The fact is, Satanism and traditional witchcraft have absolutely no link. Wiccans don't even believe in the Devil, or any totally evil supernatural entity. Some gods become capricious and lash out—like Yahweh's homicidal rage at Israel in Exodus 32—but they get over it.[20]

The larger question here is about killing someone for holding deviant religious convictions. State-sanctioned murder in support of a religious worldview is a cultural sickness that humanity has not yet overcome. The fact that today's Neopagans are by and large positive and optimistic is perhaps a tribute to the staying power of ancient pagan philosophies, which regarded human character as the solitary factor that makes us worthy to stand confidently before gods and neighbors.

Next, our study takes us afield to look for sacred space. Mystics through the ages have discovered holy places while roaming mountain, sea, desert, and forest, and most important, by penetrating deep within their consciousness.

Check Your Knowledge

1. How are Wicca and Neo-paganism related?
2. When author Patti Wigington says you can pray to "the Grand High Poobah of the Toaster Oven," what does she actually mean?
3. List a few Neo-pagan holidays and tell what they commemorate.
4. What makes *Beltane* a holiday of prosperity consciousness?
5. Explain the term *sky-clad* and tell how it relates to Neo-pagan rituals.
6. What does the author say is the difference between magic and prayer?

Discussion Starters

1. Do you believe in magic? Explain.
2. If we can create gods and goddesses for every occasion, what does that mean metaphysically?
3. Which Neo-pagan holiday appeals to you? Would you be okay with participating in ritual *sky-clad*?
4. Read aloud and discuss the *"Samhain Night Prayer to the Goddess"* and *"Yule Prayer Song."* What images capture your imagination?
5. If all other techniques were not working, would you attempt to cast a spell to help someone overcome a health or prosperity challenge? Under what conditions would you mix and deploy a love potion? Explain.
6. What are some takeaways from a study of Neo-paganism and Wicca?

Suggested Activity:
Release the Pagan in You

Sit quietly. Begin playing mood music evocative of Celtic legends and mystical nights under a full moon. Stand, stretch, move slowly ... Dance freely. Do not consider how you appear. Just let your body react to the music. You are free. You are unlimited. Raised your hands. Whirl and spin ... Any movement that feels right and respects the space of others ...

Continue for five minutes, then lower the music and unwind. Slow down. Stop. Sit quietly. Breathe deeply. Relax. Let go.

When you are ready, discuss the experience with your group, or if you are alone, write about it.

10

FIND YOUR SACRED SPACE

> When the Lord saw that he had turned aside to see, God called to him out of the bush, "Moses, Moses!" And he said, "Here I am." Then he said, "Come no closer! Remove the sandals from your feet, for the place on which you are standing is holy ground."[1]

W hether we seek holy ground or private moments of tranquility, all sentient beings share the need for sacred space in their lives. When people cannot find peaceful intervals during the information blitzkrieg of postmodern life, they eventually suffer from the spiritual equivalent of shell shock, or mental vitamin deficiency. Quiet interludes have been called many names—holy ground, Zen meditation, "waiting on the Lord," contemplative prayer, *the* wilderness experience, vision quest, or *The Silence*. As the Sacred Spaces website observes:

> A sacred space is not necessarily where answers are grasped or understood. Rather it is where questions are asked, conversations occur, rituals are perpetuated, dances are performed, songs are sung, and silence is heard.[2]

Whether following streams of thought that arose in the East or West, most religions offer techniques to quiet the mind and body. The Psalmist imagined Yahweh declaring to His people, *"Be still, and know that I am God!"*[3] Jesus walked in the desert and prayed at the Mount of Olives; Buddha meditated under a Bodhi tree until attaining enlightenment; Muhammad withdrew to his cave in the Jabal al-Nur mountain near Mecca, where he received the first revelation from God. Quiet space has nurtured many heroic figures. Even Superman needed a Fortress of Solitude. Sacred space—or at least moments of quiet—is a longing in the heart of all sentient beings, not just heroes. The Sacred Spaces website adds:

> Cathedrals stand as monuments to the universal search for meaning; they are physical embodiments of this search and, simultaneously, they reveal much about the spirituality of those who first built and used them. Buddhist temples, Islamic mosques, Hindu ashrams, Native American sweat lodges, African dance circles—all represent a similar longing to gain insights into life's deepest questions.[4]

What is Sacred Space?

But what is the nature of sacred space? Are some places more "sacred" than others? How does one find or create holy ground? Some traditions purify certain physical locations by ritual and prayer, such as the Jewish monastic Qumran community of the biblical era. Other faiths encourage the practitioner to discover sacred space through encounters with the spirit world, as in Native American vision quests, or through personal or corporate ritual. The Minnesota Episcopal Environmental Stewardship Commission says:

> Sacred Spaces evoke a feeling of a sacredness of space and time, where Heaven seems to touch Earth and we find ourselves aware of the Holy, and filled with the Spirit. A higher energy resides in a sacred space,

a power beyond human control which is part of the feeling of "awe." To find ourselves in the midst of great natural beauty is an awakening into moments of heightened spiritual consciousness. This feeling of "sacred" invokes a connectedness, a presence of the blessing of existence. It is "sacred" when it becomes for us a "window to the Kingdom of God" and a reminder of the sacredness of all space as space created by God.[5]

Are some places actually more "sacred" than others? Is it possible to find hallowed ground, a place that was holy before we got there and will remain holy after we leave? Certainly, people in the Judeo-Christian and Muslim traditions believe in holy spots. One place they agree upon—and squabble about—is Mount Zion in Jerusalem, the hilltop where the Jewish Temple stood, now occupied by the Dome of the Rock Mosque. Christians revere the places where Jesus walked: Galilee, the Jordan River, the city of Jerusalem. Muslims have the Qiblah in Mecca, Saudi Arabia, the square building covered with black cloth toward which all Muslims face in prayer five times daily. Hindus consider the Ganges River in India as sacred; they bathe ritually, drink its water, and scatter the ashes of cremated loved ones upon its surface. Mount Fuji in Japan is sacred space to Buddhists and Shintoists; the Black Hills of South Dakota are holy to Native Americans; Lourdes, France, is the Roman Catholic shrine where the Virgin Mary appeared to St. Bernadette and today is the center of worldwide pilgrimages for healing.

It cannot be denied that cross-culturally people experience heightened awareness of Divine activity in certain locations and a lesser sense of the Presence in others. Yet the question remains: *Is any place holier than any other?* Some say *yes*. There are higher vibrations in certain spots almost anyone can perceive.

> In the end, sacred spaces reveal themselves. They have a way of growing on the visitor, almost like something organic. Some would say they "breathe," and that the old stories which their walls have witnessed are somehow "whispered to those who listen." Usually sacred spaces are found in inviting places, which somehow retain the aura of those who have passed that way.[6]

However, if the Divine Presence and Power is uniformly distributed throughout the Universe, what makes one place "breathe" sacred and another profane? Let me cite an example from the grounds of Unity Village, which might shine a little light on the question. The Fillmore Chapel is one of the most historic sites on campus. It is located in the west wing of the Education Building. There is a small chamber at the south side of the Fillmore, which today must be accessed from the outside. It is known as the Peace Chapel because on the mural over the Bible stand are the words of Jesus as he stilled the storm, *"Peace, Be Still …"*

The Peace Chapel has two small stained glass windows—one with a dove, the other a scroll with the single word "Peace"—and several U-shaped wood chairs with red cushions. Visitors often report a sense of sacred Presence in that little chapel. Perhaps it is because of the historic connection to so many great leaders of the Unity movement in the past. I have prayed in the chapel, and felt something special.

What most people do not know is that the Peace Chapel has an exact, mirror-opposite chamber on the north side of the Fillmore Chapel. Two wings, exact twins, one left-handed, one right-handed. And what is the north side chapel? Well, not a chapel at all. It is the storage room for equipment used in student worship services, plus a few broken fixtures and cleaning supplies. One wing is arguably the best-known prayer spot in the Unity movement, where people feel a special sense of the holy. The other is a broom closet. A *Peace Chapel*, and a *Chapel of Pieces*.

Does this not suggest that it isn't the space itself but the expectations we bring to the experience, enhanced somewhat by reverential decorum and stained glass windows? An open-air shrine in a grassy meadow changes the space because we have dedicated it for a Divine experience, not because we have summoned more holy juice from the Beyond.

Yet the act of setting up the shrine enhances the probability of encountering the Divine. All spirituality begins with intentionality. Our ancestors at Göbekli Tepe expended enormous energies to build their megalithic temples and carve them with delicate images of animals and birds, most likely because they believed the place was holy ground. Doubtless their act of dedication furthered the sense of sacred space. We will never know what rituals their religion celebrated, but we do know they felt this place was especially holy, and we have been seeking the same sacred ground ever since. The best place to seek that which transcends words is in the Silence.

Silence Before the Mystery of Life

> The Lord is in his holy temple;
> let all the earth keep silence before him![7]

Silence before the awesome Presence and Power of the Divine is a continuous biblical theme. Elijah's encounter with the "the still small voice" of the King James Bible is better rendered by the New Revised Standard Version:

Now there was a great wind, so strong that it was splitting mountains and breaking rocks in pieces before the Lᴏʀᴅ, but the Lord was not in the wind; and after the wind an earthquake, but the Lᴏʀᴅ was not in the earthquake; and after the earthquake a fire, but the Lᴏʀᴅ was not in the fire; and after the fire a sound of sheer silence.[8]

Rabbis have long spoken about building a fence around the Torah, the first five books of the Hebrew Bible. Dr. Joseph H. Hertz, who at the time was Chief Rabbi of the British Empire, wrote in his commentary to *Pirke Avoth* (*The Sayings of the Fathers*):

Surround it (Torah) with cautionary rules that shall, like a danger signal, halt a man before he gets within breaking distance of the Divine statute itself. On the Sabbath, for example, even the handling of work-tools is forbidden.[9]

Pirke Avoth links the "fence" around the Torah to the human need for silence. "Tradition is a safety fence to Torah, tithing a safety fence to wealth, vows a safety fence for abstinence; a safety fence for wisdom is silence."[10]

Eckhart Tolle offers concrete reasons to practice quietness:

Don't apply your mind without the stillness because, if you start applying your mind without the stillness, you might very soon lose yourself in the mind and that turns into worry. Worry means the mind is controlling you. Worry is always pointless. A solution never comes out of worry.[11]

Despite the universal hunger for spirituality, silence itself can be intensely bothersome to many people. Listen as Fr. Henri Nouwen, S.J., describes the human inability to benefit from quiet time in his critically acclaimed book *The Way of the Heart: Desert Spirituality and Contemporary Ministry.*

> One of our main problems is that in this chatty society, silence has become a very fearful thing. For most people, silence creates itchiness and nervousness. Many experience silence not as full and rich, but as empty and hollow. For them silence is like a gaping abyss which can swallow them up. As soon as a minister says during a worship service, "Let us be silent for a few moments," people tend to become restless and preoccupied with only one thought: "When will this be over?" … It is quite understandable that most forms of ministry avoid silence precisely so as to ward off the anxiety it provokes.[12]

When I was studying for my doctorate at a mainline theological seminary, I had the opportunity to work with outstanding students from a number of denominations. During one course on spirituality, we divided into small teams and took responsibility for leading the class through discussions and exercises. I selected silent prayer, and when it was my turn, I set up the exercise by inviting my fellow graduate students in ministry to become still and go within for a period of contemplative silence.

"Hmmm … how long should I give them?" I thought. "Five minutes is not nearly enough to enter the Silence, but even that might be taxing their meditative muscles. Okay … two solid minutes, then we debrief the experience." I set my watch and closed my eyes.

Thirty-two seconds later, another member of my team started praying aloud, wrapping up the session with thanks and praise. I was utterly astounded. These weren't business people or school teachers or adolescents eager to get home before the kickoff. They were ministers in training or practicing clergy! If we could not sit in silence for two minutes, how could we possibly recommend meditation to others? It occurred to me the very impatience we feel during extended bouts of silent prayer is the disquiet of the mind exerting itself. My Buddhist friends call this lack of mental discipline— "monkey mind" consciousness.

> The words "monkey mind" come from a Buddhist description of the mind of a person who is not in the present moment. The mind of such a person is said to be likened to a monkey that goes from tree to tree tasting a piece of fruit from each and then dropping it and moving on to the next tree.[13]

Oceanographers say the sea remains tranquil below 25 feet. No matter how badly the storm rages on top of the ocean, the water is tranquil deep below.

Speaking of tranquility, Neil Armstrong landed the "Eagle" on the moon in July 1969 and promptly proclaimed the location *Tranquility Base*. Considering how untranquil the final leg of the journey had been, the choice was steeped in irony. When those first astronauts descended to the surface in Apollo 11's Lunar Module, boulders littered the original landing site. Armstrong took manual control and flew the LM like a helicopter to a safe spot, with less than a minute's fuel remaining.

NASA seemed to be communicating a basic principle of confident living: *You can find tranquility in the midst of turmoil.* The question is, How can we find depth of peace in the midst of storms and hazardous landings of life?

I grew up in a Pennsylvania town faraway from the ocean and walked on a rugged beach for the first time as an 18-year-old soldier in California. The mountains of the Golden State tumble down to white sands strewn with surf-pounded boulders, creating some of the most picturesque coves in the world. I loved walking its rocky coasts beside a blue-green sea.

One afternoon as I wandered at low tide, I discovered multiple pools of seawater trapped in those rocky enclaves. Sometimes the pools were deep enough to wade knee-deep, and here and there I saw little sea critters scuttling away from my toes. Water-breathers, unaware of their perilous circumstances. They were creatures of the ocean, and now sun-baked sand surrounded their world, the very definition of a desert. Yet there were forces at work beyond their imagination, which would bring back the life-giving sea. A hot star and cold moon danced and tugged at the watery skirts of the earth, which would soon reverse the emptying process. Cool, briny tidewater will flood the beach anew, releasing these tiny prisoners from their shallow grave.

Life is very much like the tidal pools—sometimes a desert, sometimes a deep ocean. As self-aware creatures, humans know the phases of life and see the tides receding. Still it is difficult in the midst of personal crisis to remember the tide will turn, life will bring its refreshing flood when the time is right. The important question about survival of consciousness is probably not answerable on this side of the final tide flow. Until the day comes when life yields to the next reality, we creatures in the tidal pool of life can find stillness and quiet in the space we currently occupy as the great cosmic tide continues its dance of sea, sky, and shore.

Quaker Spirituality: The Silent Meeting

"To sit in silence is to notice how unsilent the world is and how unstill one's body is."[14]

Quakers call themselves the *Society of Friends* and practice peaceful coexistence and respect for diversity as cardinal rules. Grounded in Christianity, the Friends are a model of inclusivity:

> The Quaker faith has deep Christian roots. Many Quakers consider themselves Christians, and some do not. Many Quakers find meaning and value in the teachings of many faiths. Quakers strive to live lives that are guided by a direct encounter with the Divine, more than by teachings about the Divine. Quaker terms for the Holy include God, the Seed, the Light Within, and the Inward Teacher, among others.[15]

Perhaps the most familiar yet least understood element in Quaker spirituality has been its tradition of Silent Meetings. This notoriety is due in part to the popular literature about Quakers, such as Mary Jessamyn West's 1945 novel *The Friendly Persuasion,* made into a motion picture starring Gary Cooper and Dorothy McGuire. The 1956 movie paints Hollywood's portrait of a Quaker Meeting, which lingers in American consciousness as the most common image of silent worship. At one point the young son of the main character leaps up and shouts, "God is love!" He is met with a scowl by an elderly gentleman. Fortunately, the boy's father, played by Cooper, redeems the moment by patting his son on the knee.[16]

Many Quakers continue the silent tradition today, although others participate in corporate worship similar to non-liturgical Protestants, with music, message, and spoken prayer. But the silent meeting is still the spiritual cornerstone of Quakerism. To understand this foundation is to grasp the Quaker theology of prayer. Birkel writes:

> Quaker meeting is simple as it is complex. The community gathers together in a waiting, expectant frame of spirit. Worship is in silence until a participant feels led to share a message with those present. There may

be many, few, or no such messages, which Friends call "vocal ministry." The meeting concludes when the person with responsibility for closing the worship discerns that the time has drawn to an end. In many parts of the Quaker world, worshippers then shake hands with those around them.[17]

Today's silent meetings are usually the traditional Protestant hour-long variety. Early Quaker Meeting Houses had a few special benches up front that faced the opposite direction, toward the congregation. People responsible for opening and closing the meetings sat in these "facing benches," although the common practice today is for the whole congregation to sit in equal rows arranged around an empty square.[18]

The leaders may or may not speak during the meeting, depending on whether they feel guided by the Inner Light. Silence itself is holy to the Friends, understood as providing space for a sacramental encounter with God. J. Brent Bill describes this theologically in *Holy Silence: The Gift of Quaker Spirituality.*

> Silence is where Quakers believe we encounter the real presence of Christ. Since we don't have rites or symbols, or use bread or wine, Jesus comes to us in the peace of the silence ... Silence, when we worship with others, becomes a means of grace. That's because it brings us into God's presence. Worship becomes Eucharistic when we sense God present with our group.[19]

Bill defines *sacrament* as an access port through which the presence and power of God becomes discernible. Silent Meetings attempt to capture the "Inner Light" experiences of the early Quaker leader George Fox, which Fox described as "openings" or messages from God. If sacraments are points in life where the normally invisible Presence and Power of God becomes discernible, Quaker silent prayer qualifies as a genuine sacramental encounter.

> And one day when I had been walking solitarily abroad and was come home, I was taken up in the love of God, so that I could not but admire the greatness of his love. And while I was in that condition it was opened unto me by the eternal light and power, and I therein saw clearly that all was done and to be done in and by Christ ...[20]

In fact, one could argue all of life is a potential sacrament to Quakers, who strive for mindfulness of the Divine Presence in all circumstances. If not every event, certainly the Silent Meeting has Eucharist-like significance.

Quaker silent worship can be simple stillness or active thinking. Birkel writes of the distinction. "Christian prayer has its *apophatic* and *kataphatic* dimensions ... Quakers have used both to centre down."[21] Sometimes worshippers let the quiet space empty their thoughts to prepare the mind and heart for God's infilling (apophatic). The goal is *not* to think but to be open and receptive to God.

Other occasions, Quakers might actively follow a line of thought, or imagine a biblical scene (kataphatic). Ironically, the kataphatic method of creative contemplation, practiced by Quakers at their starkly appointed Meeting Houses, in some ways resembles the system of self-directed guided images developed for those who worship in ornate Roman Catholic churches, the Spiritual Exercises of St. Ignatius Loyola.[22]

Whether apophatic-*passive* or kataphatic-*active*, Quaker worship is a community affair. The Silent Meeting is not simply a group of spiritually-minded people assembled to meditate as separate individuals. Quaker community practice is wholly communal, the mirror opposite of Eastern religions, notably Buddhism:

> Buddhist monks may gather in the meditation hall, but the goal is not a common experience. If a meditator were suddenly to feel that she or he has a message to offer the other meditators in the community, the urge to speak would be judged a distraction or illusion. As a group contemplative practice, Quaker meeting for worship has the group as its focus. In a friends meeting for worship, the goal is not so much achieving individual enlightenment as ministering to the gathered body.[23]

Any event that occurs during the Silent Meeting can spur the worshipper to spiritual contemplation.

> What otherwise would be distractions can be woven into a prayerful frame of mind. A baby's babbling moves one to joy and gratitude for newness of life. A neighbour's coughing inspires a prayer for her health. Gladly received, such sounds lose their potential to distract, so the task is to cultivate a disposition of grateful receptivity.[24]

Quaker Meeting Houses are holy spaces only because of the people in them; the very presence of the worshipping community hallows the grounds. Some great houses of worship—shrines, temples, mosques, and cathedrals of other religious traditions—exude a spiritual atmosphere even when vacant. Visiting an empty, candlelit Catholic church at night can evoke an awesome sense of the Holy. However, the spirituality of a Quaker Meeting House requires bodies at prayer, because the community generates its sacred space. J. Brent Bill describes a Silent Meeting he and his wife attended on a perfect autumn day.

It was a setting dreamed up by the Vermont tourism council—an 1826 era plain, white, clapboard meetinghouse its rectangular steeple-lessness tucked into a clearing halfway up a mountainside. Tombstones dotted the meetinghouse grounds. Sunlight threw the carvings into stark relief ...[25]

Inside were hardwood benches and a black wood stove. No colored glass. No bulletin. No paid preacher. They sat in silence as if anticipating a message from God, which could come from anyone. The immediacy was oddly like waiting on God's gifts to manifest in a Pentecostal service—without the music, preaching, dancing, and hand-clapping. When it happened, it was quiet and calm. The energy in the room changed.

> We became what Quakers call a *gathered meeting*— gathered together and with Jesus. We sensed Him in the electrified air. I felt charged with an awareness of the miraculous—the marrow of my bones hummed in holy recognition of the One who had stood at the dawn of creation and called the world into being. And it did not just happen to me ... Even as I tell you that story, I am struck by the absurdity of trying to write about silence.[26]

J. Brent Bill's encounter with sacred space through the Quaker Silence recalls the words of "I Am There" by James Dillet Freeman:

> I am not strange visions. I am not mysteries.
> Only in absolute stillness, beyond self,
> Can you know Me as I am,
> And then but as a feeling and a faith.
> Yet I am there. Yet I am here. Yet I answer.
> When you need Me, I am there.[27]

Silence and "The Silence"

Meditating quietly is the first step along the road, but authentic experiences in the Silence can seldom be achieved in short prayer periods. I am always amused during Sunday services when clergy announce the congregation will now enter the Silence. What we can accomplish in four or five minutes of quietude is becoming still, but probably not entering the Silence. The Silence is a deep meditation experience in which the individual consciousness grasps the oneness and connectedness of all things. While many writers have agreed with Bill about the futility of writing about the Silence, which soars beyond words, fifth-century Christian mystic Pseudo-Dionysius perhaps came as close as language can get us:

> As far as possible mount up with knowledge into union with the One who is above all being and knowledge; for by freeing thyself completely and unconditionally from thyself and from all things, thou shalt come to the superessential brightness of the divine darkness.[28]

Dionysius insisted that the only way to describe God in human language was by a method known as the *via negativa*. I discussed this problem in my book, *Friends in High Places*:

> Dionysius held that one only speaks meaningfully about God when articulating what the Divine is *not.* God is not limited, not restrained, not personal, etc. Yet, one can say accurately God is good, because Divine Mind is beyond goodness, or God is love, because the Lord is beyond loving-kindness. All statements about God must be affirmed and denied at the same time, because God is far beyond any meager effort at conceptualizing. Everything said about God is symbolic.[29]

However, Dionysius believed we can know God nonverbally by making contact with the Divine Mystery Itself. It was an oddly practical solution in a world that considered philosophy the highest form of knowledge. Dionysius was wise enough to recognize experience trumps logic. Ask anyone in love. For those who have communed with Divine Power—whether throbbing in the Cosmos beyond them, or indwelling deep within their consciousness, or both—any attempt to tell them God is not "out there" or "in here" stands contradicted by personal encounter. I do not need to prove the existence of my lover; to make any attempt would be ludicrous. Love and devotion are not rational—ask any parent who has gently tried to convince a son or daughter that the person they love has serious character flaws that will doom the relationship. As Khalil Gibran said in *The Prophet:*

> You may give them your love but not your thoughts.
> For they have their own thoughts.
> You may house their bodies but not their souls,
> For their souls dwell in the house of tomorrow,
> Which you cannot visit, not even in your dreams.[30]

Parents will try, of course, and children will usually reject parental influences and make their own choices amid the cacophony of life. Surprisingly, the unworthy young toad who is wooing Daddy's princess often turns out to be less amphibian and more prince-like over time. As the old maxim goes: "One of life's greatest mysteries is how the boy who wasn't good enough to marry your daughter can be the father of the smartest grandchild in the world."[31]

Contact with people dispels fears and overcomes obstacles; dialogue among the tribes of humanity can only reveal an essential oneness beneath the accommodations made due to culture and environment. People who get to know each other learn about flaws and strengths in themselves and others, but the process of experiencing another person's ideas, joys, worries, and hopes is in itself a journey into sacred space. When men and women encounter the Divine Mystery, similar dynamics occur. We know and are known; love and experience love. There is no rational way to explain it.

Marcus Bach described this experience-based, intuitive knowing in his book *The Unity Way of Life*, the first Unity book I ever read. Dr. Bach was visiting Unity Village on a hazy Sunday morning, musing about the nature of God. "Objective creature that I am, I was always trying to see all sides of a question."[32] He decided a cup of coffee and some breakfast might help clear his thought, then made the following observation:

> There are religions, like Catholicism for example, in which you partake of no food and enter no discussion until you have partaken of the Eucharist. After the Eucharist, you do not feel like arguing. You simply *believe*. Something has been proved to you, though you might not be able to logically explain the process and proof. You walk away from the communion rail with folded hands, *believing*.[33]

The kind of *believing* Dr. Bach experienced had little to do with *doctrine* or, to use a favorite Unity euphemism, a *teaching*. It was closer to the concept put forth by a scholar with the same first name, Dr. Marcus Borg. Faith is not about accepting the "right" religious teaching; faith means *fidelity* to God through acts of kindness and justice, *trust* in the face of adversity and obstacles to the good, and *vision* of the potential for good in every circumstance. Faith and belief are experienced, not just intellectually accepted. The experience of discovering or creating Sacred Space, internally and externally, provides people with a personalized Mount Sinai, or Bodhi Tree, or Mount of Olives, or Cave near Mecca.

Our ancestors knew Something Greater was at work in their world. Doubtless they could feel it, both inside deep and then in the furious storms breaking overhead. Maybe that was the beginning of the Silence. *Be still and know ... They* experienced *Something Greater*, and came away believing.

Eight Places to Find Your Sacred Space

Below are a series of scenarios. You can create whatever sacred space you want—pagoda temple or Grange Hall, towering basilica or tent in the wilderness. Images of potential meditation spaces begin below. Do not be confined to these examples, but think of the list as a starter kit for lifelong adventures in silent communion with your God.

1. **Walled garden**. There is something about a garden that bolsters the spirit. Look at the ancient imagery. Garden of Eden, Hanging Gardens of Babylon, Zen gardens with rock and waves of sand, Islamic dream of Paradise regained. Flowers everywhere. Red azalea bushes in bloom. White and yellow roses. You may even allow yourself a genetically engineered blue rose of Arabia, thought to be extinct. Wander the brick path through herb patch—dill, oregano, mint—and you'll find the tomato stakes. Tomatoes have a musty, earthy smell, like the wind before a rainstorm. What other edibles will be in your spiritual place? Find a bench. Rest. Drink the scents and colors. Center on the glowing, blossoming, tasty plants surrounding you. Life expresses in such splendid variety. You are life, expressing. Life flows through these plants and through you. The natural order is good, trustworthy. Relax here as long as you like, and trust life.

2. **Patio by the sea.** The sea beckons and soothes. On a stone-paved patio, a table with light refreshments awaits you. Sit awhile. Any tasty treat you want is on the table. When you have sampled the delicious fare, close your eyes and be still. Listen to whispering surf and the *caw-caw* of gulls as they swoop over rolling waves. Perhaps a sea breeze will cool your face. Feel the ocean moving in the distance; the saline content of the ancient sea flows through your bloodstream. Be still. Open your mind. Listen and know the connectedness of all life …

3. **Atop a stone tower.** You stand atop an old stone tower and peer out at the sunrise. This is the edge of the world, the farthest outpost of civilization. Beyond this point there are no cities, no legions marching, no villages with their barrel makers, bakers, and barking dogs. The sun rises over pure wilderness. Where trees have never felt the blows of an ax, meadows have never seen a plow. You are here to celebrate a holy day, appointed by your people to greet the sun over the unknown lands. What do you see in the mist, and how does the scent of an untamed world smell to you? Can you feel peace here, or does the unknown frighten you? Take a long while to walk the stone wall and communion with a pristine land that has never known human footsteps.

4. **Forest meadow.** Walk silently along this path through the forest. Here and there sunlight breaks the canopy and slants into pools of gold among the mosses and ferns. From a distant tree comes the *knock-knock-knock* of a redheaded woodpecker drilling for insects that hide beneath the bark. The occasional spiderweb stretches silver threads across the path and must be ducked under or flicked aside with a quick glance for eight-legged proprietors. Off the path now, into the trees. Leaves of yesteryear linger as brown compost underfoot, working their way into soil. Roots to

avoid and trunks to step around, all the while inhaling the brown sugar scent of an old forest, a living creature of wood and sap that lounges under its high cap of bright green like a pensioner with a day of golf ahead.

Now the tree line evaporates at the edge of a grassy meadow. A big fallen tree presides over the middle of nature's town square, offering a bench. Approaching the tree, you see you are not alone. A great spiritual teacher awaits you. Of course. What else could you expect on such a perfect day? Sit on the log and wait to see what happens. You may ask questions, or wait to hear unsolicited remarks, or simply share the perfect moment. This is, after all, *your* meadow …

5. **Old library.** The brown-robed monk leads you up two flights of winding stairs. Feel the stone steps as you walk. Your guide pushes a huge hardwood door that creaks loudly on its hinges. Suddenly you stand under an inverted u-shaped ceiling, a long, broad chamber. A glance tells you someone spent a lot of money to hire the finest painters and artisans of an earlier time. Cream colored bas-relief neatly frames the murals, which display the typical biblical scenes—Moses at the sea, David facing down Goliath, Jesus teaching the multitudes. The art is not unpleasant, but you did not come here for colors and textures. Your eyes drift to the massive bookshelves solidly braced against heavy stone walls, some offering eight or nine tiers of dusty volumes. The monk assures you this is no ordinary library. It was specially blessed by a great, unknown saint, so that any book you want is available here. Even books you didn't know existed. Do you want to read the autobiography of Jesus, including the complete text of all his sermons? It's here, in your language. Prefer something personal, perhaps a memoir written by a deceased friend

or relative? It's here. Imagine the book, and you will find it here. Past, present, or future; it makes no difference. The monk gestures to the shelves and invites you to browse. What will you find?

6. **Art studio.** You receive an invitation in gold leaf on thick, expensive paper.

> *"Your presence is requested at the Art Studio. Come at your leisure. All supplies provided free of charge.*

You follow the directions and find the sprawling, one-floor building in a warehouse district. Opening the door, you discover the place is empty of humans but stuffed with materials for creating art. Paints and canvas; big sketching pads, charcoal sticks, and pastels; spray guns and wall white space; massive marble blocks and power chisels, plus hand-tapping implements for fine work. And more. Every kind of art is here. There's even a grand piano and a recording set up. More exciting, you discover you suddenly know how to do all these artistic works with great ease. You can carve a statue, write a symphony, or paint a masterpiece. What will you create in your art studio with these new talents rushing upon you?

7. **Desert hilltop at sunset.** Lonely and remote, washed in gold from the setting sun, the hilltop overlooks a deep, dry canyon where clumps of scrub trees cling to ledges and meander downward into the shadows. The sun has not set, but a cool breeze rises from the valley floor with a taste of mesquite and darkness on its breath. Here the only sound is a rustling branch as the wind stirs. Above in the deep blue an eagle turns slowly on warm air currents that rise from the sunbaked rocks. Peaceful. Desolate. A place in the wilderness. Here your animal spirit guide might come and speak to you. Or an angel might appear in a flaming bush.

Or the sun might go down unvexed by the supernatural, giving its permission for the millions of lesser lights to appear. It's your canyon. Populate it with the creatures of your mind, or sit quietly and enjoy the sunset.

8. **House of Worship—Buildings, Grounds, and Gardens.** In the exercise at the end of Chapter 5, you designed a *Temple of the Mind*. Now let's visit your house of worship and explore the grounds. What do you see as you approach? Gardens, trees, animals, people? What does the building look like, and what kind of light illuminates it? Are there special smells, textures, sounds in the air? Is the day hot, warm, cool, or cold? Enter your sanctuary and experience it on a multisensual level. Feel the seat beneath you. Sit or kneel or stand. This is your perfect place to honor the highest ideals you cherish. Let your mind bring you surprises. Be still and know.

Other Possibilities

All eight meditation exercises will not work for everyone. If you want additional opportunities to enhance your devotional or self-awareness practices, an additional resource is Roger Walsh's book *Essential Spirituality*. Walsh, a medical doctor and Ph.D., offers page after page of individual, nonsectarian exercises with clearly written, easy-to-follow directions. The lesson I learned from my Protestant and Catholic soldiers the day we visited that cathedral in Little Switzerland is that any spiritual practice you attempt must be organically right for you. The world is full of good ideas. Surely, you have earned the right to experiment a little to find the spirituality package that works best. Long ago, Buddha said, "You can search throughout the entire universe for someone who is more deserving of your love and affection than you are yourself, and that person is not to be found anywhere. You, yourself, as much as anybody in the entire universe, deserve your love and affection."[34]

Check Your Knowledge

1. Describe the Unity Village *Peace Chapel* and its mirror opposite, which the author calls the *Chapel of Pieces*. What does this example suggest about sacred space in general?
2. Summarize the problem of "monkey mind" for meditation.
3. What are the features of a Quaker Silent Meeting, and how is it a sacrament?
4. What are the differences between *apophatic* and *kataphatic* prayer?
5. How does silent prayer differ from entering "the Silence"?
6. What alternative definitions of *faith* does Marcus Borg offer?

Discussion Starters

1. Do you believe God speaks to you when you are silent?
2. What might have prompted Quakers to reject the high ceremony of the Church of England for silent waiting upon the Lord? Why not value both experiences?
3. If God is beyond human comprehension, what is the purpose of prayer?
4. How much silent prayer can you actually tolerate before becoming fidgety or desperately bored?
5. Where is your sacred space?
6. Imagine Buddha, Jesus, Muhammad, and a few other major religious figures discussing prayer over brunch. What points of agreement and disagreement would they discover? (If you hear nothing but harmony, check your onscreen guide. You've got the wrong channel.)

Suggested Activity:
Find Your Sacred Space

Turn to the eight suggested places and pick one as your Sacred Space. Meditate for 10 minutes, spending quality time in your place.

Alternatively, go to a sacred space of your own creation for the same duration or longer.

If you are in a study group, share your insights when ready.

11

RITES OF POWER, PRESENCE, AND PASSAGE

But you shall worship the Lord, who brought you out of the land of Egypt with great power and with an outstretched arm; you shall bow yourselves to him, and to him you shall sacrifice.

—2 Kings 17:36

Religious practices generally fall under three categories: *rites of power, rites of presence,* and *rites of passage.* Given a few moments reflection, you could probably think of observances that fall outside the three categories—for example, quasi-religious celebrations of national holidays like Thanksgiving or Independence Day. However, anyone capable of a little interpretive footwork could easily shoehorn July Fourth under *rites of passage* (i.e., from autocratic rule of a king to republican democracy under "Nature's God"). Thanksgiving works as a *rite of presence,* in which the community gives thanks for fields and flocks guarded by a Merciful Providence until "all is safely gathered in/'ere the winter storms begin."[1] Acknowledging the arbitrary nature of any classification system, let's work with these broad categories to better understand the need of our species for cycles of ritual and renewal.

Rites of Power

As previously noted, before humans created governmental safety nets and nonprofits launched private food banks,

the fertility of fields, flocks, and families absolutely deter-
mined whether any group would survive. Before the domes-
tication of grain about 10,500 years ago, hunter-gatherers for-
aged roots, nuts, and wild fruit to provide the largest share of
their daily caloric intake. Traveling bands of Homo sapiens
depended on seasonally available plants, which depended
on favorable weather conditions. Lengthy dry spells, flash
floods, or early winters could destroy the largest part of the
food supply. When that happened, people starved.

The threat was so real that our species almost disappeared
70,000 years ago. According to a study published in the prestigious *American Journal of Human Genetics* and reported by
USA Today, drought conditions in East Africa lasting more
than 40,000 years pushed the human race nearly to extinction. A separate study by Stanford University estimates the
total human population shrank to about 2,000 individuals
worldwide due to primordial climate change. To put this figure into perspective, more snow leopards live in the mountains of Asia today than humans on the planet in 70,000 B.C.
Our ancestors would have made the endangered species list.[2]

Small wonder early human religious figures are female
fertility symbols, sometimes called the *Mother Goddess* or
Great Mother. Some feminist archaeologists have suggested
the existence of a multicultural female deity in prehistoric
Europe, the great Mother-Goddess of the last great Ice Age.
Excavators have discovered figurines dating from 20,000–
30,000, "… unmistakable models of women, obese, naked,
with voluminous breasts, prominent stomachs, and large
buttocks and thighs, the most well-known example being the
so-called Venus of Willendorf (Austria)."[3]

However, archaeologist Pamela Russell cautions against
presuming the figures represent a reigning female deity of
fertility. She suggests the small images may have been used

by women to ward off difficulties in childbirth, or carried by men for comfort in the hunt, or played with by children. "Or they may simply have been a protecting figure for a household, as in some Siberian dwellings today."[4] Russell warns against overzealous advocacy of the universal Mother-Goddess, especially if monotheistic theology is anachronistically read into the practice of honoring a female figure. The carved images, she says, may have been protective tokens or ritual implements in sympathetic magic for human fertility.

> While it is probable that our Paleolithic ancestors believed in the supernatural, and that superstition played a part in their daily lives, one must be cautious in assuming their religion bore any resemblance to the monotheistic religions of today. The Great Mother-Goddess of ice-age Europe is a shadowy hypothetical being. She may even be pure fiction.[5]

Even with these caveats in place, the undeniable fact is that humans across a wide range of habitats produced figurines that were in an obvious state of pregnancy, or at least suggestive of vigorous fertility. Such a repetitive practice cannot be dismissed merely as toys or pet rocks. To survive in a world without supermarkets or fertility drugs, the ancients needed healthy children, fruitful harvests of wild plants, and fertile animals. Russell rightly observes that the discovery of so many Great Mother reproductions does not mean there was a universal Mother-Goddess; it does however suggest that fertility played a big part in community religious ritual.

Throughout history reproductive rules played a central role in every culture and religion. No society on earth has ever said, *"Just do whatever you want—play house, with benefits."* When it comes to sexual access and the care for children, social mores always develop. Sometimes the rules of mating, reproduction, and kinship are so unfamiliar that no value system appears to be functioning. Blind spots blur our worldview because of the smudged lenses we bring to the study of human social systems. If we cannot easily understand the way people in world religions today organize themselves around issues of marriage and family, think how disabled we are when trying to reconstruct the value systems of cultures long ago vanished. Sometimes finding parallels among existing communities can help.

Although we cannot know what specific beliefs Paleolithic people held—animatism, animism, or early polytheistic—their worldviews are probably mirrored by surviving tribal cultures in the 21st century. A common organizing principle when studying simpler societies today is to recognize how native peoples merge nature and the supernatural into a single web of life. Indigenous forms of African Traditional Religion carry the ancient sense of intimate connection between earth and spirit world into the 21st century. Father Godfrey Igwebuike Onah, Vice Rector of the Pontifical Urban University in Rome writes:

> All the elements in the material universe are believed to be intimately connected to one another and all of them are connected to God and to the other spiritual beings. Nothing is attributed to chance or necessity. In fact the concept of chance is alien to the traditional Africans. Rather than chance, they talk of unknown invisible causes. But the orderly arrangement of things is attributed to God: day and night, the seasons, the rhythms of life, the varieties and chains of dependence and so on.[6]

Facing the storms of life, ancient men and women created spiritual technologies like they fashioned tools to deal with the tasks of daily living. Common rites of power have included celebrations of thanksgiving for productivity and security; rituals linked with success in the hunt; ceremonies for safety from injury, defeat of enemies, fertility, healing, favorable weather, and protection from malevolent spirits. People have sometimes believed the seasons will not change unless humans perform acts of worship. Others thought the divine required acts of sacrifice, performed by laypeople and priests, to restore or maintain the balance of life. In fact, until the modern era, much of religion could be seen as utilitarian. Planting and harvesting according to ritual patterns; preparing folk medicine through supplication to healing spirits mixed with preparatory directions for herbal remedies. Our ancestors developed complex rituals they believed had the power to influence the flow of events, or to help the community endure the recurrent suffering and disappointments that are a part of life.

Certain ritual acts are difficult to understand, because they involve human suffering, like the self-inflicted torture of Plains Indians Sun Dance. In the most extreme form, Aztec priests in pre-Columbian Mexico immolated thousands of human hearts after cutting them still-beating from the chests of living victims. Without attempting to justify this grotesque practice, it is nevertheless possible to understand what motivated the relentless butchery at Tenochtitlan:

> Aztec priests believed that the death of the sun could be averted if it were fed sufficient human hearts. Each day, the sun fought a battle against the moon and stars, and was victorious. The Aztecs believed they had a key role in helping the sun keep its vitality and force by providing the deity with lifeblood. In order

to provide these enormous amounts of blood, the Aztecs had to resort to wars, in order to gain enough captives whose heart was to feed the sun god. These wars, solely to gain sacrificial victims, were called the "Flower Wars."[7]

The daily jamboree of bloodletting was a ritual of self-preservation for the Aztec. Without human blood, hungry gods like the Feathered Serpent Quetzalcoatl, who was a symbol of the sun, would literally eat the world. Ritual murder became a *rite of power* by which the Aztec staved off destruction one day at a time.

Fortunately, rites of power that were gentler than whole-sale slaughter of captured armies have played a far more prominent role in most civilizations. Nevertheless, most cultures recognized some form of sacrifice as central to religion. First fruits of the harvest in ancient Israel are a good example.

On the same general principle that the firstborn of man and beast belonged to the God of Israel and were to be devoted to Him, the first fruits, including the first grains to ripen each season, were to be brought as an offering to God. Every Israelite who possessed the means of agricultural productivity was under this obligation.[8]

Standard offerings included wheat, barley, grapes, figs, pomegranates, olive oil, and dates. Some produce was occasionally burned at the altar, but usually worshippers gave the sampling of agricultural yield to the priests, who displayed the gifts publicly before receiving it as payment for their Temple service. Donors "recited the confession (Deut. 26:1-11), acknowledging God as the one who redeemed the Israelites from the Egyptian bondage, and expressing gratitude to God who brought them to the Promised Land."[9] Giving of the harvest called upon God to bless and protect fields and farms of Israel, but to receive something more personal—forgiveness of sin—required a blood offering from the flocks. I discussed the multicultural prevalence of the sacrificial system in my book *Jesus 2.1*:

> The idea of being saved by blood comes right out of temple rituals of the ancient world, where sinners paid for an animal offered by a priest to clear the worshippers' record of blood-guilt. Not just Israel but most ancient civilizations shared some variation on this theme, i.e., when a person committed certain acts he incurred a debt of sin, which must be paid in blood. It was as though they believed the laws of karma took effect in an immediate and personal way. Trespass and the Divine Justice demanded retribution, blood for sin. The believer could die or offer something else to die in his place, which was far more appealing.[10]

The practice was so common in Hellenistic cities that people took their animals for ritual slaughter by priests of this or that god rather than unceremoniously butchering livestock privately. Why waste the life of the animal, when its death could coax some god to forgive an offense or provide divine assistance? The rear entrance to pagan temples became butcher shops where the public shopped for lamb, pork, and sometimes beef. This caused a problem for early Christian communities, so that the church at Rome wrote to Paul with the question. "May we eat meat offered to idols?" He replied:

> If I partake with thankfulness, why should I be denounced because of that for which I give thanks? So, whether you eat or drink, or whatever you do, do everything for the glory of God. Give no offense to Jews or to Greeks or to the church of God, just as I

try to please everyone in everything I do, not seeking my own advantage, but that of many, so that they may be saved.[11]

Paul seems to be saying: "Who cares if our people eat meat offered in a meaningless ceremony? Well … okay. If eating food presented to idols confuses people, then don't do it. We want everybody saved before the End, which could be tomorrow!"

Sacrifice is an attempt to keep the individual in harmony with whatever God or gods or Divine Spirit holds power over the vicissitudes of life. For Paul, the One Presence and Power was the God of Israel, and the sacrifice was not an animal's life for the sake of a single worshipper but Jesus' death upon the cross for all humankind. Whether sitting here in the 21st century I agree with his logic or not, the powerful imagery of sacrifice to reconcile heaven and Earth was not something he created out of the blue. It was the cross-cultural definition of worship in most ancient religions.

The Power to Bless/The Power to Curse

Another rite of power involves spoken words rather than ritual offerings. In biblical theology, the power to *bless* is counterbalanced by the power to *curse*, which are essentially the same operation with opposite objectives. Both are prayers, which might surprise some traditional students of the Bible. Blessings invite divine benefits; curses call down afflictions from on high. For a stunning example, look at Deuteronomy 27:11-26. The passage describes a group ritual in which Moses pronounces 12 curses upon those who would violate the Law of God, followed in Chapter 28 with a reiteration of the blessings and curses. Here is a sample:

"Cursed be anyone who makes an idol or casts an image, anything abhorrent to the Lord, the work of an artisan, and sets it up in secret."

All the people shall respond, saying, "Amen!"

"Cursed be anyone who dishonors father or mother."

All the people shall say, "Amen!"

"Cursed be anyone who moves a neighbor's boundary marker."

All the people shall say, "Amen!"

"Cursed be anyone who misleads a blind person on the road."

All the people shall say, "Amen!"[12]

The ceremony most likely originated in Temple ritual from a time much later than Moses, who was probably not a historic individual but a legendary figure. Some biblical passages regard the blessing as bringing forth a living entity, like the birth of a child. Once pronounced, it cannot be taken back. This explains why Esau is so distraught after Jacob impersonates him and "steals" the blessing their nearly blind father, Isaac, was planning for Esau.

> Esau said to his father, "Have you only one blessing, father? Bless me, me also, father!" And Esau lifted up his voice and wept.[13]

The idea that a spoken or written blessing cannot be repealed sounds obsolete in today's litigious society. However, sooner or later most of us will long to take back words spoken in anger or haste and, like Esau, find that thoughts have the power to bless or curse in a way that can be irrevocable. *Blessing space* is another example of a simple rite of power.

In blessing each space we enter, we orchestrate a subtle energy shift that affects not only our own experiences in that space but also the experiences of the individuals who will enter the space after us. While we may never see the effects our blessing has had, we can take comfort in the fact that we have provided grace for those that follow after us.[14]

Some people bless public spaces in preparation for events. When I taught middle school, I performed this rite surreptitiously in my empty classroom at the beginning of every school year. Nothing formal, certainly nothing remotely liturgical in the traditional sense of the word, my simple process was to envision the desks in the classroom filled with energetic adolescents eager to learn. If you have taught grade level, you are probably smirking with jaded wisdom, knowing the quiet energy for learning that dominates the first few days of every school year quickly morphs into rowdy resistance as students settle into their daily routine. In my empty classroom I tried to see the world through their eyes, and I blessed them on their journey through the alternating flashes of boredom and excitement that is life for a 13-year-old. I called upon the Power of God to walk with them; I saw them as whole, healthy, and full of divine potential. I blessed the classroom itself and dedicated the space in service to the world of tomorrow, which the kids coming my way would one day inherit. Then I closed with James Dillet Freeman's "Prayer for Protection" and went back to my lesson plans.

Simple acts of blessing are something you can do for anyone. Resources are readily available online and in spiritual publications. For example, here is a delightful blessing from the Cherokee tradition:

May the Warm Winds of Heaven
Blow softly upon your house.
May the Great Spirit
Bless all who enter there.
May your Moccasins
Make happy tracks
in many snows,
and may the Rainbow
Always touch your shoulder.[15]

Long ago Roman Catholics originated a kindhearted practice that is becoming an annual event in many churches, the
pet blessing. The custom goes back at least 800 years to the
time of St. Francis. Medieval Church documents authorize
ceremonies to bless birds, bees, horses, oxen, and other beasts
of burden. At today's pet blessings, owners bring a wide
variety of creatures to be prayed over by priests, ministers,
and rabbis. Serving as senior minister of Unity churches, I
have blessed dogs, cats, rabbits, gerbils, ferrets, fish, turtles,
all sorts of birds, a huge spider (he stayed in his box!), large
horses and Shetland ponies, a potbellied Vietnamese pig, and
stuffed animal surrogates. Although it stretches the *pet* category, when I was an Army Chaplain a soldier insisted on a
blessing for his Jeep. (My colleagues in ministry reading this
are probably raising an eyebrow, thinking, *Oh, yeah? Lemme
tell you about the menagerie I've blessed ...)*

Pet blessings usually occur in October, since the Feast Day
of St. Francis of Assisi falls on October 4, although the ceremony is also held in January at the Feast of St. Anthony,
patron saint of animals.[16] Gathering to bless animals has
become an increasingly popular observance that goes beyond
its Franciscan origins. For example, in Mumbai, India, a pet
blessing at a Catholic church recently became a multifaith,
multispecies celebration.

Thirty dogs of different breeds, four Persian cats, fish from six aquariums, six cages with love birds, eight cages of parrots, one turtle and one rabbit were given the annual special blessing for pets. "With these prayers, we call upon God, the creator of the universe, to protect all his creatures, man's faithful friends," said Fr. Joseph D'Souza, who conducted the service. In addition to the animals, their respective owners, Hindu, Parsees, and Christians, were also blessed on Sunday in the Church of Saint Ignatius in Mumbai.[17]

The pet blessing qualifies as a rite of power because the ritual calls upon the Divine, or the Universe at large, to shield an animal from harm and give it a happy life. In all these apparently disconnected rituals—gruesome Aztec slaughter to gentle prayer over Suzy's kitten—the consistent factor is a desire to establish, reestablish, or maintain the harmonious balance of life. Rites of power are efforts to affect the events of everyday life and produce a favorable result. They differ from acts of magic because worshippers are not manipulating impersonal forces of the Cosmos into doing their bidding (magic) but attempting to coax the divine to provide assistance or aligning themselves with the will of the divine as events unfold (religion).

The notion that a believer must persuade God to render a blessing is foreign to some people who look to a scientific model of how the Universe operates. Yet billions of religionists worldwide supplicate unto the Divine, using language that suggests it is possible to convince God what His next step should be. A generation ago, rock star Jim Morrison of the Doors spoke these lyrics:

When I was back there in
Seminary school

There was a person there
Who put forth the proposition
That you can petition the Lord
With prayer
Petition the Lord with prayer
Petition the Lord with prayer

You cannot petition the Lord
With prayer![18]

The lyrics are fictional—Morrison never attended seminary—but he captured the frustration of mainstream Christian theology in those lines. Can we "petition the Lord with prayer"? If so, why did God ignore all the pleas that rose to "Him" during the World Wars and regional conflicts of the 20th century? If God ignores prayer, how powerful are the most powerful rites of power? Nothing will convince the faithful to stop filing the petitions; perhaps the very act of asking is another way of placing oneself in the heart of the Divine.

The Public Broadcasting System motion picture *God on Trial*, written by Frank Cottrell Boyce, is based on a true story from World War II. A group of Jews are grimly awaiting their fate at Auschwitz, the infamous Nazi death camp. Guards will soon arrive to cull those who will march into the gas chambers today. The prisoners decide to pass the time by holding a mock trial, naming God as the defendant. Arguments fly back and forth—about the inscrutability of the Divine Will, countered by questions about why God allows bad things to happen to the people He allegedly loves. After a powerful debate, the inmates convict God on all charges. Then they hear the camp guards coming. Someone says, "What do we do now?" And one of the chief spokesmen against God's cause says, "Now we pray."[19]

Rites of power put believers in touch with a Reality that transcends, perhaps even defies, everyday experience. Whether an animist kneeling by a swift river in homage to its ruling spirit to prevent floods, a Shinto priest invoking the goddess Amaterasu for fertility in the upcoming rice harvest, or a Jewish woman lighting the Shabbat candles—rites of power align practitioners with something greater than themselves and invoke the strength of that spiritual force in everyday life.

Rites of Presence

Religious practices need not always attempt to accomplish anything specific. Rites of Presence acknowledge what my friend and colleague Robert Brumet calls a "Greater Reality."[20] Sometimes prayer, ritual, or meditation bring increased awareness of the Divine Presence, whether understood as communion with indiscriminate spirit-power, hailing a delegate from a pantheon of gods, kneeling before the inscrutable One God of monotheism, or giving thanks to God as the Oneness containing the Cosmos and empowering everything to exist as in monistic panentheism. Rev. Kelli Isola writes:

> Prayer is one of the most powerful practices we have for creating beauty in this life. Prayer is a consciousness for co-creating a world that works for all. For me, it's less about the specific practice and more about the experience you have. If it opens you to ever-increasing connection with life, with each other, with our Higher self, then it is a living prayer. Our pains and suffering in life become softened by this opening, this living prayer, and healing leads us home to the divinity within our human experiences.[21]

Rites of presence are often closely related to holy ground, discussed in Chapter 10. Sacred groves, shrines, meditation gardens, peace parks, and houses of worship can provide meeting places for the individual and whatever Greater Reality appears.

> Everyday things like bread, water, oil, and wine can be made holy—consecrated, to use the technical term. Even an ancient method of capital punishment, like crucifixion, can become an occasion of transforming grace in the eyes of a Christian. Buddhism, on the other hand, teaches that all things are sacred, while Hinduism and Islam each represent contrasting middle grounds with respect to what is sacred.[22]

As we have come to expect during this study, various traditions have designed fascinating rites of presence to honor the sacred in their midst. Casual visitors can encounter various rites of presence simply by visiting any church, mosque, synagogue, or temple. Almost all houses of worship have public areas where people can quietly feel the Divine Presence around them. Meditation rooms, side chapels, pews, kneelers, mats on the floor, prayer rugs oriented to Mecca, and quiet gardens within the sacred building offer places where visitors can attune themselves to the Infinite.

Roman Catholics go one step further and provide a focal point for God's location in the world by the practice of the *Reserved Sacrament*. After its consecration during Mass, the leftover hosts (wafers) are placed in a metal box near the altar. A special light is lit to indicate the presence of the Reserved Sacrament, which according to Catholic doctrine has now been transubstantiated into the body of Jesus Christ. Trinitarian theology says that Jesus is divine in a unique way. Therefore, any time believers visit a church where the host is held in reserve, they can venerate the host as a localized expression of the real presence of God.[23]

Arguably, rites of presence are *sacramental encounters* with the divine, regardless of the religion professed by worshippers. To understand this concept requires a brief look at sacramental theology from a cross-cultural perspective.

What is a Sacrament?

The word *sacrament* has fallen on hard times in some Christian traditions, much to the impoverishment of the people. In his weekly online column, former Episcopal Bishop of Newark John Shelby Spong wrote the following about my home denomination:

> "Unity is just now beginning to deal with issues of biblical scholarship and it has not yet begun to look at the meaning of the sacraments. Both of those things will, I believe, come with time. My sense is that Unity often reaches those who have been hurt by or wounded in traditional Christian churches, so I am grateful for the ministry they do for all of us. They offer love and healing with no strings attached."[24]

The conventional definition of a Christian sacrament was given in the fifth century by Saint Augustine: "An outward and visible sign of an inward and invisible grace."[25] In other words, something in the outer connects with something deep inside us. Seven sacraments were eventually recognized by the Catholic Church: *Baptism*, the *Eucharist* (Lord's Supper), *Confirmation, Holy Orders* (Ordination), *Penance* (also called Confession or Reconciliation), *Marriage*, and *Anointing the Sick* (previously called the *Last Rites*). Church teaching held that the sacraments were conduits through which the grace of God flowed to the people.

Augustine pushed their indispensability even further. "Without Baptism and participation in the Table of the Lord," he wrote, "it is impossible for any man to attain either to the kingdom of God or to salvation and life eternal."[26] St. Ignatius of Antioch, fourth-century Bishop and martyr, famously called the Eucharist "the medicine of immortality, and the antidote to prevent us from dying but which causes that we should live forever in Jesus Christ."[27]

In later centuries Popes would bring down kings and rulers by imposing the *Interdict* on whole regions. The most serious form of Church discipline available to papal authorities, the Interdict closed all churches and barred anyone from receiving the sacraments until the civil authorities complied with Church decrees. No baptisms, weddings, funerals, confession/absolution of sin, or dispensation of the Eucharist. If the sacraments were absolutely necessary for "salvation and eternal life," shutting off the flow placed a powerful tool in the Pope's hand to force compliance.

More recent, the mystical qualities of a sacrament have become increasingly more important in Christian thought than its power to springboard souls to heaven. Some Protestant and Catholic thinkers want an even broader definition. Quakers, as we have seen, consider the Silent Meeting a sacramental experience. German-born theologian Paul Tillich finds sacraments dispersed throughout the physical universe.

> Christ is present in everything, in stone and fire and tree, but for us he is present only when he speaks to us. But he can speak to us through everything … In a Lutheran service during the Sundays in spring, you always find a tremendous amount of flowers and things of nature brought into the church, because of this symbol of the participation of the body of Christ in the world.[28]

Early Christian translators made a serious mistake. The Greek word indicating the encounter between individuals and God, *mysterion,* was translated into a Latin term, *sacramentum,* which had overtones of civic duty or military oaths of allegiance. Even nonlinguists can see the intent flowing from the Greek root word. Authentic experiences of God are not acts of dutiful service but mysterious, luminous theophanies.

Is a sacrament a ceremony or an encounter with Ultimate Reality? In the Hebrew Scriptures, young Samuel worked with the priest Eli, but God called to the boy rather than the veteran servant who served the altar. Was it because Eli had become so wrapped up in daily religious duties he lost the ability to feel the Divine Presence? Some say ritual cannot be the conduit for authentic encounters with the divine, but others have found the exact opposite: God, however understood, comes to our consciousness expressly through established observances. Offerings were made at the Temple daily, which brought the Lord into sacramental contact with worshippers.

Along similar lines as the Hebraic theology of Presence, Roman Catholics have adamantly defended their Sacrament of the Eucharist, and called the Lord's Supper or Holy Communion by other Christian traditions, as indispensable to their spiritual lives. Catholics believe the priest is doing far more than commemorating the Last Supper when he consecrates the host and cup; they see the Sacrament as a genuine encounter between communicants and the Divine. When a non-Catholic female writer commented at dinner that the Eucharist was a good symbol of God in the world, Catholic author Flannery O'Connor described her reply in a letter written in 1955:

"Well, if it's a symbol, to hell with it. That was all the defense I was capable of but I realize now that this is all I will ever be able to say about it, outside of a story, except that it is the center of existence for me; all the rest of life is expendable."[29]

What else could she be describing as "the center of existence" but a direct connection with God? In my book *Glimpses of Truth*, I suggested a *Sacrament* can be understood as *any occasion when God's normally mysterious, unknowable Presence breaks through and makes itself known to seeking persons.* This definition hops most religio-cultural fences, because the yearning for some kind of reverent interaction with the power of the Universe can be found everywhere. Sometimes an opportunity to encounter the Divine Presence is so ordinary that people walk right by without noticing, as the young Paramhansa Yogananda discovered while on a spiritual pilgrimage in his native India.

Yogananda requested permission of his guru, to leave the ashram temporarily on a spiritual quest. His goal would be to reach the Himalayas and "in unbroken solitude to achieve continuous divine communion." Along the way he planned to confer with Ram Gopal Babu, known as the Sleepless Saint. His master acquiesced after noting that many people "live in the Himalayas, yet possess no God perception."[30] Ignoring the deep implications of this wise remark, Yogananda took leave to fulfill his long-sought journey to the sacred mountains.

An early stop on the journey found him in Tarakeswar, where he entered a famous shrine that housed an altar made of a single, round stone. He reflected on the curved rock, which Hindus venerate for its healing power like Catholics do their sanctuary at Lourdes, France. Although others were

praying to the miracle-working boulder, Yogananda refused
to venerate any physical object.

> My own mood at the moment was so austere that I
> felt disinclined to bow before the stone symbol. God
> should be sought, I reflected, only within the soul.
> I left the temple without genuflection and walked
> briskly toward the outlying village of Ranbajpur.[31]

After a long series of poor directions given by well-mean-
ing but confused locals, the yogi in training was plodding
across a string of endless rice paddies in the burning afternoon heat when a man approached in the distance. Yogananda soon discovered the traveler was looking for him; it
was the Sleepless Saint, Ram Gopal Babu. He shook a finger
in the young man's face and chided Yogananda for attempting to pounce on him unannounced. Of course, in those days
of limited communications before World War I, the holy man
in rural India had no way to know a pilgrim was looking for
him. But if you accept Yogananda's testimony, that kind of
clairvoyance happened all the time in deeply spiritual India.
What happened next is so profound it needs to be reproduced verbatim. The Sleepless Saint initiates a new line of
conversation:

> "Tell me, where do you think God is?"
> "Why, he is within me and everywhere." I doubtless
> looked as bewildered as I felt.
> "All-pervading, eh?" The saint chuckled. "Then
> why, young sir, did you fail to bow down before
> the Infinite in the stone symbol at the Tarakeswar
> temple yesterday?"[32]

Ram Gopal Babu said that, far from limiting the divine to
inner communion, the act of discovering God within allows

us to find God everywhere. He sent Yogananda back to study under his Great Teacher with an admonition, "Mountains cannot be your guru."[33] Although he probably would not have used Christian terminology, the Sleepless Saint opened the aspiring yogi to the possibility that existence itself is a sacramental encounter with the divine. Yogananda discovered everyday life can be a rite of presence depending on your consciousness.

Rites of Passage

Everyone who approaches this study brings a well-polished set of cultural lenses through which to view each rite of passage. It is unlikely that Americans and Europeans will think of rituals of pain and endurance for the adolescent seeking adult status, or consider what kind of bride-price is appropriate to add a second or third wife to the household. As we have said before, cultures solve their equations differently, but all functional social systems provide for the health/ safety, economic well-being, and reproductive capacity of the group. Throughout history people have paused to observe the milestones along their brief journey. Yet Western civilization has moved steadily away from marking the rhythms of life with individual and community observances. Some celebrations persist, often trivialized by brightly wrapped gifts and light refreshments, but gift certificates and frosted layer cake lack the power to move the human soul. In their book *Rites of Passage: Celebrating Life's Changes*, Kathleen Wall and Gary Ferguson write:

> Our society's lack of meaningful ritual, coupled with this era of continuous and accelerating change, has altered issues of youth, marriage, childbearing, middle age, and retirement beyond what anyone would have believed possible a mere decade ago.[34]

Wall and Ferguson call for new rituals for individual and group celebration of the deep moments in life. Beginning with that simple concept, we can see how an outpouring of opportunities might present themselves: Commemorations of birth, adolescence, adulthood, community acknowledgement of increase or decrease in social obligations, attaining higher skill levels, betrothal, marriage, divorce, assumption of new roles in leadership, celebration of heroism or condemnation/punishment for criminal acts, reaching old age, special wisdom status, death, bereavement, and other events spiritualized by local practice.

For the purposes of brevity, we will take a quick look at two categories of common observances: *rites of birth* and *rites of adulthood*. They are by no means meant to be exhaustive but to sample the deep need humanity has to mark the phases of life. Let's begin with welcoming rituals for children.

Rites of Birth

Every culture celebrates the arrival of new babies, who represent the continuation of group existence and its hope for a better future. Muslim parents try to make the Call to Prayer (*God is great, there is no God but God. Muhammad is the messenger of God. Come to prayer!*) the first words a baby hears, whispered in a newborn's right ear by the father. Muslim parents want their child's first taste to be sweet, so they will chew a piece of date and rub the nectar on the baby's gums. Islam shares one newborn tradition with Hinduism; both religions shave their baby's head on the seventh day to show the child is a servant of God.

The BBC website on religions reports: "Although Hindus may take the baby's hair to India and scatter it in the holy river Ganges, Muslims weigh it and give the equivalent weight in silver to charity." There are other rituals related to birth, such as circumcision on the seventh day and the *aqe-eqah*, ritual slaughter of a lamb.[35]

Note the religious dimension to every aspect of newborn rites of passage. When I was a young U.S. Army serviceman stationed in Germany in the 1960s, an Arab couple befriended me and invited me to their home. The place was small but comfortable, and they had a newborn son whose crib took up a corner of the living room. Both Mother and Father continually leaned over the crib as they passed by to say, *"Allah, Allah, Allah, Allah!"* to him. They wanted to be sure the word for *God* was the first sound he would make.

I learned two interesting points during that visit. First, how important it was for this young couple to teach their faith to the next generation. Second, the word *Allah* does not refer to some foreign Islamic deity, because this baby's mother and father were not Muslims but Syrian Arab Christians. The word for *God* in Arabic-speaking Christian churches is *Allah*, the same name by which their Muslim neighbors call upon the Divine Presence.

Rites of Adulthood

Cultures often develop formal ways to recognize passage from childhood to full membership in the community. Actually, the word *childhood* can be misleading when looking at the history of human civilization.

> Philippe Ariès (1962) was one of the first to suggest that childhood is a modern discovery. He argued that in medieval times children, once past infancy, were regarded as miniature adults; they dressed like adults and shared adult's work and leisure. Children were not assumed to have needs distinct from those of adults, nor were they shielded from any aspects of adult life. Knowledge of sexual relations was not

considered harmful to them and public executions were a spectacle attended by people of all ages.[36]

Some scholars argue that while Ariès is generally correct, historical evidence suggests children were treated somewhat different, if only because they could not keep up with the grueling pace of daily peasant labor.[37] But until modern times most societies believed humans moved from infancy directly to full membership in society. Death penalties inflicted on children are grim reminders that no provisions existed for special treatment of youthful offenders. Rites of adulthood sometimes mitigated this severity, since tribal societies expected more of its grown-ups than those still lingering in their mother's care.

Rites of adulthood have included well-known events like the Jewish Bar Mitzvah (*"son of the commandment"*) for young men, more recent, also Bat Mitzvah (*"daughter of the commandment"*), to welcome young people to the fellowship of the Covenant with God. Unlike the Christian sacrament of Confirmation with its First Communion, the Bar and Bat Mitzvah ceremonies are not required for membership in the Jewish community. In fact, with or without the ceremony, all Jewish boys become Bar Mitzvah automatically at age 13; girls are Bat Mitzvah at 12.[38] The fact that the Bar and Bat Mitzvah rituals are not required, yet popular, suggests they are satisfying the Jewish community's need for a rite of passage into adulthood.

Among the Christian nations of Latin America, a ceremony called *quinceañera* marks a girl's passage from childhood to adolescence at her 15th birthday. The U.S. Conference of Catholic Bishops calls the celebration "a sort of bat mitzvah and debutante ball combo."[39] Quinceañera "expresses thanksgiving to God for the gift of life" and "asks for a blessing from God for the years ahead." A form of the ritual has been officially approved by the Church for inclusion in the Mass.[40]

Not every rite of adulthood is as charming as those described above. Some cultures require rituals of physical deprivation to demonstrate endurance; management of pain, fear of death, or injury to show courage; or ingestion of drugs and other intoxicants to induce visions. Occasionally, the procedure is lengthy but not necessarily painful. For example, the *Festa das Mocas Novas* is a ritual of separation for young women of the Tukuna people in the Northwest Amazon. Seclusion begins at the onset of menstruation and lasts four to 12 weeks. This initiation into womanhood requires girls to enter a small chamber built within the family dwelling to protect them from demons called the *Noo*. The rite of separation ends with family and community all-night dancing, after which the initiate throws a fire brand at the Noo, which breaks their power and releases the Tukuna girl safely into womanhood.[41]

In the United States today, high school graduation marks the boundary between childhood and full adult status. Most young Americans graduate at 18, the age at which they become emancipated from the control of their parents. Graduating seniors gain the right to vote, join the military service, and marry without parental approval about the same time they walk in cap and gown to receive their diplomas.

The religious aspect of a graduation ceremony is obvious. Although it is not officially a service of worship, high school graduation is arguably an outgrowth of American civil religion, like Independence Day, Thanksgiving, or Memorial Day. Graduation ceremonies usually include a musical prelude, processional march (invariably featuring "Pomp and Circumstance"), congregational singing (the school song and appropriate hymns to *Alma Mater*), inspirational readings, testimonials ("Valedictorian" address), an exhortation to greatness by a wisdom speaker (sermon?), altar calls (receiving the diploma), and recessional.

The important takeaway from this discussion is that people need rituals to mark the high and low points of life— joyful weddings to tearful tragedies. Individuals and communities have the power to create new rites of passage that celebrate the mileposts along their journey through the mystery and terror and joy that is life on this planet.

Check Your Knowledge

1. Describe *Rites of Power,* giving several examples. Do the same with *Rites of Presence* and *Rites of Passage.*
2. Why has fertility been such an important religious theme since primordial times?
3. Explain how *curses* and *blessings* are closely related in the Bible.
4. Unpack the definition of a *sacrament* given in this chapter.
5. What is the "Reserved Sacrament" in Roman Catholic practice? Which of the three rites does this offer?
6. Describe Paramhansa Yogananda's experience with the Sleepless Saint. What did this teach the Aspiring yogi about where God is found?

Discussion Starters

1. The late rock star Jim Morrison shouted, *"You cannot petition the Lord with prayer!"* Do you agree?
2. What Rites of Passage have you attended in your life?
3. Bishop John Shelby Spong believes many progressive religious groups, like Unity, have "not yet begun to look at the meaning of the sacraments." What do you think?
4. Why do people celebrate passages in life with ritual? What are the milestones in life you have observed with some sort of ceremony? (Yes, blowing out the candles counts.)
5. How pervasive is ritual in your world? List and discuss some of the public rituals you have attended. Examples might include Independence Day fireworks shows, political rallies, lighting of the community Christmas tree, Halloween trick or treating (think about it), and others.
6. If you could eliminate one holiday or holy day from the calendar, which one would it be, and why? (Don't say "Birthdays"—that's cheating!)

Suggested Activity

Note: This can be done as an individual or group activity, or as a meditation exercise.

Create a New Rite of Power, Presence, or Passage.

Think of an event in your life others may have experienced in their lives yet is currently not commemorated in ritual. How would you celebrate this experience? Does it call for a Rite of Power, Rite of Presence, or Rite of Passage? Or could it be some combination of the above—Power and Passage, or Presence and Power? Specify what materials, props, settings, liturgical tools (music, readings, etc.) you will need to create a genuine spiritual observance. Don't piggyback on existing holidays or established rituals. Find new thoughts and bring them into celebration. Design your new rite for individuals, groups, or both.

As before, if you are in a study group, you may choose to work separately or in small groups. Match notes when complete.

PART
FOUR

MASTERING THE RHYTHMS OF LIFE

Getting to the Still Center

First you must dance
in the language of prayer.
You must use your entire body
including your knees.

You must lift your arms
and let them open your spirit.
You let your mind float
in the vocabulary of wordlessness.

You must learn to light your way
by the flame within the flame—
the beacon that blazes like a rose
surrounded by darkness.

You must empty yourself
of everything but silence, peel
away the garments of doubt
until you're naked as a stone.

You must practice silence
of even the eyes. You must turn
your palms upward, lift them
like empty plates—and wait.

You must learn to listen with even
your toes to what you've been told
simply isn't there. Only then,
will you hear it call your name.

—Fredrick Zydek[1]

12

DECLARATIVE PRAYER

There is one Supreme Being, the Eternal Reality, the Creator, without fear and devoid of enmity, immortal, never incarnated, self-existent, known by grace through the Guru. The Eternal One, from the beginning, through all time, present now, the Everlasting Reality.[2]

—Mul Mantra, Sikh Morning Prayer

Declarative statements on spiritual matters—e.g., proclamations about the nature of the Divine; Ultimate Reality; humanity's potential and eternal destiny—pepper the religious literature and daily practices of all religions. The reading above, quoted from Sikhism's *Mul Mantra*, presents an example of declarative prayer from a radically monotheistic theology. Judaism, Christianity, Islam, and Baha'i offer similar pronouncements about the human relationship to the Supreme Being. For example, Baha'is recite the "Remover of Difficulties" when facing challenges or danger.

> Is there any Remover of difficulties save God? Say: Praised be God! He is God! All are his servants, and all abide by his bidding![3]

Declarative prayer is also found in religious traditions without a solitary Creator-God. The following "Meditation of Sri Krishna" is from polytheistic Hinduism:

> I know not any other Reality than the lotus-eyed
> Krishna with hands adorned with flute, looking like
> a heavy-laden cloud in lustre, wearing a yellow silk
> garment, with His lower lip like a ruddy bimba fruit,
> and with face shining like the full moon.[4]

All declarative prayers share a basic engineering platform; they are statements of perceived spiritual truth announced in the Presence of the numinous. The grammatical form of this announcement may actually be *interrogatory* or *imperative*, even though the prayer practitioner is neither asking a question nor ordering God to do this or that. Here are two examples from the Hebrew Bible, one interrogatory and the other imperative:

> When I look at your heavens, the work of your
> fingers,
> the moon and the stars that you have established;
> what are human beings that you are mindful of
> them, mortals that you care for them?[5]

> Summon your might, O God;
> show your strength, O God,
> as you have done for us before.[6]

Declarative prayer is ordinarily not used in confession or supplication, which usually requires addressing the Divine Power directly. Although declarative prayer muses, invokes, proclaims, laments, and celebrates, its practitioners are essentially speaking to themselves in the Presence of the Divine. The apparent minimal goals of declarative prayer include comfort and self-assurance, plus a sense of connection to Something beyond themselves by a testimonial of fidelity despite appearances to the contrary. However, stakeholders frequently expect concrete results in the world as well. The Judeo-Christian Bible and the Quran overflow with declarative verses about the world-shattering power of their solitary, Abrahamic God.

Like the library full of doors mentioned in Chapter 1, there are too many examples of declarative prayer in world religious literature to attempt a comprehensive study. Therefore, this chapter will briefly survey a nonsectarian, declarative technique used across the religious spectrum, *affirmative prayer*. Our study will focus on the variation of affirmative prayer found most prevalently in the Metaphysical Christian tradition, specifically the syncretistic movement known as Unity. We have already examined some of these concepts. However, when dealing with the vast subject of how humanity meets its spiritual needs, there are always depths and heights yet to explore. Because this is a journey of reconnaissance and reflection, we shall continue to raise critical issues and ask tough, appreciative questions along the way.

In that spirit, let's start with a quick background check on the Unity movement.

Background Check

Metaphysical Christianity and its kissing cousin, the New Thought movement, emerged as a hybrid of 19th-century Transcendentalism, New England Unitarianism and Universalism, and the work of early practitioners in the "Christian sciences." Ralph Waldo Emerson and other 19th-century progressives provided the theology; Phineas Parkhurst Quimby, Warren Felt Evans, Mary Baker Eddy, and Emma Curtis Hopkins applied Transcendentalist theory to spiritual healing, prosperity teaching, and God-consciousness. The migration away from traditional theology toward pragmatic applications of the *God-within* concept came to be called *New Thought*. Its theology was built upon trust in the *imago Dei*. New Thought teachers took seriously, some would say literally, the Genesis model of humanity as made in the image and likeness of God and paired this concept with the definition of God in John's Gospel:

> Then God said, "Let us make humankind in our image, according to our likeness (Genesis 1:26)."[7]

> (And Jesus said) "But the hour is coming, and is now here, when the true worshippers will worship the Father in spirit and truth, for the Father seeks such as these to worship him. God is spirit, and those who worship him must worship in spirit and truth (John 4:24)."[8]

Flexibility and openness propelled New Thought to radical universalism. No one was outside God's kingdom, even though some people refused to avail themselves of its blessings. Applications of practical principles based on the New Thought Christian perspective—whether discovered anew or recovered from the ancient faiths—required a fresh, breathtaking understanding of the untapped potential in prayer, which flowed from the premise that God dwells within. The New Thought worldview provided the human family with a new way to find common holy ground (i.e., the spark of divinity we share with every sentient being).

Charles and Myrtle Fillmore, Unity founders, believed this new insight was applicable and adaptable in all religious traditions, so they strove mightily to avoid setting up a denomination. The Fillmores held study and prayer meetings Sunday afternoons and specifically encouraged people to continue attending morning worship services in the Kansas City area. Eventually, the afternoon study group became the central religious experience of the week and members demanded a Sunday morning option.

Echoes of the original reluctance to establish a new "church" can be heard occasionally in Unity publications, which sometimes still attempt to claim a *nondenominational* label. For example, a Midwestern Unity Church describes itself as "a nondenominational, interfaith community."[9] This tendency to use the term *nondenominational* is surprisingly resilient, even though published by a movement with ordained ministers, licensed teachers, local spiritual leaders, seminary students, ministers' organizations, hymnals, churches, and worldwide headquarters.

One can only speculate that the toxicity of religious discord in Western culture has driven open-minded people to call themselves *nondenominational*, even while belonging to an established Protestant Christian denomination like Unity. Perhaps a better word picture can liberate Unity from this contradiction. Mr. Fillmore called the movement *Practical Christianity*. While claiming his Christian heritage, Fillmore read broadly in other traditions, because he believed truth was not the private property of any religion. Unity was built on Fillmore's Christian universalism, a concept I have described elsewhere as *"Culturally Christian, Spiritually Unlimited."*[10] Other candidates for a summary term might be *Inclusive Christianity*, *Metaphysical Christianity*, or *Progressive Christianity*.

Early in their work, Unity founders Charles and Myrtle Fillmore, who had studied with Eddy and Hopkins, established an ongoing service for anyone who requested prayer. Begun modestly in 1890, the Fillmores quickly renamed this soon-to-be worldwide prayer ministry the following year.

Silent Unity began as The Society of Silent Help when Myrtle Fillmore urged readers of *Modern Thought* (magazine) to "meet in silent soul communion every night at ten o'clock all those who are in trouble, sickness, or poverty, and who sincerely desire the help of the good Father."[11]

From a few isolated individuals in the Kansas City area who paused in their homes each night at 10 p.m. Central Time to join in distant prayer, Silent Unity® has grown to a world-embracing, 24/7 ministry that receives 2 million telephone, mail, and Internet prayer requests per year. Callers reach an operator who answers: "Silent Unity. How may we pray with you?" People from every religion on earth have called this nonsectarian prayer ministry for comfort, celebration, and consolation. (1-800-NOW-PRAY/1-800-669-7729; outside USA: 01-816-969-2000)[12]

Affirmative Prayer

Silent Unity will pray with anyone; its protocols guide Telephone Prayer Associates to language that addresses the needs of the caller. The central concept behind Silent Unity's method is called *affirmative prayer*.

> To affirm is to state positively; to pray is to speak to God. When we are using affirmative prayer, we are using positive statements of Truth and thanksgiving to speak to God.[13]

The technique works whether praying to God in the Cosmos or the Divine-Indwelling, both of which are widely practiced in Unity today.

> *Daily Word*®, Silent Unity's magazine, begins each day's message with an affirmative statement. These affirmations can easily be used as prayers that establish a positive mind-set. For example, a *Daily Word* affirmation reads: *The ever-present life of God heals my body and renews my soul*. To personalize it for our

prayers, we can say, "Dear God, thank You for healing my body and renewing my soul."[14]

Rather than attempting to *"petition the Lord with prayer,"*[15]
which is telling God what Omnipotent Mind should already
know, affirmative prayer reminds us of what God already
knows.

If, for example, one were to pray traditionally, one might
say: "Please God, help me find a job." By contrast, an affirmative prayer might be: "I am now guided to my right and perfect employment." Affirmative prayer reflects the certainty
that we are each being led to our highest good, despite any
temporary appearances.[16]

There is nothing particularly new about prayer built on
declarative statements. In fact, one of the oldest recorded
prayers uses a combination of negation and affirmation. The
Egyptian Book of the Dead contains a "Negative Confession" of
42 sins of which the dying person proclaimed his innocence
before passing beyond this life.

> I have not blasphemed a god,
> I have not robbed the poor.
> I have not done what the god abhors,
> I have not maligned a servant to his master.
> I have not caused pain,
> I have not caused tears.
> I have not killed,
> I have not ordered to kill,
> I have not made anyone suffer.
> I have not damaged the offerings in the temples,
> I have not depleted the loaves of the gods,
> I have not stolen the cakes of the dead ...
> I have not added to the weight of the balance,
> I have not falsified the plummet of the scales.
> I have not taken milk from the mouth of children,

I have not deprived cattle of their pasture.
I have not snared birds in the reeds of the gods,
I have not caught fish in their ponds.
I have not held back water in its season,
I have not dammed a flowing stream,
I have not quenched a needed fire.
I have not neglected the days of meat offerings,
I have not detained cattle belonging to the god,
I have not stopped a god in his procession.
I am pure, I am pure, I am pure, I am pure![17]

Note the movement as the prayer shifts from entering pleas of *not guilty* of specific offenses to a sweeping, repetitive proclamation of virtue: *"I am pure, I am pure, I am pure, I am pure!"* Metaphysical Christianity has historically called this arrangement *denials and affirmations.* However, the word *denial* has fallen on hard times, taking on a wholly different meaning than the Fillmores intended at the turn of the 20th century. To be *in denial* today means, "To be in a state of denying the existence or effects of an ego defense mechanism."[18] What the Unity founders meant by *denial* was to reject the *power* of sickness and suffering over the individual, not to assert bad things never happened. A better expression that recaptures the original intent of Metaphysical Christian prayer might be *to negate* that which is counterproductive. If neither word— *deny* or *negate*—works for you, try an alternative such as *eliminate, renounce, let go, abandon,* or *release.*

Negation (Denial) and Affirmation

For centuries, variations of this simple prayer method have attracted people at all levels of spiritual practice, beginner to advanced metaphysician. It is an easy gateway to starting or expanding a lifelong habit of prayer and meditation. In fact, negation and affirmation is a bridge technique that employs principles of prayer in a meditative pattern. A well-known

Zen story about the value of an empty cup provides a good foundation for our discussion.

> A university professor went to visit a famous Zen master. While the master quietly served tea, the professor talked about Zen. The master poured the visitor's cup to the brim, and then kept pouring. The professor watched the overflowing cup until he could no longer restrain himself. "It's overfull! No more will go in!" the professor blurted. "You are like this cup," the master replied. "How can I show you Zen unless you first empty your cup?"[19]

Prosperity guru Catherine Ponder says cleaning out the clutter is fundamental to demonstrating prosperity in life. And she is not speaking figuratively.

> Get rid of what you do not want in an outer way. Clean up, clean out the closets, desk drawers, house, car, office. Forming a vacuum in an outer way makes a believer out of your subconscious mind, which goes to work in inner ways to manifest greater prosperity for you. There has to be a release of the old to make way for the new. You can unblock your good by forming a vacuum.[20]

Note the two steps in Ponder's dance of prosperity: *release the old (negation), make way for the new (affirmation).* The enigmatic biblical parable of the "Unclean Spirit," shows what happens when cleaning out the clutter is not linked to filling the space with positive good. The Gospels of Matthew and Luke both record this strange parable. Here is Matthew's version:

> When the unclean spirit has gone out of a person, it wanders through waterless regions looking for a rest-

ing place, but it finds none. Then it says, 'I will return to my house from which I came.' When it comes, it finds it empty, swept, and put in order. Then it goes and brings along seven other spirits more evil than itself, and they enter and live there; and the last state of that person is worse than the first.[21]

The Unclean Spirit seldom shows up in the greatest hits of the parables anthologies when competing against scriptural darlings like the Prodigal Son or the Good Samaritan, but it occasionally turns up in the work of diligent biblical interpreters. A United Methodist pastor from New England wrote about the parable:

Why are spiritual disciplines such as prayer, study, and worship so important in our lives? One reason is because they help establish God-like patterns of behavior that pushes out ungodly things. Scripture tells us that we are like containers. What are you filling your container up with? If we are not intentionally filling ourselves with the things of God, then the things of this world will rush into that empty space and begin to take over our life.[22]

Whatever you might believe about discorporate gremlins bumping around the arid Judean countryside, the basic idea of this story is founded on a cliché of good science: *Nature abhors a vacuum.* How many reformed alcoholics pick up other habits when clearing booze from their lives without filling the gap with something beneficial? How many friends of yours have broken off one bad relationship, only to bounce into another, even more hurtful situation? Jesus specified the clean space was too tempting for the returning, unclean spirit to resist; even worse, it recruited "seven other spirits more evil than itself" to occupy the tidy but empty "house" of its momentarily free human landlord.

One night in the late 1970s when I was a U.S. Army Chaplain serving at Fort Leonard Wood, Missouri, I received a call to go to the family quarters of a soldier who was being held by the Military Police for domestic violence. His wife had packed a bag and was ready to leave, so I volunteered to drive her to the bus station. Along the way she told me how he had beaten her regularly. Military families represent a cross section of middle-class America, and since battering occurs with alarming frequency among all populations, it would occasionally happen among soldier families.

I didn't know this family before tonight; I was duty chaplain and caught the call. She was quietly reflective, still traumatized from the slapping and pushing that drove her to call the police. During our ride to the Greyhound station she mentioned she had been married four times. That set off an alarm in my head. When I asked if any of them had hit her, she said sadly, "Oh, yeah. All of them." Normally, I would have tried to schedule further counseling to explore her situation, but this was the last time we would ever speak. I made the decision to toss nondirective counseling out the window and become a Dutch Uncle. After asking her to please listen carefully, I said something never repeated again in my ministry, something intentionally designed to scare her into action.

"You married four batterers in a row. That is not an accident. It suggests there is something in the battering personality which attracts you. If you don't find a good counselor and explore why you are making these choices, you are going to do it again. And sooner or later, one of them will probably kill you."

She got very quiet, but when we arrived at the station, she said, "Thank you." Her eyes told me more than the simple words conveyed. I have no idea what happened to her, but I came away praying she would fill the cleansed space with positive self-esteem with the help of a competent professional.

Psychiatrist William Glasser, author of acclaimed `70s-era books such as *Reality Therapy* and *Positive Addiction,* told about an alcoholic monk who made an offhand remark about being addicted to chanting and how this filled his need to drink.

> He'd been alcoholic at age 18 and drunk heavily for the next 6 or 7 years. Then at age 25, he reevaluated his life. He concluded he was going to kill himself with drink, and desperately decided to chant in some effort to help himself. He couldn't explain how he'd chosen chanting, but he reported that gradually he lost all desire to drink. Within six months, he believed he was as firmly hooked on chanting as he had been on drinking, but now his whole life was changed. He had always wanted to be a monk and began to study to be one. He is now (30 years later) chief monk of a small monastery in Southern California.[23]

Although he used the language of psychiatry rather than theology, Glasser had rediscovered the meaning of the *Parable of the Unclean Spirit.* After expelling bad habits from their consciousness, people can fill the empty spaces with *positive addictions,* which effectively hangs a "No Vacancy" sign for any unclean spirits wandering the neighborhood. Glasser prescribes a powerful replacement for serious addictive behavior, something that becomes a compulsion to rival the urges for drink or drugs or other self-destructive behaviors. Lesser demons might succumb to reprogramming away from negative, cleaning out the self-denigrating thoughts or behaviors and replacing them with healthy affirmations of the person's worthiness and value. The following meditative ritual, based on the above paradigm, might be helpful.

Evicting the Negative/Welcoming the Positive—
Permanently

My personal "demon" is _____.

To get rid of it, I must _____.

But if I don't fill up the empty space with good things, such

as _____, the injurious condition will return

and bring a gang of fiends to keep him company, for example:

_____.

Therefore, my inner space now overflows with the following

blessings and unlimited possibilities: _____

_____

_____.

From Books of Psalms to Alcoholics Anonymous

Beyond the obscure and seldom-preached *Parable of the Unclean Spirit,* some of the most popular passages in Judeo-Christian scripture feature *negation* and *affirmation.* The 23rd Psalm is an excellent illustration. We have turned to the Shepherd's Psalm frequently in this study. Watch how effortlessly the psalmist glides between the two poles of Negation/Affirmation in the first four verses:

> The Lord is my shepherd (*Affirmation*), I shall not want (*Negation*).

> He makes me lie down in green pastures;
> he leads me beside still waters;
> he restores my soul.
> He leads me in right paths
> for his name's sake (*Affirmation*).

Even though I walk through the darkest valley,*
I fear no evil (*Negation*);

for you are with me;
your rod and your staff—
they comfort me (*Affirmation*).[24]

What is the author's goal in this prayer? Certainly it offers self-comfort, which is how many people read the psalm today. However, look closely at the strong language of the Shepherd's Psalm. The text reveals a person reaching out for actual assistance, not just a herdsman whistling in the dark. The psalmist claims protection and prosperity by telling himself—consequently reminding God, Who listens always—about the mighty power of YHWH the God of Israel to defend and supply daily sustenance for those who call upon His Name. It is a prayer that *denies* lack and *affirms* plenty. What other belief was possible for the henotheistic Hebrews? Any other point of view would call into question the fundamental justice of the Lord, which was unthinkable for God's Chosen people. Charles Fillmore operated from the same premise while expanding the concept to all humankind.

We must faithfully and persistently deny the appearance of that which seems to be inharmonious and silently and faithfully affirm the omnipresent peace, love, and harmony that we want to see manifested.[25]

Again, it is important to stress that use of negation/affirmation does not compel the prayer practitioner to deny the *experience* of sickness, poverty, personal danger, or broken relationships. Alcoholism is the poster child for the danger of *psychological denial* and value of *spiritual denial* in overcoming a chronic condition that is both physical and spiritual. Unity author J Douglas Bottorff cogently describes the difference:

> They (alcoholics) may think that they are doing just fine; it is everyone else who has the problem. Of course, this form of denial is not confined to the disease of alcoholism. Most chronic suffers tend to see themselves as victims of either someone else's shortcomings or just plain old bad luck and they categorically deny any involvement in the production of their dilemmas. This is psychological denial. Spiritual denial means release. Using denial to deal with certain problems means you are to release the energy you have been pouring into the appearance. It does not mean you are to act as if it's not there. Like the alcoholic, as long as you refuse to acknowledge that you have a problem, you cannot do anything about it.[26]

More than a century ago, H. Emilie Cady attacked what she considered the burdens of erroneous beliefs by suggesting four denials for daily silent repetition. Note how carefully she avoids denying the experience of suffering while pronouncing it powerless over the spiritual nature of humanity:

- There is no evil.
- There is no absence of life, substance, or intelligence anywhere.
- Pain, sickness, poverty, old age, and death cannot master me, for they are not real.
- There is nothing in all the universe for me to fear, for greater is He that is within me than he that is in the world.[27]

Not all affirmative prayer contains lines that explicitly renounce error-beliefs. Sometimes, negation plays as a background theme without open expression of denials. In a "Life Is a Wonder" column for *Unity Magazine*®, James Dillet Freeman told the backstory of his best-known work:

Let me tell you how I wrote Unity's "Prayer for Protection."

When World War II was raging in Europe, we received many letters and phone calls from people caught in the conflict, but for a long time we did not have a prayer for protection that we were all satisfied with. This is how one came.

Silent Unity has always written a special Christmas Prayer Service just for Silent Unity workers. And in 1940 I was asked to prepare this service. We had never before needed a prayer for protection, but in 1940 we needed one, so I wrote one to go with the Christmas service. What I wrote was a little four-line verse:

"The light of Christ directs me; The love of Christ enfolds me; The power of Christ protects me; The presence of Christ upholds me."

I had hardly finished this Christmas service before Silent Unity came to me again and asked me to write a protection pamphlet that we could send to people, so I did. It was called *His Protecting Spirit*. They told me they wanted affirmative prayers for protection on the back page. Among these was the verse from the 23rd Psalm: "Yea, though I walk through the valley of the shadow of death, I will fear no evil: for thou art with me" (Ps. 23:4 KJV).

One of the young women who worked in Silent Unity was reading my manuscript as I wrote it, and as she finished it, she came up to me and said: "Jim, if I were a woman in England and they were dropping bombs on my roof, or if I were a soldier and someone was pointing a loaded gun at me, I wouldn't want to feel like I was walking through the valley of the shadow of death. Can't you do better than that?"

I thought, *You want me to do better than the 23rd Psalm? You have to be out of your mind.* But rolling around in the back of my mind was the little verse I had written as a prayer for protection at Christmas. I had written it just for Silent Unity, but now it came rolling up to the front of my mind and demanded that I pay attention to it. It enticed me to see what I could make of it. First I took the rhymes from it. I felt it would be more universally received if it was not a rhyme. Then I changed Christ to God. It had been Christ because it was a Christmas prayer, but I felt if we were going to send it around the world, God might be more acceptable to more people. So the little prayer became:

> "The light of God surrounds me, The love of God enfolds me, The power of God protects me, The presence of God watches over me."

That is the way we first printed it. Then a line came to me that I felt would make the prayer even more powerful. The line was:

> "Wherever I am, God is."

I added it as the fifth line. The "Prayer for Protection" first appeared as a four-lined prayer in 1941, but when we reprinted it in 1943, it appeared in the form it has had ever since.

> "The light of God surrounds me; The love of God enfolds me; The power of God protects me; The presence of God watches over me. Wherever I am, God is!"[28]

The prayer was an instant success. Freeman built his theme on *affirmations*, yet he never attempted to deny the reality of danger soldiers, carrying the prayer in their packs, would face on the battlefield.

It makes no attempt to rationalize why bad things happen to good people, arguably the most reoccurring religious question of all time. Nor does it assure the individual of magical safety while in harm's way. The words simply reminded soldiers, consequently reminding us, about the Omnipresence and Omnipotence of God. Freeman's implicit universalism—there are no doctrinal requirements to invoke God's Presence and Power—hints at a Buddhist-Christian attitude to life's challenges. While we cannot always control external events, a response of faith despite tragedy or triumph is completely within our power. The message works so universally that people around the globe display Freeman's words without the slightest notion of its origin. Freeman said his work even found a home in space.

> On the very first flight to the moon, on Apollo 11, astronaut Col. James Aldrin carried Unity's "Prayer for Protection" with him. He did not know me or Unity.

Other churches that share the New Thought heritage with Unity—notably Religious Science and Divine Science—give affirmative prayer a central place in their spiritual practices. While not all readers will agree with every aspect of the theology undergirding Metaphysical Christianity, the experience of Silent Unity's century-old prayer ministry demonstrates the broad applicability of affirmative prayer. One could argue that the techniques of negation and affirmation offer ways to refresh spiritual experiences across the diversity of religious traditions today.

Check Your Knowledge

1. What is Declarative Prayer? Give examples.
2. Summarize Unity's struggle to maintain its openness while retaining historical tethers to progressive Protestantism. What did Unity cofounder Charles Fillmore call the movement all the days of his life?
3. Describe the interplay of Negation (Denial) and Affirmation in prayer.
4. Evaluate the author's interpretation of the Parable of the Unclean Spirit. What other biblical examples are given to illustrate Affirmative Prayer?
5. How did the story of the battered Army wife illustrate the need to fill empty space with positive changes?
6. What prompted James Dillet Freeman to write the "Prayer for Protection"?

Discussion Starters

1. Do you believe saying a prayer actually protects you from harm?
2. What gives "Practical Christianity" the right to call itself Christian?
3. Have you ever called Silent Unity? What was your experience like?
4. The Alcoholics Anonymous recovery program asks people to affirm they are powerless to control their addiction, but "Came to believe that a Power greater than ourselves could restore us to sanity." Some have criticized this as giving power to the negatives. What do you think?
5. How could your church help people meet their needs to rid their lives of "demons" and fill the vacated space with something positive? Think beyond AA and recovery; plenty of people suffer in silence without being addicts.

6. What spiritual practices do you fall back upon in times of difficulty? Any new ideas to share?

Suggested Activity:
Evict the Negative/Welcome the Positive

Note: This can be done as an individual or group activity, or as a meditation exercise.

Work the exercise on "Evicting the Negative/Welcoming the Positive—Permanently" found in this chapter. Do it individually as a personal negation-affirmation drill. If you are in a small group, share your feelings but *not* the specifics of your experience. Do not feel compelled to go public, and don't hold back on the real "demons" you want to exorcise because you're worried you may have to read the worksheet aloud. You won't. Hold up this page and allow me to remind the group this is a *personal* discipline.

13

LECTIO DIVINA

Lectio divina is a slow, contemplative praying of the Scriptures. Time set aside in a special way for lectio divina enables us to discover in our daily life an underlying spiritual rhythm. Within this rhythm, we discover an increasing ability to offer more of ourselves and our relationships to the Father, and to accept the embrace that God is continuously extending to us.[1]

People read Scripture many different ways. Take for example, *comfort reading*. When I was a child, my very Germanic grandmother would read the 91st Psalm "over me" at bedtime like a protective incantation. Perhaps Mom-Mom Quell, as everyone called her, performed this ritual to counterbalance the standard *"If I should die before I wake ..."* prayer she taught me to recite each night. The King James Version of Psalm 91 has all those ominous, archaic phrases about deliverance from "the snare of the fowler, and from the noisome pestilence (harmful disease)." She read me the comforting words that promised God will "... cover thee with his feathers, and under his wings shalt thou trust: his truth shall be thy shield and buckler." I hadn't a clue what a *buckler* was (small shield), but I liked the image of God as a gigantic mother hen who tucked Her chicks under wing. Alas, that was before realizing I am allergic to feathers.

I have never seen a statistical analysis of motivators for reading Scripture, but after four decades in ministry, I'm fairly confident that comfort reading is the most frequent habit among partakers of biblical nourishment. Mom-Mom Quell read the Bible silently at night, because she believed the words came from God, and therefore, gave her a private line to Jesus' Father in heaven. She was not the slightest concerned about historical context, or deeper meanings behind Hebrew and Greek words from which *The Good Book* (her words) was translated into King James English exactly 300 years before her birth. She read the Bible because it brought Jesus Christ Himself to our redbrick row house on Mulberry Street in Reading, Pennsylvania, which made her feel like God had everything under control.

Other people—including Mom-Mom Quell's insatiably curious grandson, Thomas—hunger for more information about the biblical text and context. Some students of the Bible are called to explore deeper/higher/more complex levels. We cannot keep ourselves from looking into historical backgrounds, investigating nuanced meanings sometimes clarified by side trips to Hebrew and Greek roots, analyzing theological positions held by this or that biblical author, asking the hard questions, and wrestling with angels of the mind until they give their blessing. Or not.

There are people who read the Bible for personal guidance, moral direction, information about the Judeo-Christian heritage through recorded stories about Israel and the events of the New Testament; doctrinal support for individual and community religious beliefs; prophetic tools to interpret the events of our day or of the days to come; tools for instruction of youth and adults in the faith; and source materials for creating and/or leading prayer, ritual, public exhortations (sermons), and various other forms of worship.

People read Scripture for countless reasons; none of the above is superior to any other. Think shopping at a supermarket for dinner makings. Are the salad fixings *better* than Idaho potatoes or Pacific salmon? It's a matter of taste. Some people dig into the smorgasbord of biblical information; others nibble around to savor the numinous.

Hallowing the Written Word

One of the great contributions of Judaism to world religious thought was the process of *canonization*, by which humans recognized some written texts as more than inspirational; they were *authoritative*, the actual words of God. It became clear to their Hellenistic neighbors that Jews did not mean their scriptures presented words *about* the Divine Power, like Greek and Roman philosophers had done. Jews believed a small collection of sacred texts were authentic communication *from* God, preserved in written form to read and study later. It was a revolutionary concept in a world overflowing with countervailing philosophies and practitioners of rhetoric, the art of shaping one's argument to prevail in legal and political proceedings. No documentary evidence from heaven was available to the Greco-Romans. Inspirational writings, yes—but nothing like tablets of divine guidance lowered from heaven in a basket.

Before the written text of the Torah gained recognition in Hebrew religion as authoritative, Israelites sought "the word of the Lord" from oracles, later called prophets. Like the Greeks, Romans, and countless other ancient peoples, Hebrews seeking guidance or hints about the future sought advice from a specially attuned professional (נְבִיא, Navi, *spokesperson)* who delivered the forecast. Consulting a prophet was not unlike soliciting a reading from a psychic or visiting a stereotypical Gypsy fortune-teller today.

However, the mavens of the Divine Will went beyond soothsaying and began delivering unsolicited oracles, delivering moral and political advice, and generally issuing the equivalent of a *fatwah* against rulers whom they felt were violating the Law of God. Understandably, the Hebrew kings were unhappy with the editorial hammering they were getting in the Old Testament. In the following passage, Ahab King of Israel and Jehoshaphat King of Judah are shopping for prophets. They need to find somebody who will tell them good news about their upcoming war against the Arameans.

> But Jehoshaphat said, 'Is there no other prophet of the Lord here of whom we may inquire?' The king of Israel said to Jehoshaphat, 'There is still one other by whom we may inquire of the Lord, Micaiah son of Imlah; but I hate him, for he never prophesies anything favourable about me, but only disaster.'[2]

With a little adjustment for time and technology, the above passage sounds remarkably like two party leaders having coffee in Washington, D.C., as they lament the endless, unwarranted lambasting their administration has taken on the Op-Ed page. Writers get the last word, and many of the historic figures who come down to us as bad guys may have simply had the misfortune to offend a Scribe of Israel. For example, a terse, two-verse reference from Second Kings summarily dismissed Joash King of Judah. The unknown prophet who wrote the review declined to elevate Joash from obscurity, but tagged his name for infamy with formulaic brevity: *"He also did what was evil in the sight of the Lord."*[3]

What the typical king wanted was a staff of prophetic yes-men who would put the Divine Seal of Approval on whatever

hazardous decision he was contemplating, or at least warn
the sovereign of impending catastrophe in time to prevent
it. Early Israelite religion was set up to meet this need three
ways: through the prophets' inspired utterances, by their
interpretation of dreams, and through prophetic readings.

The third option required special tools of divination, spoken of as casting *lots*. Sometimes a priest of the Israelite religion performed this oracle instead of a prophet. The ceremonial implements he used were called the *Urim* and *Thummim*
(םוהתתומי and האורים), *doctrine* and *truth*. No translators have
had the courage to render the term in what may be its best
descriptive expression, *sacred dice*.

> Like other peoples, ancient Israel recognized the
> efficacy of magic (Ex. 7:11-12), acknowledged the
> power inherent in blessings and curses (Num., Chap-
> ters 22-24), and assumed the ability of some men to
> ascertain God's will through dreams, sacred dice, and
> oracles.[4]

Scholars are uncertain what the *lots* looked like. It's possible they could accommodate just one question at a time,
like tossing a coin—heads or tails, true or false, loves me/
loves me not—which meant divination technology forced the
prophet or priest to render a *yes-or-no* decision.[5]

It is not difficult to imagine how this system of living
truth-tellers with special power to contact the supernatural
might go back to shamans dancing around community camp-
fires. From what social scientists know about indigenous
peoples today, our distant ancestors must have lived an interconnected, hands-on existence. The natural world was far
from natural. Good and evil spirits brought rain or drought;
sickness or cures. Humans craved the security of a balanced
world where evil was kept at bay by charms and ritual, and

helpful spirits guided the tribe to food and shelter. Interfacing with Spirit required a specially attuned individual who could speak with the invisible powers. The first shamans were probably not full-time religious leaders but paraprofessionals, members of the tribe who displayed paranormal perception and the ability to work magic and communicate with the spirit world. The shaman provided a link between the tribe and the unseen world of spirit in which they were immersed.

This distance widened as paraprofessional leadership became full-time priesthood. It is unlikely the early religious professionals forced themselves on the people; someone had to tend the sacred fires and perform the rituals that kept life going. Rites of Power, Rites of Presence, Rites of Passage—all demanded by the people for emotional comfort and spiritual needs in a world that could be harsh and meaningless. The gulf between priest and worshipper widened with time. Abuses sometimes occurred, as we know today from various church-related scandals. However, as religion became cult and culture, rabble-rousers occasionally arose to call their communities to account for moral and political lapses, to demand a return to basic teachings of the faith, or to call people to strike out on an entirely new course.

Quasi-legendary leaders like Moses; historical figures like the Jewish prophets, Jesus of Nazareth, Muhammad, Guru Nanak, and Baha'u'llah—all these leaders had different approaches to life, but they also had something in common. Their communities produced a body of religious writing in support of the wider faith. Today those writings are considered authoritative by many of their followers. Effectively speaking, Scriptures of these religious traditions are regarded as God's Word on paper.

Huldah's Decision

It might surprise those of us in the Jewish-Christian-Islamic tradition to learn the concept of a written "Word of God" is not universally held among religions today. Hinduism, Buddhism, and Tribal Religions have inspirational literature, but their documents are not regarded as divinely revealed, authoritative truth. The wellspring of this belief in sacred texts probably flows from a source of origin in the Hebrew religion and a decision rendered by a relatively unknown woman who lived 2,700 years ago. Her name was Huldah; she was a bona fide prophetess of Israel.

I first learned about Huldah's importance from lectures by Dr. Bruce Rahtjen, who taught Old Testament Studies at Saint Paul School of Theology in Kansas City and was a frequent guest speaker at Unity Village. In a series of audio cassettes published by Unity School in the 1970s, Rahtjen described Huldah's role in the theological revolution that followed the discovery of a scroll of the Law in the Jerusalem Temple during the seventh century BCE.

King Josiah (r. 641–609 BCE) decided the Jerusalem Temple needed renovations and a general clean up. Solomon had built the Lord's holy sanctuary in the 10th century, so spring cleaning was past due. During his lectures at Unity School, Dr. Rahtjen remarked with a chuckle that it clearly showed men were in charge of the Temple, since they cleaned up the mess every 300 years or so.[6] As the job progressed, workers found a scroll somewhere inside the Temple building. They took it to the priest Hilkiah, who gave it to the King's Secretary. Eventually, he read it aloud to his master. "When the king heard the words of the book of the law, he tore his clothes."[7]

The situation was grave. This scroll claimed to convey decrees from God in written form. Since a ruler has the power to dictate messages his subject must obey, the same kind of communication from *Josiah's* Master, the God of Israel, made sense to the King. But was this message really from God? Josiah ordered his staff to find a prophet who might inquire of the Lord, which probably meant, *Ask the question and do the sacred coin-toss.* Apparently, all the male prophets were at a convention or otherwise unavailable. But King Josiah was in no mood to suffer failure cheerfully.

> So the priest Hilkiah, Ahikam, Achbor, Shaphan, and Asaiah went to the prophetess Huldah the wife of Shallum son of Tikvah, son of Harhas, keeper of the wardrobe; she resided in Jerusalem in the Second Quarter, where they consulted her. She declared to them, "Thus says the Lord, the God of Israel: Tell the man who sent you to me, Thus says the Lord, I will indeed bring disaster on this place and on its inhabitants—all the words of the book that the king of Judah has read.[8]

That was it. The scroll was authentic; it presented God's decrees in writing. Neither Huldah nor her King was aware of the revolution in world religious thought she had just initiated. Taking the authority of a sacred text as a given, all subsequent words spoken by prophets and teachers of Israel must conform to the template of God's Word. The decision provided the basic syllogism upon which revealed religions of the Abrahamic lineage would rest. Here are two examples phrased in Aristotelian logic.

Major Premise: The Torah is the Word of God in written form, therefore true.

Minor Premise: A new opinion in our midst *conforms* to the Torah.

Conclusion: Therefore, the new opinion *is true.*

Major Premise: The Torah is the Word of God in written form, therefore true.

Minor Premise: A new opinion in our midst *contradicts* the Torah.

Conclusion: Therefore, the new opinion *is not true.*

Huldah's decision to acknowledge the scroll in hand as a dispatch from God established sacred literature as the basis of Judaism, moving away from the age of prophecy and into the beginning stages of rabbinic interpretation of the meanings found in the sacred text. Paradoxically, a prophetess had sounded a bell, warning of the impending death of prophecy, that is, the end of living, professional intermediaries as the indisputable link between God and humanity.

Other religious traditions had produced written works that taught spiritual truths as understood by the culture of the day. The written works of early Israel told *about* the mighty acts of YHWH and catalogued His decrees, but the texts were not themselves considered the Word of God. The Divine Word came live-streamed from the LORD to His prophets, and from the prophets unto the people. The Word of God was an event—for example, when Moses encountered God at Sinai—not the book that recorded it. Something of this original viewpoint lingered into the Christian era, when the Gospel of John boldly declared:

In the beginning was the Word, and the Word was with God, and the Word was God. He was in the beginning with God. All things came into being through him, and without him not one thing came into being. What has come into being in him was life, and the life was the light of all people. The light shines in the darkness, and the darkness did not overcome it.[9]

Obviously, John is not speaking of a written text, floating around in the superheated singularity that exploded into the Big Bang, but a living Presence and Power through which "all things came into being" and burst forth as "the light of all people." However, once the message appears on a written page, it is tempting to conflate the message with the medium. The Bible becomes the Word of God; instead of containing someone's description of Divine Truth, the text takes on the authority of God's revealed word.

Something important happened when the prophetic door to immediate contact with God closed. In a strange way, establishing scripture as a conduit to God took the specialist out of the loop and democratized access to the Divine. Even though the "official" religious teachings would move from the self-appointed prophet to an educated priesthood, people through the ages have recognized their need for intimate contact with the Divine Mystery without intermediary. Often those with the closest affiliation to formalized religion were in the forefront of mystical experimentation, seeking God intimately rather than strictly through the study of official texts. And ironically, the hunger to experience God led people to develop simple ways of *reading scripture as acts of encounter* with the Mysterious Presence and Power that moves through the Universe and expresses as amazing grace. With these thoughts held in mind, we move to the technique for encountering Sacred Space known as *Lectio Divina.*

"Holy Reading"

Lectio Divina is devotional contemplation of sacred scripture, first expounded by Benedict of Nursia (480–547 CE). Although originating among Catholic ascetics, *Lectio* is not limited to celibate Christian orders; it's a technique anyone can master quickly. Carmelite Father Joseph Chalmers credits his order with reviving the ancient practice:

> Lectio Divina is the Latin for "Holy Reading" and was a form and approach to praying with Scripture that was common among medieval religious orders. The value of Lectio Divina was rediscovered by the Carmelite Family (and indeed the wider Church) in the twentieth century. Essentially Lectio Divina involves taking a short passage of Scripture and pondering it. This can be done alone or in a group, and normally involves prolonged periods of silence.[10]

The method originated in the monastic discipline of daily reading from scripture and the writings of early Church Fathers, but contemporary *Lectio* has expanded to include all spiritual books. When reflecting on passages from the Old or New Testament, *Lectio Divina* differs from historical-textual studies because its goal is not educational but devotional. The process treats selected readings as holistic literary works with personal applications for the reader. Gabriel O'Donnell, O.P., says the key concept is to approach the text like a gateway to God:

> When early monks and nuns went about the business of *lectio,* they believed that there was in each text a personal message *for them in particular.* They did not assume that the message indicated the meaning of this scriptural text for the whole Church for all time but felt "Right now, here, today, at this moment, God has something to say to *me.*"[11]

The goal is not about *learning*; it is about *experiencing*. Fr. O'Donnell says the difference is crucial. For example, he says Catholic clergy have…

> … never used *lectio divina* for some utilitarian or prag-
> matic purpose, such as preparing a sermon, learning
> more "about" the Bible, or even for what might now
> call spiritual self-improvement. *Lectio* is a disciplined
> form of devotion and not a method of Bible study. It
> is done purely and simply to come to know God, to
> be brought before his Word, to listen.[12]

Non-Christians should find the *Lectio* technique easily
adapts to any tradition, especially those with a strong foundation in sacred texts, whether Jewish, Islamic, Sikh, or Baha'i.
Under this broad application, *Lectio* can apply to extracanoni-
cal Christian texts like the *Gospel of Thomas* or the *Teaching
of the Apostles* (Διδαχή, *Didache*), esoteric writings like the
Jewish *Kabbalah* (קַבָּלָה), or virtually any inspirational literature—from the Hindu *Vedas* to *Jonathan Livingston Seagull*.
Some people prefer to move beyond language to commune
with God nonverbally. "Although the text used for lectio divina is traditionally a passage from the Bible, any inspiring text
or art form may be used to reflect upon—a poem, a drawing,
a painting, a quote, a song, etc."[13]

The method proposed in this chapter requires no doctrinal
test for religious literature. Any writing that raises your consciousness to a "higher" level—to a place where you begin
to experience the presence of Divine Spirit, God, Ultimate
Concerns, Indwelling Divinity, the Oneness of the Cosmos, or
whatever you call the top floor of your pantheon—qualifies
as worthy material for *Lectio Divina*.

Steps in Lectio Divina—The Four Rs

The four traditional steps of *Lectio Divina* offer a conve-
nient pattern based on four Latin words: *Lectio, Meditatio, Oratio, Contemplatio* (see chart on page 263). These words roughly

correlate to *Read, Reflect, Respond, Rest*. The sequence is not inflexible, just an effective guideline.

> Prayer is rather like soup. Good soup (prayer) has these four elements as basic ingredients, but each cook will have a different recipe. The soup will have a different taste according to the quantity of each ingredient and according to what other ingredients are added. We have a great freedom in our relationship with God but Lectio Divina contains the wisdom of centuries of living the Christian life. Lectio Divina is not a rigid method but changes according to the person who follows its rhythm.[14]

Now that we've done our background study in the "Word of God" and the general goal of *Lectio*, let's warm up the stove and make prayer soup. Advocates of *Lectio* say it works best as a daily discipline. Although not specifically referring to text-based experiences, Linda Martella-Whitsett calls for quiet time every day. "Daily prayer practice builds spiritual muscle in much the same way physical exercise builds muscles in the body."[15]

If you decide on a daily routine, it's a good idea to select readings that continue at length—perhaps the Gospel of Matthew or a series of well-known Psalms. You will pick up the flow more easily tomorrow if you're continuing an ongoing journey rather than a single, cherry-picked incident—unless you'd rather hop around among favorite passages. Good guidelines help, not hinder; follow Spirit wherever you're led.

Steps in Lectio Divina

Lectio—Read aloud until encountering a key passage.

↘

   Meditatio—Reflect on the text; imagine freely.

   ↘

      Oratio—Respond by prayer; talk to Divine Spirit.

      ↘

         Contemplatio—Rest in silence with your key passage; expand your mind to God Mind.

Step 1—Lectio (Read)

After selecting a spiritual text and finding a comfortable body position, simply begin reading, preferably aloud. If your physical surroundings make oral reading impractical, silent reading works fine. Remember, you are reading *devotionally*, looking for an encounter with God. Not information, not even spiritual insights. Let the text wash over your consciousness until you begin to feel an elevated sense of the Divine. Father Luke Dysinger, O.S.B, describes the first step in the language of his Catholic heritage:

> Turn to the text and read it slowly, gently. Savor each portion of the reading, constantly listening for the "still, small voice" of a word or phrase that somehow says, "I am for you today." Do not expect lightning or ecstasies. In lectio divina, God is teaching us to listen to him, to seek him in silence. He does not reach out and grab us; rather, he gently invites us ever more deeply into his presence.[16]

You can experience the Divine Mystery in whatever configuration your faith cherishes—whether you understand God as Supreme Being, Force of Nature, multitudes of divine beings, an expression of human potential, the Presence and

Power that causes the Universe to exist, or any other God concept that works for you. This isn't about theology, doctrine, or even clarified insight.

If you have taken advanced courses in biblical studies or the comparative scriptures of other faiths—great! Now, lay it all aside. As important as historical-critical studies are in providing context for religious writings, now is the time to move past critical thinking and to drink deeply from the same inspiration stream that irrigated the minds of the original authors. Like Yogananda's lesson from the Sleepless Saint, Ram Gopal Babu, after the aspiring young yogi had refused to bow before the Infinite in the stone symbol at the Tarakeswar temple, you are not reading the text to affirm some abstract principles. You are reading to recognize the all-pervading Presence and Power of God in your specific location, to browse the pages for a chance to tread upon holy ground.

Many religious traditions define *faith* as *encounter* and theology as an attempt to make sense of the experience later— Moses on the mountain, Jesus at the Jordan, Muhammad at the cave, each followed by centuries of interpretation and reflection. Holy Reading proceeds at a slow, comfortable pace. *Lectio* redirects spiritual exercises away from athletic mental events toward a stroll through God's garden. Father Gabrielle O'Donnell says:

> If *lectio* becomes something that *has* to get done, then we have lost the sense of sacred reading that leads to meditation. It must remain a leisurely activity.[17]

Step 2—Meditatio (Reflect)

Read the passages you have selected until something snags your attention. It could be a phrase like, "The Lord is my shepherd," or a familiar story. See the hillside up ahead?

A shrub tree appears engulfed in flame, yet the blaze does not consume its fuel. What's going on here? Don't you want to park the sheep and check it out? Wonder what you will find …?

This is *meditation* in the ancient understanding of the word. *Meditatio* begins when a word, phrase, or story connects with your thoughts at a deeper, intuitive level. It need not directly attach to the specific words of the text, which would limit your possibilities. A passage from Eastern scriptures might transport you to Buddha under the Bodhi Tree, and summon you to sit beside Gautama Siddhartha and feel the peace of enlightenment. Or a verse from the Quran may invite you to travel with Rumi the medieval Sufi mystic, who said upon his first encounter with dancing dervishes, "What I had thought of before as God, I met today in a person."[18]

Follow the images that arise until the hiatus drifts back to the text again. If special people or characters from your pantheon appear, you might walk with them and have a quiet conversation. Or not. Personally, my favorite meditation scene in *Lectio Divina* occurs when I read the Nativity from the Gospel of Luke. I hear the angels, then wander into Bethlehem with my fellow shepherds under the silver-white light of the Christmas Star. When we arrive, the Wise Men are offering their gifts to the Virgin Mary, with Joseph, the proud papa, standing behind her. Intellectually, I know this conflates Matthew and Luke into one Christmas crèche postcard version, but I don't care. I want to experience it all. Rough wooden manger cushioned with fresh straw. Animal sounds and scents, camels standing like statues while their royal riders kneel before the Baby Jesus. I have visited this scene many times, and have never spoken a word or heard anyone break the silence of the holy night. Although the scene I visualize is legendary, I always come away feeling like I have walked upon holy ground.

Step 3—Oratio (Respond in prayer)

Sometimes *Meditatio* images beckon you to more than observe; you want to respond in prayer. Communion with the Divine flows easily inside sacred space, which may be why religions continue to recognize holy ground in a postmodern world. Wiccans today still cast a circle to begin Neo-pagan rites. In antiquity, Romans established a Shrine to Vesta with cloistered virgins to care for its sacred flame; Jews cordoned off the Jerusalem Temple to prevent non-Jews from penetrating beyond the outer Court of the Gentiles. Christians have erected churches with nave/sanctuary segments to separate the special domain of clergy from their congregants. Muslims veil, with black silk and gold embroidery, the building toward which the Islamic world turns in daily prayer, the cube-shaped *Kaaba*, while forbidding all unbelievers from entering their holy city of Mecca. The Church of Jesus Christ of Latter-Day Saints requires an elaborate series of credentialing rituals—to include recitation of exact responses in a liturgical catechism and secret handshakes through slots in a gossamer curtain—before allowing even faithful members into the Celestial Room of Mormon temples.[19]

Many faiths have such elaborate rituals of entry to special places. Sometimes, but not always, members in good standing alone are qualified to visit the inner sanctum. While special admittance can accelerate the participant's sense of the numinous in the sacred place, on the downside, restricted access can generate spiritual elitism, a feeling one has passed from the realm of the ordinary into holy spaces reserved for the uniquely qualified, or the worthy few who are saved, the Elect. Groups whose theologies require such fences between themselves and the rest of humanity often point to the gates in the fence through which anyone can become a communicant member, while universalist groups point to the fence itself as an error in consciousness.

However, with the process of *Lectio Divina*, you have entered holy ground through a wide-open door. Any number can play. You don't have to be a Jew or Christian to stroll into the Book of Psalms. In fact, all sacred texts of the human family transcend their clannish origins and offer sanctuary to everyone. Like the psalmist who narrated a soul-restoring journey through green pastures and beside still waters, now might be the time to respond to Divine Spirit in prayer. Father O'Donnell says:

> Such "rumination" on the Twenty-Third Psalm may well lead to a desire to speak to the shepherd, to speak to God. Our heart and mind move toward the Lord, who is the Good Shepherd, and this movement of the heart toward God is the beginning of prayer.[20]

Let me reiterate my Universal Prayer Rubric: *Pray any way that works for you*. Do not worry about technique, or whether anyone else will approve or disapprove of how you pray. As Mom-Mom Quell liked to say to unsolicited advice, "Mind your own beeswax." The human family has solved its religious equations countless ways; spiritual diversity is your birthright.

Step 4—Contemplatio (Rest in Silence)

The traditional name for the fourth moment or ingredient of Lectio Divina is contemplatio or contemplation. This is a concept with a lot of history behind it and not a few difficulties connected to it. I prefer to use a more common term that is easily understandable: rest. At this point we are invited to enter into the mystery of God. It is no longer necessary to think holy thoughts, or to speak but simply to rest in God.[21]

Contemplatio is *rest* in the sense of peaceful awareness of the Presence, like two old friends sitting together at sunset without needing words, or two lovers lingering in the afterglow of powerful, joyful sex. This is not the time to *do*; it is the time to *be*.

Father Chalmers says, "There comes a time when we must leave behind our beautiful words because they cannot express what is in our heart." *Resting* is akin to Quaker Silence, but seeks no message, no "Word of the Lord" like the Hebrew prophets handed down from the Divine Judge. *Contemplatio* is closer to Eastern meditation, or the high state of consciousness sometimes called *entering the Silence*, which we explored in Chapter 10.

It is even possible for *Contemplatio* to become a mystical experience in which people transcend everyday thinking and see the Oneness. However, do not judge the quality of your *Lectio Divina* effort by comparing what others have experienced. Spiritual exercises are better when effortless, and whatever happens will be part of your journey.

I can conceive no better summary of the process known as *Lectio Divina,* but let's fly over and look at the gateways to sacred space.

Lectio (Read): Breathe in the sacred text. Move among the words and make them your own by converting black marks on a page into audible, living sound. You might also try handwriting the text as you read aloud. Nothing personalizes Scripture more vividly than seeing it appear in your handwriting. Sooner or later, a word or phrase will speak back to you, and you are ready for the next step.

Meditatio (Reflect): Let the word or passage, or perhaps a whole parable or story, take you by surprise. Follow it wherever the path goes. If images appear, play or observe or dance along, but let them lead. Let go and follow the imagery without trying to understand. You are a mega-fan with a front row seat, perhaps even a backstage pass. So celebrate! Embrace, sing, play an instrument even if you have trouble mastering the kazoo. Bathe in the moonlight; swim a tropical sea; fly with eagles or seagulls; sail among the stars. Go where Spirit takes you, boldly and with joy. You will reach a place where the delight or beauty or awesome majesty rouses you to push beyond participant-observer. Then you must respond.

Oratio (Respond): Speak, sing, or chant. Let your prayer tumble jubilantly, like a cool mountain brook. Say whatever you need to say; express yourself in this sacred ground you have claimed by rite of participation. Pray any way that works for you.

Contemplatio (Rest): Move beyond words. Rest in the Presence and Power of whatever you understand to be Ultimate—the Divine Spirit, the Universe, God. If possible, move beyond thought itself into the Silence in which you experience the mystical awareness of the Connectivity of the Cosmos, the Oneness of all things.

One final advantage of *Lectio Divina* today is popularity across denominational lines. *Lectio* applies to all sacred texts because it is theologically indifferent to doctrinal issues, so this technique has the potential to bring diverse peoples together for personalized meditative encounters in the symbols and scriptures of their faiths. *Lectio* began in the Christian monastery, but its potential as a platform for multifaith, nonsectarian, shared spiritual experiences looks encouraging.

Check Your Knowledge

1. Describe the *canonization* of Hebrew Scriptures and tell what role the Prophetess Huldah played in the process.
2. Who rediscovered *Lectio Divina* after a long hiatus?
3. What is the primary goal of *Lectio Divina*?
4. Explain the "Four Rs" of the method.
5. How much training in biblical studies is required to practice this method?
6. Why is *Lectio* such a flexible practice?

Discussion Starters

1. Can a written document speak with authority as the Word of God?
2. How different might Judaism and Christianity be today if Huldah had not confirmed the Josiah scroll as God's word?
3. Has a "sacred word" ever leapt off the page while reading the Bible or *Daily Word*? What words carry extraordinary spiritual meaning for you?
4. Have you experienced heightened awareness of the Divine while reading or reflecting on sacred texts? Describe what happened.
5. What other sacred texts might work in a *Lectio Divina* repertoire?
6. Do you think this method has possibilities for finding common ground with people of other faith traditions? How might that work?

Suggested Activity

Note: This can be done as an individual or group activity, or as a meditation exercise.

We cannot visit this process without trying it. Follow the steps in this chapter and do experiment with *Lectio Divina*. If you are in a group, discuss your experience after the final quiet moment. You might also want to journal or simply write stream of consciousness notes about what you encountered during *Lectio*. As always, share what you choose, but keeping holy secrets is perfectly okay too.

14

CENTERING

*The teaching of the Divine Indwelling is a fundamental
doctrine for the spiritual journey.*[1]

—Fr. Thomas Keating, O.C.S.O.

Most world faiths teach some variation of the ancient
concept known as *Centering*. The oldest name-brand religion
on the planet, Hinduism, has taught mind-body Centering from antiquity. The Japanese martial art *Aikido* features
Centering as an integral part of its discipline.[2] More recent,
Emmett Fox proposed a variation of active Centering in his
"Golden Key" exercise, which we shall review shortly. Practi-
cally everywhere the student of religion looks, some form of
Centering can be found. The best-known application in Western culture, *Centering Prayer*, probably traces back to the Desert Saints of the early monastic movement.[3]

However, any technique that aspires to higher consciousness by focusing on a key word, concept, state of mind, bodily
function (such as breathing), feeling (love, joy, gratitude,
release), or silence in the absence of thought or emotion arguably qualifies as *Centering*. As often the case, itemizing what
Centering *is not* helps to define what it *is*.

• Centering is neither active communication nor meditative
  waiting for new ideas.

- Centering is not intellectual reflection, supplication, adoration, praise, or petition.
- Centering is not conversation with God, or with your higher self.
- Centering is not listening for messages like the Quaker Silent Meeting.

The objective of Centering Prayer closely resembles *Lectio Divina*, to enter sacred space by discovering it everywhere. In its simplest form, Centering Prayer works by finding a prayer word and repeating it in your mind like a mantra. As stray thoughts come to the surface, return to your word at center. Eventually, Centering leads to a place beyond words where praying persons are caught up in connectivity—with God, Holy Existence, the Universe, Ultimate Reality, or whatever serves as your highest level of consciousness. If the mind begins to stray from this lofty place, return to the Centering word for stability until the mystical process takes over again or your time allotted for Centering Prayer expires.

That's the whole technique. Uncomplicated though it may sound, advocates of Centering Prayer say it has the potential to turn the mind toward divine melodies that silently fill the soul with the music of the spheres. An architect of the modern Centering Prayer movement, Father Thomas Keating, O.C.S.O. (Order of Cistercians of the Strict Observance, known as Trappists), began his work after hearing the Pope encourage a renewal of spirituality in the Church.

> As abbot of St. Joseph's Abbey (Spencer, Massachusetts), Father Thomas Keating attended a meeting in Rome in 1971. At the meeting, Pope Paul VI called on the members of the clergy to revive the contemplative dimension of the Gospel in the lives of both monastic and laypeople. Believing in the importance of this revival, Fr. Keating encouraged the monks at

St. Joseph's to develop a method of Christian contemplative prayer with the same appeal and accessibility that Eastern meditation practices seemed to have for modern people.[4]

Since those early days, Keating and another Trappist from St. Joseph's Abbey, Basil Pennington, have become well-known authors in spiritual literature and closely identified with the movement to revitalize the ancient technique of Centering. Keating and Pennington have led Centering Prayer "prayershops" worldwide, to include work with the novices of Mother Teresa of Calcutta. Pennington writes:

> Today it is used in all parts of our small world ... This precious part of our heritage, which, like the fire of the Temple, was hidden in a deep well of a few monasteries, is burning brightly again, within all parts of the Christian family ... truly an ecumenical movement.[5]

This is essentially the same theology that underlies all the "practicing the presence" methodologies. However, because Centering Prayer functions by silently repeating a key word over and over again, questions invariably arise among those who grew up in churches or traditions with less formal structure. For example, when does repetition become "vain repetitions" of the King James Bible:

> But when ye pray, use not vain repetitions, as the heathen do: for they think that they shall be heard for their much speaking. Be not ye therefore like unto them: for your Father knoweth what things ye have need of, before ye ask him.[6]

Today most scholars recognize the King James as a much beloved, but highly inaccurate translation, partially because it was based on corrupt manuscripts, which were the only Hebrew and Greek texts available in post-Elizabethan England. The modern New Revised Standard Version clarifies some of the archaic language.

> When you are praying, do not heap up empty phrases as the Gentiles do; for they think that they will be heard because of their many words. Do not be like them, for your Father knows what you need before you ask him.[7]

To the nonparticipating observer, this is exactly what continuous repetition of a mantra or prayer word sounds like—trying to be heard by flooding the ethers with message traffic. The argument has been with us a long time. Among its other complaints, Reformation Protestantism of the 16th century rebelled against church liturgy which, to the reformers, had become rote. As late as 1639 the British government considered burning a tradesman as an example to other secret heretics. The crimes for which he was charged included studying the Bible at home and opposition to printed prayers. He escaped the stake, but the government was clearly unhappy with the idea of "vain repetitions" in their official liturgy.[8]

Meanwhile, on the other side of the world, Buddhists were spinning prayer wheels and heaping up Himalayas of prayer with each turn. In the Middle East, Muslims were facing Mecca, repeating their ritual prayers five times daily, and moving from kneeling to standing to touching the forehead to the carpeted floor. There is also an Islamic practice known as "Reciting the 99 Most Beautiful Names of Allah (God)." Highly specialized benefits are believed to accrue from recitation. Here is an example—Name No. 38—Al-Kabeer (God as the Greatest) from a Muslim website:

ألْكَبِير

38. Al-Kabeer (The Greatest)
If you have been dismissed from a post, then fast for seven days and each day recite this name of Allah 1,000 times. Allah will reinstate you to your post and grace you with honor and dignity. Insha-Allah.[9]

That amounts to 7,000 repetitions of *God the Greatest.* After watching the zeal with which Muslims throw themselves into daily prayer, nothing like *vain repetitions* occurs to most observers.

Repetitive prayer is more than a means to escape from some unpleasant circumstance like unemployment; it can be an excellent spiritual discipline with no particular goal in mind. As a young man, I became a follower of the Baha'i Faith, which has its origins in Islam, just like Buddhism emerged from Hinduism and Christianity from Judaism. We often recited the "Remover of Difficulties" in times of crisis. (See Chapter 12.) The prayer was *revealed* (Baha'i term) by the John the Baptist figure of the Faith, Siyyid `Alí Muḥammad Shírází, who was called the *Báb,* which means *gate* or *door.* Then I learned Baha'u'llah, Prophet-Founder of the Baha'i Faith, had told his biographer, Nabil, to ask his disciples to say the prayer relentlessly.

Tell them to repeat it five hundred times, nay, a thousand times, by day and by night, sleeping and waking, that haply the Countenance of Glory may be unveiled to their eyes, and tiers of light descend upon them.[10]

I tried to do this, with mixed results. However, I knew other Baha'is who chanted the "Remover of Difficulties" on continuous loop as they went about their daily chores. One young farmer told me he logged 10,000 repetitions of the prayer while driving a tractor during his very long work week. Although my spiritual path took me away from formal membership in the Baha'i Faith decades ago, I still treasure the zeal they hold for God and keep their prayers and ideals in my heart today.

From *"Hail Mary"* to 南無阿弥陀仏

The key word in the text from Matthew's Gospel—*"vain repetitions"* or *"empty phrases"*—suggests vacuous, perfunctory activity. *Vain* has two meanings, *conceited* or *futile*. The first definition found musical voice in a Carly Simon classic hit:

> You're so vain, you probably think this song is about you. You're so vain, I'll bet you think this song is about you. Don't you? Don't You?[11]

The KJV's *vain repetitions* seem to mean *babbling without connection,* or *useless and futile clamoring,* which the NRSV renders *"empty phrases."* This has been an ongoing critique by liturgical reformers since the days of the Hebrew prophets. In the eighth century BCE, the Prophet Amos leveled a *"Thus saith the Lord"* blast against meaningless Temple worship in the face of religio-political corruption throughout the land. In the following passage, Amos delivers a withering, sermonic oracle that shook Israel to the foundations. YHWH of Sinai is speaking through his prophet.

> I hate, I despise your festivals,
> and I take no delight in your solemn assemblies.

278 of The Many Faces of Prayer

> Even though you offer me your burnt-offerings and
> grain-offerings,
>   I will not accept them;
> and the offerings of well-being of your fatted
> animals
>   I will not look upon.
> Take away from me the noise of your songs;
>   I will not listen to the melody of your harps.
> But let justice roll down like waters,
>   and righteousness like an ever-flowing stream.[12]

The next time politicians publicly proclaim their faith in God while supporting policies that abuse the poor and neglect most vulnerable citizens, quote the Book of Amos to them. To the Hebrew prophets, rituals without compassion were a way to "heap up empty phrases," as Jesus would call them.

If repetition can be *mindless* in the sense of vain and empty phrases, what about its counterpart, *mindful* repetitive prayer? Children in every culture are taught to speak their native tongues by endlessly repeating patterns of speech from their elders. Singing the same Christmas carols each December usually expresses heartfelt joy of the holiday season. In many traditions, liturgical funerary rites express the solemnity of mourning in prescribed language that comforts the grieving by its very familiarity. The opposite of mindless is *mindful,* and we have already reviewed how important that term is in Buddhism. Could the concept apply to all acts of religion, even reciting mantras and repetitive prayer? Certainly, prayers that feature repetition can be hollow sounds or rich melodies, depending on the consciousness of the practitioner. From Catholics praying the Rosary to Pure Land Buddhists chanting 南無阿弥陀仏 (*Namu Amida Butsu ... I venerate Amida Buddha*), mindfulness determines whether prayer is autonomic or intentional.

Distinguishing Centering From Repetition

As we have seen in our scanty study of Buddhism, mindfulness requires more than bare attention, because the Eightfold Path goes beyond mere intensified perception or deep comprehension of religious themes. Mindfulness heeds the cry of the Hebrew prophets; it is an orientation to life that includes ethics and compassion. As mentioned earlier, when visiting Colombo, Sri Lanka, on a recent trip, I discovered rules posted at the Vishva Niketan Buddhist Retreat Center that asked visitors to "Look After Plants as Living Beings."[13] Like the prophet-founders of many world faiths, Buddha and Jesus shared a concern for ethical issues that stand at the center of life.

Mindful prayer, therefore, must transcend attention to spoken words in favor of the Ultimate Reality beyond (or within) the individual. The words themselves are just a vehicle to achieve higher consciousness, and the way such insight will manifest is largely dependent on the religious tradition from which a person approaches Centering. God-consciousness, however defined, remains the goal, not deeper understanding of the meaning attached to the prayer word. Centering follows the pattern of *Lectio Divina,* which calls the meditative reader of spiritual texts beyond the stories, parables, koans, teachings, and assorted mythologies that dot sacred literature to a place where the individual encounters God firsthand rather than through words attributed to another. While Centering Prayer requires discipline, there is also a certain effortlessness to the process, which is captured in the following historical yarn from Sister Melannie Svoboda, S.N.D.

> Being a person of prayer is not something we achieve by our own strenuous effort. I am reminded of a story from the desert fathers, early Christian hermits who

lived in the Egyptian and Palestinian desert, that illustrates this point. A young monk asked the old Master, "How long will it take me to achieve enlightenment?" The Master replied, "Five years." The young monk asked, "But what if I work really, really hard?" The Master replied, "Ten years."[14]

The anecdote humorously illustrates the point we have been exploring. Centering Prayer is a discipline without severity; its benefits cannot be stormed and seized by force of will. There is something of the porch swing on a lazy afternoon in the rhythms of Centering. Let the world stroll past; I am content to rest here in the breeze of the Holy Spirit. Although I have difficulty explaining the connection intellectually, Centering Prayer reminds me of the second verse of the old hymn *This Is My Father's World.*

This is my Father's world,
The birds their carols raise,
The morning light, the lily white,
Declare their maker's praise.
This is my Father's world:
He shines in all that's fair;
In the rustling grass I hear him pass;
He speaks to me everywhere.[15]

Shamelessly anthropomorphic, gender insensitive, yet magnificently peaceful lines I have loved all my life, the hymn does not have to be taken literally to experience its transcendent imagery. One need not subscribe to a monotheistic Creator-God in order to grasp the mystical symbolism of a Divine Presence moving through the world.

Centering on Your Prayer Word

To center is to find quiet space to be present to the Divine. Centering Prayer is like riding a word-steed into the forest of your mind. When you arrive at a clearing that offers sacred space, dismount and move beyond words into silent communion. The prayer horse will wait patiently, because your mind will probably start to wander from silence to stray thoughts. Mount up, Centering on your word, and find holy ground again.

Because Centering Prayer usually begins with a specific word, we need to examine ways to select it. Although non-Christians practice the technique, Centering Prayer advocate Thomas Keating comes to the process from his experience in the Trappist order. In chapel services at Trappist monasteries, the monks often chant from the Psalms and reflect upon Old Testament/New Testament readings *seven times a day.* So not surprisingly, Fr. Keating recommends finding prayer words from biblical sources.

> The practice of Centering Prayer, built upon *lectio divina,* is based on a millennium of Christian contemplative tradition. The barriers that we have created and our own internal "noise," however, must be overcome before we can fully allow the silence of God to well up from within and heal us.[16]

Certainly, *Lectio divina*—reading and reflecting on Scripture—offers a good way to access the powerful tools of Centering Prayer, but the same procedure works with any spiritual text. Here are the four-step guidelines Keating recommends to start a lifelong practice of Centering Prayer.

1. Choose a sacred word.

Centering Prayer begins with a *sacred word* rather than unintelligible utterances from an ancient language or resonant syllables. The word must have personal significance, because you want to tap into the root system of meaning beneath the organic sound. It can be anything with deep significance. Spirituality is connective, which is why Centering Prayer links to a sacred word rather than neutral sounds. The effect is self-evident. How could anyone repeat *peace* or *light* or *joy* without becalming the mind, or illuminating the path ahead, or rising above sorrow to rejoice in the Lord, even briefly? If the word flows like a cool, natural spring from within you, drinking deeply from its living water will carry you beyond yourself to a firsthand encounter with God, the wellspring of life.

Fr. Keating suggests images from his Catholic heritage: *Lord, Jesus, Father, Mother,* or *Mary.* Words with significance from other languages also work: *Abba, Adonai, Agape, Amor, Jesu, Jeshua, Kyrie, Mater, Maria, Shalom.* Anything conveying a sense of the Divine Presence will suffice: *peace, love, mercy, silence, stillness, calm, faith,* or *trust.* To this list you could add Metaphysical Christian terms, for example: *light, healing, prosperity, harmony, oneness, unity, faith, strength, love, wisdom, power, imagination, understanding, will, order, zeal, elimination, life;* or expressions from other religious traditions like *Ahura Mazda, Allah, Allahu Akbar, Brahma, Buddha, Chih, Compassion, Gaia, Great Spirit, Kami-Sama, karma, Khalsa, Mindfulness, Naam, Sangha, Shiva, Vishnu,* or *Yin-Yang.*

Any word that evokes a sense of God-presence or heightened spirituality will do nicely. Keating says it is important not to change it during the prayer period. He also suggests an alternative to word-based Centering.

> A simple inward gaze upon God may be more suitable for some persons than the sacred word. In this case, one consents to God's presence and action by turning inwardly to God as if gazing upon him. The same guidelines apply to the sacred gaze as to the sacred word.[17]

Substituting an inward, *apophatic* gaze toward God instead of focusing on a word is probably too advanced for the beginner in Centering Prayer. Word-based Centering is a *kataphatic* technique for achieving mystical awareness, not unlike slapping training wheels on a child's first bike. Advanced meditators may be able to slip into the Silence beyond thought without effort, but most of us will probably need to find the door to the place within, which the King James Version called our inner *closet*, rather than walk through the walls that form this sacred space. The New Revised Standard Version modernizes the Greek idiom to *"go into your room and shut the door,"* but the same principle applies.[18] Centering Prayer can open the door "into your room" where God awaits like a patient Parent. Once you have selected your sacred word, it is time to begin.

2. Sitting comfortably, repeat the word inwardly.

Keating says get comfortable, but not so comfortable you fall asleep. He recommends a position that keeps the back straight. Closing eyes helps to let go of external distractions. Sit comfortably and close your eyes. Introduce the sacred word "as the symbol of your consent to God's presence and action within."[19] When speaking the word inwardly, Keating recommends doing it "as gently as laying a feather on a piece of absorbent cotton."[20]

3. Let stray thoughts drift away; return to center.

"Thoughts" include feelings, images, memories, reflections, commentaries—anything that beckons you away from

Centering on your word. Buddhists call this "monkey mind" after the branch-to-branch flittering of monkeys in search of fruit. How common is the problem, and how quickly can it be permanently overcome? During a recent visit to Unity Institute® and Seminary, Bhante Wimala told my students he struggles with Monkey Mind even today, after a lifetime of spiritual discipline. If the mind of a 50-year-old Buddhist monk, formally addressed as *the Venerable*, still wanders during meditation, what is the likelihood you will encounter similar distractions? Father Keating says stray thoughts are a part of Centering Prayer, requiring no Herculean effort to exorcise them.

> By "returning ever-so-gently to the sacred word," a minimum of effort is indicated. This is the only activity we initiate during the time of Centering Prayer.[21]

Keating says the sacred word may actually become vague or disappear. Not a problem. In fact, the goal of Centering Prayer is to move through language to mystical awareness. Sit in the Silence, experience the Oneness beyond words, or simply relax into thought-free, uncluttered space. Return to your sacred word when other thoughts rush into the quiet time.

4. End with silence.

Like fresh-baked bread, Fr. Keating's recipe for Centering Prayer calls for a restful, cool-down period at the end of the process. He advises a few minutes of silence with eyes closed before returning to everyday life and conversation. If Centering Prayer is a group activity, someone could lead the "Lord's Prayer," 23rd Psalm, or some non-Christian expression such as the Muslim *Shahadah,* declaration of faith in God and the Prophet. Other appropriate ending thoughts include Freeman's "Prayer for Protection," or other well-known prayers, like the following from the 14th-century spiritual classing *The Cloud of Unknowing*:

> GOD, unto whom all hearts be open, and unto whom all will speaketh, and unto whom no privy thing is hid. I beseech Thee so for to cleanse the intent of mine heart with the unspeakable gift of Thy grace, that I may perfectly love Thee, and worthily praise Thee. Amen.[22]

The group leader could also recite something more exotic, like the opening lines of the Christian-influenced "Maasai Creed" of East Africa.

> We believe in the one High God, who out of love created the beautiful world and everything good in it. He created man and wanted man to be happy in the world. God loves the world and every nation and tribe on the earth. We have known this High God in the darkness, and now we know him in the light.[23]

Variations on Centering Prayer

The above is the formula for Centering Prayer as a 20-minute activity. However, my favorite use of the sacred word is an abbreviated application that incorporates the benefits of repetitive prayer within the framework of Centering. Simply take your word with you and play it as a meaningful mantra throughout your week. Whether driving to work, pausing between chores, walking the shopping lanes at Wal-Mart, or watching the kids play soccer, let your sacred word be the mental default you return to whenever you find an opening. If you go long periods without remembering to play the word in your mind, don't feel disgruntled. Just hit the restart button and *gruntle* yourself again.

Some people—myself included—find their sacred "Word for the Week" from the well-known source of the "daily word," *Daily Word*® magazine. You can locate today's word at *www.dailyword.com*.

Check Your Knowledge

1. Why does Centering use a well-known key word rather than a sound from an unfamiliar language like Sanskrit?
2. How does Centering work when biblical texts warn about "vain repetitions"?
3. Explain "mindful prayer" as a goal of Centering.
4. What story does Sr. Melannie Svoboda tell about hard work in Centering?
5. Describe the four-step Centering Prayer process.
6. How does the author use Centering during the week?

Discussion Starters

1. Have you ever meditated on a single word? Describe the experience.
2. Make a list of 20 words to use in Centering. Look at the list—any surprises?
3. What might happen if you taught your non-Unity friends and relatives how to do Centering Prayer? Could this be a common spiritual meeting ground?
4. What do you think about repetitious prayer? Discuss the examples cited from Islam, the Baha'i Faith, Roman Catholicism, and Pure Land Buddhism.
5. If you spent a week affirming *peace* or *light* or *joy,* would it affect your attitude?
6. Can you imagine a world in which vast numbers of people go about their daily tasks with their prayer word playing in the background? What kind of a world might we become?

Suggested Activity:
Centering With Music

Note: This can be done as an individual or group activity, or as a meditation exercise.

Centering prayer as described in the chapter is an excellent activity. Let me add one further element to the mix with this add-on. Try "centering" with music rather than a single word. Find a recurring musical theme or sonorous, repetitious sound—Native American flutes, Taizé chanting, classical organ music that floods space with light and turns a closet into a vaulted cathedral. Play your music and be present to it. If stray thoughts come to mind, release them like monkeys playing through. Return and center on your music.

After 10 to 15 minutes, slowly return … gradually turn down the sound. You might want to sit in silence a few moments more. Then write, or talk with others.

Remember, there is no need to attempt meditative acrobatics. You cannot get it wrong, even if the monkeys prevail. At least you will have playtime.

15

A GOLDEN KEY FOR PRIVATE FRANKLIN

Scientific Prayer will enable you, sooner or later, to get yourself, or anyone else, out of any difficulty on the face of the earth. It is the Golden Key to harmony and happiness. To those who have no acquaintance with the mightiest power in existence, this may appear to be a rash claim, but it needs only a fair trial to prove that, without a shadow of doubt, it is a just one. You need to take no one's word for it, and you should not. Simply try it for yourself, and see.[1]

Emmett Fox's *Golden Key* exercise is a modified, nonverbal form of repetitious Centering on the Divine Presence and Power for use during times of trouble. I like to think of Fox's brief essay as the second phase of the Baha'i "Remover of Difficulties" prayer. Although they are theologically unrelated, both promise relief from any sort of problem by persistent application of spiritual principles. Like the Baha'i writings, Fox is quietly adamant about the effectiveness of Centering on God. He guaranteed results in the preamble to his short composition, featured above.

When I read those words early in my career in ministry, I'll have to admit my response was flagrant skepticism. *Maybe that was hyperbole to get the readers' attention.* Not so. Fox doubled-down on his opening with an even bolder assertion:

Beginners often get startling results the first time, for
all that is essential is to have an open mind and sufficient faith to try the experiment. Apart from that, you
may hold any views on religion, or none.[2]

*All right, Rev. Fox, let's have this magical solution you've dis-
covered to fix problems great and small.* I continued to read.

As for the actual method of working, like all fundamental things, it is simplicity itself. All that you
have to do is this: Stop thinking about the difficulty,
whatever it is, and think about God instead. This is
the complete rule, and if only you will do this, the
trouble, whatever it is, will presently disappear. It
makes no difference what kind of trouble it is. It may
be a big thing or a little thing; it may concern health,
finance, a law-suit, a quarrel, an accident, or anything
else conceivable; but whatever it is, just stop thinking about it, and think of God instead—that is all you
have to do.[3]

I reread the passage three or four times, thinking I'd missed
something. Turn from worry over difficulties to thoughts of
God instead? Isn't that denial, in the negative-psychological
sense of the word? I went back to the opening and reread an
important line I had skipped over in haste to get the package unwrapped: *"You need to take no one's word for it, and you
should not. Simply try it for yourself, and see."*[4] After trying the
Golden Key on a few occasions, I discovered turning my
thoughts away from worry toward the Presence and Power
of God proved a good strategy. Most of the problems melted
away during the redirection process, which could have been
a coincidence.

I remained mildly skeptical.

Then I met Private Franklin, and everything changed. Let me tell you her story.[5]

Five prisoners came to my Chapel that sunny Monday morning. I glanced down the row of manacled soldiers—two males, three females—and nodded at the uniformed guard.

"Thank you, Sergeant. I'll take good care of them. Please remove the shackles."

He shook his head. "Can't do that, Chaplain. They're in custody."

"This is an Army chapel," I reminded him. "They'll behave."

"I dunno, sir." He hesitated, blue eyes darting from face to face, as if inspecting them for signs of flight risk. "Don't want to be responsible for nothin' going wrong."

"Don't worry. I've been in the Army long enough to know that if anything goes wrong, it's on the guy who signs the papers." I jotted my name in the proper box and returned the clipboard and watched as he carefully unlocked each of the five soldiers' green pant legs.

I was serving as a U.S. Army Chaplain assigned to the Fourth Mechanized Infantry Division at Fort Carson, Colorado, and I talked the powers-that-be into reopening a battered, World War II vintage wood frame chapel near the back gate. Although it apparently had a long and distinguished history as a religious facility, when I received the keys to the place, it was immediately obvious the only creatures meeting in this battered house of worship were the church mice. And they scampered everywhere.

My dog came to work with me in those days, an old female border collie named Missy. She reverted to puppyhood as soon as she saw the target-rich environment of Wildmouse Chapel, as we called the place. Missy never actually *caught* any mice, but she loved to chase the little varmints, who suddenly seemed eager to relocate.

My enlisted Chaplain Assistant—a sharp-eyed woman—took one look at the mud-crusted floors, dirty pews, and grimy, colored-glass windows and announced, "Chaplain, we need some help here."

That's when I called the Post Confinement Facility and arranged for a cleaning detail to be assigned to us every day until further notice. Most prisoners were for AWOL (*Absent Without Leave*) or minor drug offenses; they usually served their sentences of three-, six-, or 12-month increments followed by discharge to civilian life.

This particular morning, I noticed one of the female soldiers loitering in the chapel near a rack of pamphlets, lifting a pamphlet and looking at it briefly, replacing it and then repeating the procedure with the next one. As the rest of the work crew scuttled to their tasks at the urging of my Chaplain's Assistant, this young woman lingered. She was about 19 or 20 with black hair and dark eyes. Her name tag read *Franklin*.

"So, Private Franklin, how's it going today?"

"Not so good, sir." She put another pamphlet back in the rack.

"Anything I can help with?"

She told me her story. My best recollection is that Franklin was incarcerated for one of the typical minor offenses. To be honest, I don't remember exactly what she did to land her in the Post Confinement Facility, but that Monday morning she had another six months left on her sentence. At first I thought she was just feeling depressed about the idea of spending half a year of her young life in custody; to a woman in her late teens, six months represented a significant percent of her brief lifespan.

But that wasn't her problem. She explained that she had broken some minor rule of the Confinement Facility and was awaiting the determination as to what her punishment would be. As one might imagine, military prisons are strictly disciplined. However, despite several inexcusable incidents that have recently caught public attention, I can honestly say after 20-plus years in uniform that I've never known of any prisoners who were abused by guards or other soldiers. *Tough but fair* was the rule. Nevertheless, corrections personnel have ways to maintain good order and discipline among those already incarcerated, and doing so without slipping into abuse presents an ongoing challenge for prison staff.

One common solution is to segregate disruptive or disobedient offenders from more cooperative ones, a kind of advanced form of "time-out" as punishment for prison violating rules. Anything not serious enough to add more jail time to the sentence was usually handled by depriving the prisoner of privileges, with levels of deprivation becoming more severe according to the severity of the transgression or the number of repeated occurrences.

Like her initial offense, I don't recall what stockade rule this young woman had broken, but Private Franklin felt she had done something that could get her the ultimate punishment, short of adding more time. She suspected they were going to send her to Disciplinary Segregation, or D.S., and the thought terrified her.

As I recall it, D.S. was also arranged in a gradient of severity. Everything from being held alone in a row of other single-person jail cells, to the nuclear option of in-house punishment: total disciplinary segregation. There was a bunk with the typical metal-net suspension—no mattress or bedding provided until bedtime—plus a sink without mirror and toilet without a seat. Thick, plaster walls, as well as the ceiling, floor, and door were all painted black. A solitary window, closed and sealed, was also painted black. There must have been some kind of electrical lighting overhead, but I don't recall whether it was a fluorescent tube or dangling bulb.

Unruly soldiers could be locked up in this extreme form of D.S. for up to two weeks! Their only break was getting out, once a day, for a five-minute shower. No radios, reading, or writing materials were allowed, although the prisoners were permitted religious books. Chaplains provided Bibles, often motivated not so much as a way of spreading Christianity as by the need to give the confinees something to do. One soldier I visited told me matter-of-factly he had read *the whole Bible four times* during his 14 days in D.S. He said reading the "Good Book" passed the hours and kept him from the anguish of insufferable boredom, which of course carried the brunt of the punishment of D.S.

Later, I found the guards would allow other religious literature, so I began slipping the prisoners copies of *Daily Word* and *Unity Magazine®*. To give equal time to a variety of religious traditions, I also handed out copies of other Protestant journals such as *Our Daily Bread* and *The Upper Room,* as well as *Catholic Digest.* Bibles remained the most requested, so I got copies in English and Spanish and made a run to the stockade regularly with my sack of spiritual goodies. To my recollection, we had no Buddhists, Hindus, or Muslims in jail during my tenure as a prison-visiting chaplain back in the 1980s. Even so, I probably could have provided any religious book—the Bhagavad Gita, Quran, or the 6,200-plus pages of the Jewish Talmud—and it would have been snapped up for the chance to read something new.

It was on these trips I learned about prisoner details being signed out to work around the Post, and that was how Private

Franklin and her associates arrived at Wildmouse Chapel one sunny morning.

"And I'll find out about my sentence tonight," she said. I noticed a tear forming in her eye, but she looked away, trying not to show her feelings. Up to two weeks in Disciplinary Segregation—two weeks in a black room with a bed without a mattress, a toilet without a seat, and nothing to do but read the Bible. It was a scary proposition for a young person. I am not so old as to not remember how hard it was for me to sit still at that age, and I've never been incarcerated.

So what do you do, Chaplain? The dye is cast. It's not like I could have called the stockade and asked them to reconsider the verdict. Military Chaplains don't have that kind of power. We are marginal people in a highly structured, vertical-power system. There was nothing I could do to keep her from the fate which she, after all, brought upon herself by the choices she made. No matter how slight the offense might seem to a civilian—after all, you can walk off the job at a Burger Barn, and they won't send the police after you, unless you take the cash register with you—*but this is the Army*, and Private Franklin knew she was surrendering some civilian rights when she took the oath of enlistment.

Still … Metaphysical Christians are supposed to believe in the power of prayer to work wonders regardless of circumstances or appearances to the contrary. My eye caught a yellow booklet on the top row of the pamphlet rack. *The Golden Key*. What would this frightened young woman think of Fox's outrageous ideas, when she might have to spend the next two weeks in a black cubicle thinking about her problem? True, the *Golden Key* had usually worked for me, whenever I had the faith to try it. But it is such an audacious claim—all problems, regardless?

I looked at Franklin, took a deep breath, and handed her the booklet. "Here's a little essay which has helped me. Why don't you sit down and take a minute. In fact, take as long as you need to pray and get your thoughts together."

She thanked me and accepted the yellow pamphlet. I returned to my office as she slid into a freshly dusted and polished pew. The sanctuary was quiet because my Chaplain's Assistant had taken the work crew outside for some yard work. A few minutes later, I noticed Franklin was still at prayer, but within an hour when I passed the sanctuary again, she was gone. Checking outside to make sure she hadn't decided risking a jailbreak was preferable to solitary confinement, my fears were immediately alleviated. The Army has an old saying about how to beautify a military environment: *"If it doesn't move, pick it up. If it's too big, paint it."* I was glad to see Franklin painting rocks along the front lawn, and I thought she actually smiled.

To this day, I don't know if she read the *Golden Key*, much less tried its simple principle. I *do* know I placed that yellow booklet in her hands and gave Franklin more than enough time in the quiet coolness of Wildmouse Chapel to read, pray, and meditate. Fox's opening words—*"prayer ... will enable you to get yourself, or anyone else, out of any difficulty on the face of the earth ..."*—must have sounded like a church bell in the night to Franklin.

Late afternoon came, and my Chaplain's Assistant said we needed to get this crew back again tomorrow, because they were the best workers we'd ever had. So Missy the Border Collie climbed into the back of my car and we followed the two-and-a-half-ton Army truck back to the Post Confinement Facility. My dog waited patiently with her nose out the open window while I went inside to see the NCO in charge. He was a Sergeant First Class, E-7, the kind we called an "old soldier." A fellow Vietnam veteran, he was standing ramrod straight and checking off the names of prisoners as they came back from various work details around Fort Carson. When I requested this same group tomorrow, he said no problem.

"Except for one." He looked at his clipboard. "Can't let you have Franklin."

I nodded. "I know. She's got Disciplinary Segregation."

He chuckled. "Naw, that ain't the reason."

"So, why then …?"

My frown must have betrayed the confusion, because the sergeant motioned for me to follow him a few paces away from the small knot of prisoners. He held up the clipboard and showed me a thin sheet of paper, unmistakably torn from the kind of flimsy newsprint that scrolled from a military tele-communications printer in those last days before computers took over.

"We just got this message. Franklin's sentence has been reduced to time served. She's getting out tomorrow."

My voice was barely audible. "But she has six months left …"

He laughed. "Not anymore, Chaplain. Looks like God gave this one a *'get out of jail early'* card."

When I returned, speechless, to my car, Missy looked at me with a doggy glance that seemed to say, *"I could've told you."*

As I write these words, over a quarter of a century later, I still find my eyes filling with tears. Was this a coincidence, or a demonstration of the power of Omnipotent-Omnipresent Spirit? The message was already in the system. Private Franklin would have been released no matter what happened at Wildmouse Chapel that day. However, irrational as some may find my conclusion to be, I am certain to the center of my being that God engineered and executed a "miracle" through the ordinary events of an ordinary day.

"You need to take no one's word for it," Emmett Fox had written, "and you should not. Simply try it for yourself, and see." I am not ready to go all the way and affirm that Centering on thoughts of God will *always* have positive results, but whether the "Golden Key" unlocks the doors of your prison cell like Private Franklin, or swings open an upstairs window to higher possibilities in your life, I am now a certified advocate of Centering as a spiritual discipline.

Check Your Knowledge

1. Summarize Emmett Fox's *Golden Key* exercise.
2. What does Fox say about how to prove the method works?
3. Who was Private Franklin, and how did the author meet her?
4. Why did the author introduce Private Franklin to the *Golden Key*?
5. What was the outcome of their encounter?
6. How did this incident convince the author about the value of Centering?

Discussion Starters

1. How does the story of Private Franklin work in your belief system?
2. What might the author have decided if things turned out differently when Franklin went back to the Confinement facility?
3. Do "miracles" happen? Was this true story an example of one?
4. Have you had any experiences like this chapter? Miraculous deliverances after prayer?
5. If you believe Divine Spirit is capable of working in the tangible world, why doesn't Spirit help more people? Why do the innocent suffer? (*Theodicy*)
6. Do you believe Private Franklin's fate was altered because she read about and presumably tried Emmett Fox's "Golden Key"?

Suggested Activity:
The Golden Key

Note: This can be done as an individual or group activity, or as a meditation exercise.

Following Emmett Fox's formula, become still and think of some difficulty you, a friend, or loved one is facing. After fixing the problem in mind, let it go. Release all thoughts of trouble, all anxiety about outcomes. Turn your attention to thoughts of God, however you conceive Divine Spirit to be. Center on thoughts about Divine Presence and Power. Your prayer cannot fail—no matter the outcome—because it is not you alone but the Father-Mother-Spirit that works in and through all things. Think of the line in Philippians: "I can do all things through God who strengthens me."

If your mind begins to wander or if anxieties arise, return to thoughts of God's Presence and Power. No matter whether you conceive of God as Supreme Creator, or Divine-Indwelling, of the Power of the Natural Universe; many gods, may spirits, many saints and many angels; you get the Whole Package, or at least as much as you want.

Carry these thoughts with you as you go forth. If you are in a group, you might want to discuss any results of your *Golden Key* exercise in future meetings.

16

MEDITATIVE EXPLORATION AND ONE-PERSON RITUALS

Every culture on earth … has produced some sort of mental practice which might be termed meditation. It all depends on how loose a definition you give to that word. Everybody does it, from Africans to Eskimos.[1]

When Westerners hear the word *meditation*, a likely stereotype pops up: Robed practitioners sitting cross-legged on a bamboo mat, emptying their minds of conscious thought by an assortment of taxing mental disciplines—concentration on breathing, fixing their gaze on a candle flame, or reciting a mantra. Some observers classify meditation under the two broad categories mentioned earlier, *apophatic* or *kataphatic* (sometimes *cataphatic*). Normally, these refer to any attempt to define God by saying what He/She/It *is not* (apophatic) or what God *is* (kataphatic). In other spiritual disciplines, such as prayer and meditation, the words take on slightly different nuances. The Venerable Henepola Gunaratana—octogenarian Buddhist monk from Sri Lanka with a Ph.D. from American University in Washington, D.C.—explains the two terms:

In the Christian tradition there are, broadly speaking, two kinds of prayer. "Kataphatic" prayer has content; it uses words, images, symbols, ideas. "Apophatic" prayer has no content. It means emptying the mind of words and ideas and simply resting in the presence of

God. The word "meditation" can be used in reference
to both kataphatic and apophatic prayer.[2]

Meditation advocate Josh Davis says the skill required is
not the ability to prevent stray thoughts, but learning how to
respond effectively when they invariably occur.

> In apophatic meditation one empties the mind, while
> in cataphatic one fills it with a visualization, an object,
> a mantra, or a feeling. The object of focus expands by
> virtue of one's attention until it fills one's entire uni-
> verse ... As a witness of thoughts, understand that
> you will not stop thoughts by reacting to them—it is
> precisely reaction that is holding you back, as reaction
> requires attention. Simply be aware of your thoughts
> as they appear and disappear, always returning to
> your point of focus, be it some thing, or nothing at
> all.[3]

For the purposes of our discussion, we shall say *apophatic*
receptivity offers powerful tools for achieving peace of mind
through passive stillness, while *kataphatic* activity expresses
through meditation that requires creative input from participants. This latter category includes various techniques that
can be grouped under the heading of *meditative exploration*.
Perhaps the most mentally vigorous method of all, meditative
exploration lets the kataphatic content out of its creative bag.

Spiritual Exercises

Meditative exploration has deep roots in the Christian
faith. Reflecting on spiritual imagery dates at least to St. Ignatius Loyola (1491–1556), founder of the Society of Jesus (the
Jesuits). Inigo de Loyola was born in 1491 in the Basque country of northern Spain. The youngest of 13 children, the family dispatched Inigo to Arevalo, a town in Castile, where he

served as a page for Juan Velasquez de Cuellar, one of King Ferdinand's provincial governors.[4]

Like Harry Potter at Hogwarts, life at this late medieval court agreed with him. Young Inigo found himself at home in the world of knights, chivalry, and highborn ladies. Unfortunately, he fell madly in love with a woman whose social caste towered far above him. Some historians have speculated the object of his affection might have been a member of the royal family, an impossible match for a member of the lesser nobility like Inigo. Based on the romantic notions of chivalry, he took to fantasizing about her, living in his mind the life they could not have together. Later, after Ignatius declared his intent to seek a spiritual path by entering the priesthood, the habit of fantasizing about deeply cherished ideas continued in his devotional life. Creative visioning became the backbone of his *Spiritual Exercises*, the education program Ignatius created for initiates to the Jesuit Order, which he and his friends founded.[5]

> The Spiritual Exercises are divided into a series of four "weeks"—not literally seven 24-hour-day weeks, but "movements" or "stages"—with accompanying prayer, visualizations, reflections, and spiritual exercises for each week … [Exerciants] attempt to get out of God's way in our hearts, deepen our sense of interior freedom from the hero-system of popular secular society, and allow God's own impelling Spirit to lead us in taking action, out of this new freedom, which is authentically emancipatory for other men and women.[6]

But things moved slower centuries ago, and not everyone can take a month, or even a week, from working to attend an extended program like the Spiritual Exercises. How can super-busy, 21st-century people find time for spiritual activity? The Jesuits offer modified programs for busy *exerciants* (participants in the *Exercises*):

> These Exercises are usually made in one of three different ways: first, extended over approximately thirty days in a silent retreat away from home, which was its original form; or second, as condensed into a weekend or an eight-day retreat based on Ignatian themes; or third, in the midst of daily life, while living at home, over a period of several months.[7]

Even if you can't spare a vacation-sized block of time, there are ways to inject spiritual breaks into harried schedules. Tom Zender, former CEO of Unity School and author of *God Goes to Work,* says a brief period of meditation can improve your day.

> Perhaps the first point is why do it. Some key benefits include more creativity, focus, patience, teamwork, energy, and feelings of wellbeing. There are many ways to meditate in the workplace. Just being quiet for a few moments with eyes closed, focusing on breathing and relaxing. Thinking of something beautiful and serene, connecting with our own understanding of a spiritual higher power, and listening to some soft music can be helpful—while gently releasing any negative thoughts. Brief times are good and longer times are better. St. Francis de Sales said, "If you are too busy to meditate for a short time, then meditating for a longer time is essential."[8]

We need better ways to find the kind of instant, postmodern "desert spirituality" which Fr. Henri Nouwen addressed in his book, *The Way of the Heart.* How can a busy person discover sacred space in urban or suburban settings? Why not brief, coffee-break meditation at work, as Tom Zender suggests, or listening to meditative music in the car? Find a Centering word and let it play in mind as your default mantra ("*Peace ... peace ... peace ...*") during the work week.

An excellent resource is Zender's book, *One-Minute Meditations at Work*, which like the general *Daily Word* format, provides 365 spiritual and inspirational messages for working people of all faiths. Each day focuses on a different Word and offers an affirmation, a meditation, and an inspired quotation.[9]

We've Covered Lots of Ground

In this study of prayer, we have paused several times to allow for self-guided meditation. The *Temple of the Mind* exercise in Chapter 5 invited participants to design their ideal house of worship, much like someone might build a "dream home" by working with architects and contractors. Chapter 11 encouraged a follow-up visit to this customized sanctuary to explore the grounds, gardens, fountains, and temple itself. Chapter 13 suggested walking into a biblical scene, such as the Nativity, during the *Meditatio* step of *Lectio Divina*. Finally, in the previous chapter we looked at Centering and discussed methods for discovering the Presence and Power of the Divine through repetition of sacred words and holding images in mind.

Now we push beyond those examples to examine more possibilities for self-guided, image based, kataphatic meditation. We'll sample the techniques of meditative exploration with four good examples: *Time Travel, Vision Quest, Encounter With the Great Teacher*, and *God's In-Box*. The chapter concludes with a bonus fifth activity, a hybrid blend of introspective meditation and hands-on contact with a sacred object, which I call the *God Rock* exercise.

We'll begin with a nighttime visit to Carmel Bay, 50 years ago.

1. Time Travel: *Run the dark beaches.*

With the use of your power of imagination, it is possible to travel back in time and "visit" yourself as a younger person. Think of an experience in childhood, perhaps with a parent or loved one no longer alive. Cast your mind across the decades to elementary school, or your first encounter with young love. You can even comfort yourself at a moment of disappointment or pain in the distant past. Tell that shy adolescent what a marvelous, beautiful, radiant person you behold. Then give yourself a hug.

Because you are always changing and growing, the progression works both ways in time. You can project your mind back, or look ahead and give yourself a *"well done, thou good and faithful servant"* as your life on this world draws to a close. Your life is a process, not merely the slice in time seen in today's mirror.

Let me share a deep memory. I was an 18-year-old army private attending the prestigious Defense Language Institute in Monterey, California. Luckily, I made friends in the community and was able to spend weekends as their houseguest in picturesque Carmel-by-the-Sea, wandering the courtyard shops and lanes of cypress trees that overlooked a white sand bay. It was October, 1964. The air was clean, salty, and cool. The California coast at Monterey-Carmel offers an invigorating Mediterranean climate—warm afternoons, cool nights, sea breeze. At that time, I had never been to sunny Crete or the humid tropics of Southeast Asia or the Austrian Alps, so it was all new to me.

I recall one perfect evening when the sun went down over the Pacific like an orange fireball dipped into a lake of liquid silver. The night came rushing after the departing sun, and brought millions of stars on its back like a jeweled compensatory offering for the vanishing light. I stood on the tide-smoothed beach near the water's edge and felt strong and young. Thinking about the day just passed, I started jogging, slowly, the *Airborne shuffle, along the* wet sand.

My mind drifted forward in time and sought myself in the distant future. What would I be like as an old man? In those late-teen years, "old" meant 50 or 60, which today doesn't seem so old at all. I let my imagination wander down the corridors of time and I found myself in the gray years ahead. I remember thinking, *When I am old, I want to remember how it feels to run along a dark beach on youthful legs.* Feet slapping the wet sand, I ran with arms raised to a starry sky and listened to the symphony of crashing surf. *Remember this …* I said to my future self.

Decades later, I complete the circle through meditative exploration, traveling back in mind-time to that night in 1964. The Carmel Beach experience was before marriages and children, before war in Southeast Asia, before trekking the globe and learning vast new information about life and religion and human history. My solidarity with the younger *me* flows from viewing life as a process rather than a snapshot.

I am not just the 60-something seminary professor who today pecks at the keyboard to write these words. I am the infant in the crib of a working-class home; I am the little boy who recited his memorized Bible verse on Palm Sunday at Zion's United Church of Christ; I am the young soldier scrambling from a crashed, burning helicopter on the slopes of a hillside near the Vietnamese-Laotian border. I am the seminary student learning about world religions and gaining a new perspective of the Christian faith. I am the mature man, raising children, experiencing divorce and remarriage, teaching public school, pastoring churches, writing for publication, teaching graduate school, slowing down with advancing years but still active enough to earn a doctorate in my early 60s.

Furthermore, I know there is more to come. Today's vigorous schedule will seem like running on young legs to the truly "old" man I will one day become. Exploring memories of that dark beach beside the pounding surf half a century ago, I realize the journey has been, is now, and always will be *good*, regardless of the pain or difficulties, because the whole sweep of life in its majesty and mystery is a good and trustworthy process. Run the dark beaches; commune with the ongoing story of life. However changed externally, your inner self is the good person you will always be.

2. Vision Quest: *Find your animal spirit guide.*

Cultural anthropologists have encountered the phenomenon of vision questing among indigenous peoples, from the polar regions to the tropics. Sometimes vision-seeking governs the rite of passage to full adulthood, but other practices feature visioning for special guidance, which is unrelated to any phase of life. Maurizio G. Smith, speaker and author on Native American subjects, said in a lecture on the "American Indian Vision Quest" he presented to the Theosophical Library Center:

> The Vision Quest helps the seeker to realize his oneness with all life and that all creation is his own relative. It helps him to pray to the Great Spirit for further knowledge of the One who is the source of all things yet vastly greater ... [Most seekers expect] to see in vision one or more guardian spirits, usually in the form of an animal, a bird, or as a natural force like thunder and lightning. This guardian spirit is a reflection of the Great Spirit in each seeker, and will remain with him all his life to help and protect him, especially if he keeps his heart purified.[10]

While most cultures allow everyone to seek assistance from the spirit world—males and females, young and old—tribal Shamans commonly serve as either star players or sideline coaches. To receive guidance from the spirit world, these proto-professional religious leaders might ingest large quantities of tobacco or hallucinogenic plants, or deprive themselves of nourishment and sleep for long periods, which often induce dream-states. The resulting delirium provides phantasmagoric encounters later interpreted for magical or divination purposes, or to receive answers to questions that are perplexing the tribe or its leadership.

With or without physical deprivation or chemical bolstering, shamans frequently seek visions to obtain healing remedies, or to discover spells to ward off or break the power of evil spirits, or incantations to bring luck, love, fertility, and protection from enemies. And before we as 21st-century sophisticates *tut-tut-tut* too smugly, let's power up our computers and Google for *psychic readings.* When I ran the search, more than *5.6 million* hits came back. Presumably, not all of them are websites posted by shamans of indigenous people.

Authentic vision quests practiced by native societies are organic to a particular culture, like food taboos, language dialects, or rules of sexual access and kinship. It is not possible for an outsider to clone the sweat lodge, Sun Dance, or peyote ritual without omitting vast stretches of cultural DNA, invariably committing massive faux pas of ignorance. In a similar context, it's obvious a band of suburban neo-pagans meeting in a room above the local New Age bookstore is wholly incapable of recreating the spirituality of Stonehenge. However, there is arguably some merit in honoring the ancient Britons through creative approximations of pre-Christian ritual, which celebrates the gods and goddesses of many cultures.

This is the tendril of connectivity that tenuously reaches from the inspired imagination to the soil of imagination from which both ancient ritual and postmodern recreation have sprung. A similar desire for cross-cultural contact, this time with the future, leads otherwise reasonable men and women to don futuristic military garb, make themselves up with head ridges, and swagger around *Star Trek* conventions muttering, *"These humans have no honor ..."* in the Klingon language.

The value of imaginative simulations based upon indigenous vision-seeking has the potential to connect participants with an imaginary past. Creating parallel rituals modeled on the vision quest—yet designed without dangerous or illegal components—can move the *exerciant* beyond speculation to an exploration of their own depths. In that spirit, knowing full well the inadequacies of replication by Native American wannabes, let's allow the bare elements of the Plains Indian vision quest to serve as a template for meditative exploration.

Like many native peoples, Lakota men and women traditionally set aside time at key moments of their lives to "cry for a vision."[11] Although cast in a Native American mold, the following description should not be viewed as an anthropological field study but as *inspirational fiction*. Imagine the scenes and events unfolding like a drama of the mind, with you as its central character. Today, you will *cry for a vision* and receive your Animal Spirit Guide.

> **Preparatory Notes:** You cannot choose your guide. It will choose you. I have led this exercise many times, and I have yet to discover anyone who imposed a preselected, favorite animal on the process with success. Keep your mind open, in the words of the old hymn, to "All Creatures Great and Small." Frankly, many people are surprised—some even shocked—at the critter who finally shows itself.

Your Animal Spirit Guide might speak, or might not. Keep an open mind. If you work the exercise with receptivity, your results will likely be profound. Sometimes no Animal Guide appears. This is not a personal failure. The exercise does not work the same for everyone, and even those who are not visited can benefit from a meditative pause in pristine wilderness.

Begin by reading the descriptive text, below, pausing where indicated to participate through your power of imagination. Although the narrative covers many hours of activity, the whole exercise need not take more than 20 minutes, or 30 at the very most. **Note:** This exercise is meant to be *meditative only*, as it contains some elements that could be dangerous if attempted without proper supervision, notably the sweat lodge experience and venturing alone into wilderness places.

Vision Quest for Animal Spirit Guide

Early. Dark before dawn. You rise from your lodge, a conical tipi fashioned of bison skins supported by wood poles. The scent of smoke floods the air as cooking fires are lit for the warriors who will hunt today, but you will not eat or drink today or tonight. To cry for a vision requires sacred fasting. Walk through the early dawn and experience this awakening Lakota community. Hear the rustlings of tipi flaps, barking dogs, a crying baby. Feel the roots and soft earth through the soles of your moccasins. Take a moment to explore the scents, sounds, and sights of this multisensual world.

Your first stop is the sweat lodge, where you will sit in silence and purge your body of impurities. It is sultry in here, like a sweltering summer night after much rain. You are fully clothed, as is traditional. In the center of the lodge are hot stones, which the shaman who tends the sweat lodge has heated for hours in a special, sacred fire outside the tipi. He periodically pours gourds of clean water over the steaming stones. The words of Lakota elder Black Elk come to mind. "The sweat lodge utilizes all powers of the universe: earth, and things that grow from the earth; water; fire; and air."[12] Sit quietly in the hot, wet space. Cleanse your body and mind.

After a good, long sweat, you emerge into the cool morning air. Gathering your bundle of buffalo robe, sacred pipe, eagle feather, and other items you wish to carry to the visioning ground, you leave the hoop of tipis and walk upslope until the sun is nearly at its zenith. Inhale the clean air, sweet with the smell of grass from the plain wafting around you. The land rises steeply now. Arriving at the summit, you reach a ledge where the land abruptly drops away to a vast canyon. Stand at the rim and peer into the canyon awhile.

Walking along the rim, you soon find a rectangular patch of ground covered with cut sage, prepared by the shaman for your quest. A stout pole marks the center and smaller poles for each of the four directions. Placing your bundle on the sage, spread out the buffalo robe and arrange your sacred objects.

Pray to *Wakan Tanka*, the Great Spirit, at each of the four directions. Take a few moments now to arrange your sacred place, and then send out a prayer to the North, South, East, and West …

Sitting on your robe, the musty scent of sage engulfs you. Repeat your prayer to the Great Spirit. Clear your mind. Be present to the natural world. Cloud and sky. Stone canyon dropping away from grasslands. Caressing breeze to relieve the afternoon heat. Watch the shows grow long as the sun passes to the western horizon. Experience the sunset, the darkening sky with its first star. Play your flute. Send a lingering melody down the canyon. Hear its notes echo back in the gathering darkness.

Stars appear in the clear sky, crisp as diamonds on black velvet in the clean night air. A silver slice of moon arises slowly. Far in the distance a wolf howls. Take up your flute and answer him.

The shaman has said it is permitted to sleep on the bed of sage with your head at the center pole. Play your flute until drowsy, and then nap under the stars and crescent moon.

Awake with the sunrise, stretch toward the light. Now wait patiently for your Animal Spirit Guide, if it has not already appeared. Follow your guidance about what to say or do. Take as long as you need.

After your Animal Spirit Guide departs, roll up your sacred items in your buffalo robe. The shaman comes to the canyon rim and together you walk in silence downslope toward the hoop of lodges. You return to the sweat lodge, where the shaman listens to your story about everything that happened. If you did not receive an Animal Spirit Guide, report that without hesitation. The vision quest does not work for everyone. Tell the shaman what your guide said or did.

When the final cleansing is complete, you may eat and drink. Perhaps you will want to step out of character and journal about the experience or simply write notes while they are fresh in your mind.

The Vision Quest can be adapted to any environment. For example, rescript the story from the Great Plains to a night atop a skyscraper in Manhattan, or an alien planet with six moons and two suns, or a fantasy world with castles and flying dragons. The exercise works best when adjusted to a setting you create. Most important, remember this is an exercise you can revisit whenever you choose, experimenting with locations and times and settings. Convert the indigenous peoples experience to an ancient, urbane Greek encounter with the Oracle at Delphi, or hear the voice of God inside the Jerusalem Temple's Holy of Holies. The possibilities are limited only by your energy and imaginative zeal.

If you found the vision quest an appealing possibility, let me introduce you to another method for receiving guidance from another source of wisdom.

3. Encounter With the Great Teacher

The difference between vision questing and the Great Teacher exercise is more form than substance. Both are encounters with sources of wisdom, except the Vision Quest looks for guidance in specific circumstances, and the Great Teacher exercise seeks a more generic experience with a guru or prophetic figure of your choice.

Preparatory Notes: As with the Vision Quest, read the following example of a Great Teacher scenario, pausing for reflection whenever needed.

A Walk in the Forest

Clear your mind by centering on a gentle word, such as *peace.* Repeat the calming word as you follow a grassy path into the cool shadows of a great forest. As gladness sweeps over you, look around at the thick trunks and scattered underbrush. Notice how the morning sun slices through green canopy to hurl shafts of light between the trees. Now and then a bird flitters from branch to branch, while others sing their melodies to attract feathered lovers. The scent of pine above mingles with aromatic mint from the tiny leaves underfoot.

Continue through this enchanted forest and experience it with all your senses.

After a few moments, leave the trail and stroll among the soaring trees. The air is alive with buzzing insects, but they go about their business and ignore you.

Reaching the tree line marking the forest edge, you discover a wide meadow with knee-high grasses dripping with dew. A low outcropping of erosion-smoothed bedrock dominates the middle of the clearing like a natural altar. Raising a hand to shield your eyes from the sudden onslaught of bright light, you now see someone seated upon the sun-drenched stone. As you cross the wet field, you realize who awaits. It is the Great Teacher. You approach reverently and sit upon the warm rock. Take a few moments to bask in the morning sunlight and absorb inner light from the presence of this special personage.

When ready, engage the Great Teacher in conversation as long as you want. Ask personal or theological questions. Raise an argument. Request specific healing or simply a blessing. The choice is yours.

When you are ready, bow respectfully to the Great Teacher and return through the forest to the path leading home …

After remaining quiet for a few more minutes, you might want to journal or make notes about the experience. If you are in a group, discuss the exercise as you feel guided. Always remember, the forest meadow is always there, and the Great Teacher awaits your next visit with serene patience. Return any time you want.

4. God's In-Box

A very simple meditation for groups or individual groups is an exercise I call *God's In-Box*. This is closely related to the Burning Bowl Ceremony and a distant cousin to other rites of reconciliation found in traditional and indigenous religions— sacrificial offerings, Yom Kippur; Confession, Penance and Absolution; infant and adult Baptism, plus many others.

> **Preparatory Notes:** The scenario begins with the assumption that the *exerciant* has something to release into God's hands, the troubles, concerns, fears, healing needs, and difficulties that need to be removed. The scene begins in the hallway outside God's Office in heaven, where the *exerciant* awaits entry.
>
> Theological permission slip—Don't be overly concerned about the anthropomorphic, dualistic elements of the exercise. It is a *story*, so give the scenario dramatic license, which playwrights call the *will-*

ing suspension of disbelief. It is an old practice without which fantasies, fairytales, and fables would be impossible. When Aesop's frustrated fox gives up trying to reach high-hanging fruit, she departs with the story's punch line: "The Grapes are sour, and not ripe as I thought."[13] If you push the story to behave rationally, Aesop loses the chance to deliver the moral of his fable, because foxes can't talk. Give the fanciful scenario of *God's In-Box* the same courtesy you might extend to a Road Runner cartoon, or we'll never see Wile E. Coyote get clobbered by the inevitable anvil from the sky.

So get a manila folder, stuff it with problems, challenges, celebrations, and requests, and let's begin …

God's In-Box

You are in the hallway outside God's office at Celestial HQ, at the corner of Presence and Power Streets, Heavenly City (or anywhere you want to locate it). Your hands grasp a thick manila file packed with notes about things you have been carrying around with you for a long time. Budgetary challenges, health care glitches, interpersonal relationships that are not up to code, and many other items you have brooded about in secret.

Think about your file folder for a few moments. What is in there? Be fearlessly honest with yourself. You never have to speak these thoughts aloud, but allow them to surface without shame or guilt. At this moment, realize troubles are what they are, but limitations and mistakes are not who *you* are. Wait in the corridor and review your file.

The door opens. Not surprisingly, an angelic being smiles—God's Executive Secretary, no doubt—and welcomes you into the reception office.

Enter, take a seat, and look around. Remember to open all your senses, not just the visual. What does this outer office smell like? How does the seat feel beneath you, the floor below? Are there sounds? Sit quietly and experience the space outside God's workplace.

A few minutes later the angelic Executive Secretary says, "God always approves of you, and, of course, you may go in."

You open the door and enter God's office.

God rises to greet you warmly. You may decide whether to raise your eyes to look at God, but do look at the desk and it's old-fashioned In-Box. Also, take notice of this office like you did the reception area. Scents, textures, sounds, flavors, colors?

After a long hug, God speaks. *"I believe you have something for me?"* A gesture toward the In-Box on the desk. *"Please put the file in there, and we're done."*

You place the folder full of joys and concerns atop a short stack of similar files in God's In-Box. Then you must step back, releasing the package you have delivered. (This may prove to be the hardest step of all.)

God says, *"Thanks. I've been trying to get you to send that to me for a long while. Now, get back to business. I'll take care of these matters."*

You ask for specific guidance, but God repeats the pledge to *"take care of these matters,"* then adds, *"But don't expect me to solve your problems by magic. Be open and receptive to possibilities that present themselves. You know the old preacher's story. This time, get in the boat, climb up to the helicopter. Don't drown on the roof."*

You leave feeling … (describe how you feel).

During the days and weeks ahead, whenever you begin to think about the problem(s) or challenge(s), remember where they are. God has promised to *"take care of these matters"* as long as you are *"open and receptive to possibilities that present themselves."*

As with other exercises, a quiet period for a few more minutes can be helpful, followed by journaling or writing notes about the experience. If you are in a group, discuss the exercise as you feel guided.

As with all meditative exploration, the experience may be repeated as frequently as needed.

During my Creative Spirituality retreats, I often teach the technique and add a tangible meditative exploration by sealing a shoebox with heavy tape, cutting a slot on the top, and encouraging participants to jot down problems, challenges, or celebrations on slips of paper. After prayer over the "offering," we take the cardboard box outside and safely immolate their problems. The ritual is reminiscent of the annual Burning Bowl Ceremony observed around New Year's Day by a growing number of progressive churches.

After working with soldiers and their families on retreats during my years as an Army Chaplain, I found this exercise quite popular among people of different religious backgrounds. I remember a few couples who especially enjoyed the technique and decided to create a home-based version of "God's In-Box" for family members to release concerns and proclaim celebrations privately during the daily routine. One family periodically took their box outdoors to burn safely, replacing it with a new one. Another clan of enthusiasts put their *In-Box* on top of the refrigerator, which the NCO husband said with a grin, "Gets it up there closer to God."

5. One-Person Rituals (OPRs) and "The God Rock"

One-Person Rituals (OPRs) spotlight visual imagery, tangible objects, and kinesthetic activities to heighten mind-body awareness to the connectedness of all things. "One-Person Ritual" describes what they offer: Sacred rites performed in solitude. At home, this could mean establishing a personal altar to decorate the space with meaningful objects, as suggested in Chapter 5. Displaying fruit and grain offerings might represent the ancient tie to your hunter-gatherer ancestors. Those offerings, of course, can be eaten after briefly reposing on the altar, thus providing opportunity for another ritual, not unlike Christian communion. Setting aside a meditation space, or planting a rock garden can offer space for OPRs.

Simple events easily translate into an OPR with a slight adjustment in mindfulness. Strolling down a country lane can become a prayer walk; a half-hour in the tub can be a prayer bath with inspirational music, or reading spiritual literature. Regular journaling, exploring one's credo, or singing in the shower—any activity that brings a sense of the Divine Oneness could be a One-Person Ritual. I pray inside my car while driving down the highway, and the opportunity for spiritual discernment as the vehicle passes through color-sprays of an auto-wash should not be overlooked. Mystical awareness transforms an ordinary event into a sacramental experience.

As the Sleepless Saint, Ram Gopal Babu, showed young Yogananda, the Divine Presence can be recognized everywhere if our vision is expansive enough to see how "all-pervading" it is. As part of my *Creative Spirituality* workshop, I developed an activity to demonstrate this principle. I call the exercise, "The God Rock." Although it is highly individualistic when performed, the practice works surprisingly well as an OPR or with a group.

To make this both an OPR and a group activity takes some planning. The goal is to lure participants beyond their ordinary perceptions into a sacramental, One-Person encounter with all-pervading Spirit. With only slight modification, you can use the exercise later in private meditative exploration.

Assume you are the group leader in the following exercise. Because of the individual participation of this activity, it is best done in groups of 30 or less. You now have a backstage pass to watch the sneaky way it is set up.

The God Rock

Before beginning, you will need a rock. Not a pebble, something substantial, but small enough to fit easily inside closed hands. Nothing too smooth. Not a worked stone or anything semiprecious. Go from the building and find your *show-and-tell* somewhere on the grounds, and do not let participants see you locating it. Take your stone to a restroom and wash all the dirt away, dry thoroughly, and hide the rock at a handy place in the room where you will lead the activity.

Begin with introductions, if necessary, and then ask people where God can be located. Within a short time, they will probably arrive at, "Within me and everywhere." (Yogananda's answer to the Sleepless Saint, but don't tell them yet.)

Hold up the God Rock and say something like this: "So if God is everywhere, then God must be in this rock, right?" After a moment of reflection—someone will invariably say *"not just in the rock,"* to which you agree and repeat the basic formula: God is everywhere, which means God is in this rock. At this point most people get what you are saying and are willing to give you the benefit of the doubt, if only to see where this is going.

Next, explain the exercise itself. You will pass the rock to the first person, who holds it for 20 or 30 seconds, centering on the Presence and Power of God within this solid object in hand. Without getting too specific, you might mention this is similar to Eastern disciplines to see the all-pervading nature of the Divine in every location.

Then softly play gentle, nondescript, instrumental music as the rock passes from hand to hand.

After the rock has passed through the group, retrieve it and ask them to slowly return to this time and place. When you stop the music, solicit remarks about what happened. Some people are unable to "feel" the Divine Presence in the stone, but most will report an experience of heightened mystical awareness. Occasionally, someone will comment about how powerful the God Rock felt. Was it used in other rituals? What special significance does this particular rock have that allows them to feel God within it so readily? When you tell them where you got the rock, they are often amazed, which is the whole point of the exercise. They have discerned the divinity in a common stone, just as people celebrating the Eucharist can experience the "real presence" of the Christ in the bread and cup.

Tell them the God Rock is a sacramental encounter. It will open their minds to a new way of thinking.

Create Your Own

Meditative exploration allows participants to experience any spiritual tradition more deeply. Sit with Buddha under the Bodhi Tree; listen from the crowd by Galilee as Jesus teaches his disciples from the stern of an anchored boat; ride with Muhammad as he departs from Mecca to Medina and the *Hijra* begins. These are a few scenarios, but your mind is capable of designing and exploring many more. Nineteenth-century skeptic Robert Ingersoll called for free exercise of the imagination in every human life, to include spirituality:

> Surely there is grandeur in knowing that in the realm of thought, at least, you are without a chain; that you have the right to explore all heights and depth; that there are no walls nor fences, nor prohibited places, nor sacred corners in all the vast expanse of thought.[14]

Humanity has made straight paths into the wilderness since our ancestors climbed down from the trees in Africa around 2 million years ago. Perhaps our time-distant relatives already had the rudiments of spirituality in the reverence for the earth's majesty, which Jane Goodall has discovered among the great apes. We can only speculate, and that ability to think backwards and forward in time is the key component in human awareness of ourselves as part of something grand, ongoing, and beyond imagination itself.

Check Your Knowledge

1. How did St. Ignatius Loyola contribute to the techniques of guided meditations?
2. Author and former Unity CEO Tom Zender suggests brief interludes of spiritual renewal are possible at the workplace. What does Zender specifically suggest?
3. How did the author use "time travel" to connect with his elder self?
4. Describe the imaginary Vision Quest for an animal spirit guide in this chapter.
5. What is "God's In-Box" and how can it help release burdens carried too long?
6. If you were told to find "the God Rock," where would you go?

Discussion Starters

1. Have you gone on a Guided Meditation retreat? Do you think St. Ignatius Loyola's "Spiritual Exercises" might be a worthwhile experience for you?
2. What kind of "time travel" meditation exercise would you like to try?
3. If you decided to go on a Vision Quest, would you make it a mental exercise only, or add some safe physical disciplines? Do you already know your Animal Spirit Guide, or are you prepared for a surprise? (One participant in a retreat led by the author wanted an eagle and got a much humbler creature.)
4. Have you had experiences with Burning Bowl Ceremonies? How does "God's In-Box" provide a portable version of that exercise?
5. Find a rock and meditate on the Presence and Power of God within it. The rock can be small, medium, or cliff-like.

Zen gardens sometimes feature big rocks in the center of a ring of sitting places, so meditators can focus on the strength and texture of the stone from many positions during different times of day.

6. If you were to choose a biblical scene to explore, what would it be? Why not go there soon?

Suggested Activity:
Create Your Own Meditative Exploration

Create your own Meditative Exploration exercise. Something wholly original. One-Person Ritual or group activity. You may use materials from sacred scripture, spiritual or secular literature, movies, or music. Follow the loose guidelines in this chapter.

Discuss the activity with others. Will you try it, or simply create and let it go?

17

FINAL THOUGHTS FOR AN
ENDLESS JOURNEY

What connections, if any, do the religions of humanity share in regard to spirituality and prayer? During this work, we have noted the temptation among progressives to leap over or kick down the fences that mark community boundaries for the sake of harmony among faiths. The first chapter of this work noted that lumping human faiths into a syncretistic omni-religion paradoxically denigrates its representative traditions by discounting the rich diversity of spiritual choices on the planet.

One result of the hunger for harmony is the movement to create "Interfaith" ministries in the USA. While motivated by a healthy desire for inclusiveness, synthesizing an *Interfaith* denomination is both a wistful glance at the potential for concord among religions and a misunderstanding about the role of geography, history, and culture in the evolutionary process that made us who we are today. People who attend meetings of interfaith alliances are not homogenized members of some emerging "Interfaith" religion, but are comprised of representatives of distinctive faiths, which grew organically.

Religious offshoots have naturally occurred in human history; Buddha was born a Hindu, Jesus was a Jew, and Baha'u'llah, founder of the Bahá'í Faith, was a Muslim. History suggests the Prophet-Founders were not entrepreneurs. The great spiritual teachers rarely intended to launch new brand-name belief systems; they wanted to reform the *dharma*—the doctrine and lifestyle taught by their inherited faiths. Assembling a new religious preference by drawing from various world religions is an ambitious project to say the least. I suspect what is more likely to happen in the long run is traditional religious communities will become increasingly more open to diversity in devotional practices, theology, and their canons of scripture, effectively morphing into an "interfaith" Catholicism, Protestantism, Judaism, Islam, and so forth, without unplugging from the lifeline of their distinctive traditions and history.

Not all differences separate; not all similarities unite. The fundamental differences among religious traditions define who we are. Muslims are not monotheistic Hindus; Jews are not Old Testament Christians. The Japanese Shinto priest offering prayer to the kami at a shrine in Kyoto is not addressing the same deity as a Lutheran minister serving communion in St. Paul, Minnesota.

Even among members of the same faith group, long-standing differences of belief and practice prevail. When researching this book, I asked my friend and sometimes mentor, Bhante Wimala, what he understood about Buddhist prayer. He said thoughtfully, "We don't use the term, *prayer,* because prayer asks somebody outside for help. We have meditations, affirmations. We don't pray to Buddha." Bhante said certain words, sometimes translated from Buddhist writings as *prayer*, actually mean recitation of a mantra, meditation, or connecting with inner wisdom.

However, when I pressed him gently about Buddhist practices in China, he agreed Chinese Buddhism addresses "higher beings," which are "like angels." Bhante said these are actual living beings that may not be visible to the naked eye, yet they watch what we do and send out their influence to us. He also spoke of *Bodhisattvas*, spiritual beings who are fully committed to purifying their minds beyond self and yet delay their release from the cycle of birth, death, and rebirth because of their compassion for all living beings. All these and other supernatural entities exist in a cosmology that does not feature a unitary, high god. One could argue that Buddhist *principles* by which existence itself operates fulfill the function of the Creator-God in monotheistic religions.[1]

In Chapter 7, we looked at the spiritual practices of Pure Land Buddhists, who pray to a supernatural entity, *Amitabha Buddha*. Pure Land Buddhists believe calling upon this divine being will grant immortality and final rebirth in the "Pure Land" to the west. How different is this concept from the Christian idea of salvation by faith?

Buddhism may seem monolithic to outsiders, but there are layers upon layers of traditions, major and minor schools of thought, and profound dislocations of the body of faith. The same is true about every major religious group, and minor ones as well. What, then, do we share in common with our brothers and sisters in the separated families of human religions?

Cave and Thunderstorm

During the studies that led to this book, I continually found myself returning to a vivid, central image. I imagined one of our primordial ancestors as he stood at the mouth of the tribal cave, peering into a thunderstorm. His family was safe and dry for the moment, but his eyes beheld the awesome power of this world he inherited at birth. What did he feel as lightning crashed and trees burst into flames? Surely, he wanted to protect his mate and children and others in the family circle. How could he prevail with so many forces arrayed against him? His world was simultaneously majestic and terrifying.

Changing seasons, the need to forage constantly and gather food; large, quick-moving game animals to hunt, and powerful predators that could kill him; people from other groups who wanted this good shelter—what chance did he have against such forces?

Were there unseen powers out there, moving like the unseen wind? Perhaps some invisibles wish to harm and must be avoided or placated, while others may offer assistance, if properly approached.

How about the people in his tribal circle? Many died young; others lived until their bodies gave out. Why did they stop moving and turn to dust? What was life, which could depart abruptly, never to return? Why did living people sometimes shout at each other and act cruelly? How did he stop hurting those closest to him? If he could not find peace with his smaller circle, how could he ever get along with people of other circles beyond the family?

When placed in the mind of an imaginary prehistoric ancestor, the above thoughts are glaringly anachronistic. Yet questions like these may have arisen fairly early in human mental evolution. This ongoing reflection over the meaning of life can be seen in the religious traditions extant today. As I reviewed various world religions, it became apparent any attempt to homogenize beliefs and practices today was both naïve and doomed to fail. Early in this work, I summarized the problem:

> Critical thinking about spiritual practice clears the underbrush and asks, "*What is actually happening here? What are religionists really saying? What points of similarity-dissimilarity are present?*" Metaphysical theology loses its credibility when it succumbs to the New Age fantasy of "all religions are the same" and

attempts to homogenize ideas that are contradictory and unmixable.[2]

Once more, images of the cave dweller in the thunderstorm came to mind, and suddenly it occurred to me I was looking for similarities at the wrong end of the process. *It is the questions we share, not the solutions.* All religio-cultural groups have grappled with the same issues about life, death, love, truth, falsehood, and ethical conduct. Who has not asked the greatest human question, both trivialized and aptly summarized in the 1965 song lyrics by Burt Bacharach and Hal David: *"What's It All About, Alphie?"*[3]

Humanity's religions represent different ways to answer the same questions, much like physicists will work out an assortment of equations to solve common problems. If we demand conformity of solutions reached by world religions, failure cannot be avoided. However, if we approach interfaith dialogue as *representatives of different ways to answer shared challenges*, we have found common ground in the sacred space where all people wrestle with the surly angels of life. More than discovering a meeting place, our pooled solutions to widely faced challenges may provide tools to address problems back in our home communities.

To work together for a better world and a healthier future for all the children of our common African ancestors, we must surrender thoughts of hostility toward the threat of the outsider—alien, gentile, heretic, skeptic, nonbeliever—and embrace the magnificent diversity that human ingenuity has created to meet its spiritual needs. We shall still disagree, and that is a good thing. Tolerance is not approval, and understanding is not endorsement. Something like *cultural relativism, or Star Trek's* Prime Directive, must become the operating manual for intercultural, interfaith, and eventually interspecies communication and cooperation.

But the practices of prayer, meditation, and ritual are more than avenues for bliss, salvation, or peace of mind. There is an ethical dimension in the religions of humanity. My imaginative meditation on the cave dweller and the thunderstorm had him wondering about how he would get along with blood relatives and those beyond the circle of family. It is a theme many traditions would share through history.

The Hebrew prophets and wisdom teachers of all faiths have recognized the need for reconciliation with neighbor, protection of the weak, and equitable distribution of the resources necessary to sustain the quality of life. Jesus was not crucified for heresy. Like other prophetic figures in human history, he had been making claims outside the boundaries of religious orthodoxy for years without fear of the religious establishment. However, when he upset the economic system by overturning the tables of corrupt money handlers, the Romans executed him promptly. Arguably, Muhammad was forced to flee to Medina because the monotheism he preached threatened the economics of Mecca and challenged the city's status as a pagan pilgrimage center, not because he was a heretic against polytheism.

Religious and ethical factors are inexorably bound with economics and social issues because human life is forever an integrated whole. Spirituality often has a prophetic edge that moves beyond words of comfort. For religious tolerance to prevail, we must allow ongoing, critical analysis of values and practices that claim a spiritual foundation. Although people must be allowed freedom of *belief* in a world society, some *practices* are clearly harmful and must be opposed by people of good conscience. Take the following "religious" declaration by Jefferson Davis, president of the Confederate States of America:

> [Slavery] was established by decree of Almighty God ... it is sanctioned in the Bible, in both Testaments, from Genesis to Revelation ... it has existed in all ages, has been found among the people of the highest civilization, and in nations of the highest proficiency in the arts.[4]

When Abraham Lincoln rebuked 19th-century slavery in America, he went to the words of Jesus: "'A house divided against itself cannot stand.' I believe this Government cannot endure permanently half slave and half free."[5]

Surely, tolerance does not mean allowing people to be treated as property, or awarding a religious exemption to every crackpot idea or hateful expression that clothes itself in pious language. The views of faith communities large and small, like political parties, should be fair game for hard, respectful questions, especially on ethical issues. Suicide bombers do not get a pass simply by claiming a divine mandate as an excuse for homicide, any more than we would allow a serial killer to get away with his string of murders by avowing they were ordered by the Voice of God. Al-Qaida, the Ku Klux Klan, and the NAZI party have used religious symbolism, cynically guided or seriously misguided, and have sometimes convinced true believers that indiscriminate violence and hate crimes are doing the work of God.

Interaction among people of diverse backgrounds must begin with tolerance, but we must retain the right to oppose evil that masquerades as an act of religion. However, I believe it is a workable paradox. One solution to this dilemma could be frank, honest dialogue across the fences that separate us, guided by an ethical foundation built upon the cross-cultural standard of the Golden Rule.

The Morovian Church, arguably the first Protestant denomination, was organized in 1457 in what is today the Czech Republic. Among its contributions to world religious thought is an early version of the Bible in the common language of the people and a spirit of liberty among its followers. Moravians shared their sense of religious freedom by popularizing a saying known as the dictum of the Fathers: *In Essentials, Unity; In Nonessentials, Liberty; In All Things, Love.*[6]

This one-line summary is sometimes attributed to St. Augustine of Hippo or the scientist-skeptic Marco Antonio Dominis (1566–1624), although no definitive author has been identified. It has been the Morovian watchword for centuries. The task of theology is to discuss what constitutes the essentials and nonessentials; the task of spirituality is to constantly remind ourselves that the greatest of these is love.

To Boldly Go ...

Looking back over the concepts presented in this study, I am struck by how much more we could have explored, from simple ideas like *prayer partners* to more complex configurations like Unity's annual *World Day of Prayer*. We never touched on efficacy studies, some of which support the power of prayer to affect outcomes in healing, others which show no positive correlation whatsoever. This raises the broad issue of religion and science, and any honest discussion of the relationship between faith and empiricism must concur with Carl Sagan, who famously said, "Extraordinary claims require extraordinary evidence."[7] Too many religionists climb aboard new sciences that seem to verify their beliefs, only to discover themselves out on a vanishing limb once scientists revise earlier theories. Newton's mechanical "cause and effect" universe crumbled into ruin with the rise of quantum physics, which now has its new generation of challengers. As Harry Emerson Fosdick observed:

> The fact that astronomies change while the stars abide is a true analogy of every realm of human life and thought, religion not least of all. No existent theology can be a final formulation of spiritual truth.[8]

The role of *grace* and the providence of God could be stand-alone volumes, and whether the goal of prayer is to *comfort* or to *cure* is a long-standing controversy in religious thought. The crowds did not come to Jesus only to hear philosophy; they brought their sick and blind and physically handicapped to his traveling spiritual healing clinic, to the point of disassembling the roof on one occasion to lower an invalid through the ceiling.

What can prayer do? Are we praying into the thunderstorm to ward off its effect, or to bolster our courage? Buddhists do not attempt to shape results; they shape their responses to whatever results. Christians, Muslims, Jews, and people of many other traditions want hands-on divinity that can spring open the prison doors, heal the sick, and bring relief in the tangible world. Answers to the questions raised by the challenges of life are neither simple nor dispensable, and if they seem otherwise, it is probably because you have not looked into the depths of human suffering.

In the Genesis legends, God hovers over the face of the waters, does His Creation thing, and pronounces it *good*. Surely a Creator so powerful must have known future Adams will eat the fruit, and future Cains will kill their brothers. Yet the beneficial progression of life—the long, deep, natural history of the Cosmos, which began billions of years before humans brought forth their multiple families of gods and goddesses, which eventually would include the desolate Yahweh of Sinai—continues an evolutionary process that produced the dance of roses and honeybees, prey and predator, lover and betrayer, child and rejected parent, sinners and spiritual teachers. Life's lessons, studied well, teach us how to find peace of mind when the systems we embrace crash around us. Better still, reflection upon the great teachers of humanity can clarify ways to fix the damage before catastrophic collapse occurs, by offering alternative paths to reconciliation and a more peaceful world.

What will humans do for spiritual nourishment when they set foot on other worlds? Doubtless our descendants, as they look up at new constellations and perhaps multiple moons hanging in the night sky, will feel a sense of awe, not unlike our ancient ancestors as they looked skyward. As long as humanity retains that impulse to raise its vision to higher possibilities, the inward spiritual journey will continue no matter where we go.

BENEDICTION

My Love to Thee
(Adapted From "The Rosary")

By Myrtle Fillmore

The hours I've spent with Thee, dear Lord,
Are pearls of priceless worth to me.
My soul, my being merge in sweet accord
In love for Thee; in love for Thee.
Each hour a pearl, each pearl a prayer,
Binding Thy presence close to me;
I only know that Thou art there, and I
Am lost in Thee.
Oh, glorious joys that thrill and bless!
Oh, visions sweet of love divine!
My soul its rapturous bliss can ill express
That Thou art mine, O Lord! That Thou art mine.[1]

SELECTED BIBLIOGRAPHY

"Affirmative Prayer." Unity School of Christianity, www.unity.org/prayer/inspirationalArticles/affirmativePrayer.html.

Aldrete, Gregory S. *Daily Life in the Roman City.* Norman, OK: University of Oklahoma Press, 2008.

Al-Jazeera News Service. 09-12-12. "US envoy dies in Benghazi consulate attack." http://www.aljazeera.com/news/middleeast/2012/09/20129112108737726.html.

All About Philosophy website. "Cultural relativism," http://www.all-aboutphilosophy.org.

Altizer, Thomas J. *The Gospel of Christian Atheism.* Louisville, KY: Westminster Press, 1966. _____. *The New Gospel of Christian Atheism.* Aurora, CO: The Davies Group Publishers, 2002.

Anderson, C. Alan and Whitehouse, Deborah G. *New Thought: A Practical American Spirituality.* NY: Crossroad Publishing Company, 1995.

Angelline, Ravenna. "Samhain Night Prayer to the Goddess." http://www.angelfire.com/wa3/angelline/samhain_night.htm.

Armstrong, Karen. *Islam: A Short History.* NY: Modern Library, 2002.

Atheist Revolution. http://www.atheistrev.com/2008/01/atheist-spirituality.html.

Aubin, Christina. "Beltane—Holiday Details and History," *Popular Pagan Holidays* website, http://www.witchvox.com/va/dt_va.html?a=usma&c=holidays&id=2765.

The Báb. "Remover of Difficulties," http://www.bahai.com/Bahaullah/prayers.htm.

Bach, Marcus. *The Unity Way of Life.* Kansas City, MO: Unity Books, 1962.

Baha, Abdu'l. *Divine Philosophy.* http://www.earth2844.net/2.5Work.htm.

Baha'i Library. "God Is One." http://bahai-ibrary.com/compilation_bahai_songs#29.

Baha'u'llah. *The Gems of Divine Mysteries*. Haifa, Israel: Baha'i World Center, 2002.

_____. Baha'i website, http://www.bcca.org/bahaivision/prayers/20.html.

Barth, Karl. *Prayer, 50th Anniversary Edition*. Louisville, KY: Westminster John Knox Press, 2002.

BBC Website *Religions*. "Four Noble Truths," http://www.bbc.co.uk/religion/religions/buddhism/beliefs/fournobletruths_1.shtml#h5.

"Biography of St. Ignatius of Loyola," http://norprov.org/spirituality/lifeofignatius.htm.

Bennett, David. *De Peccatorum Remissione et de Baptismo Parvulorum by St. Augustine*. *Ancient and Future Catholics Website*, http://www.ancient-future.net/eucharist.html.

Bill, J. Brent. *Holy Silence: The Gift of Quaker Spirituality*. Brewster, MA: Paraclete Press, 2006.

Birkel, Michael L. *Silence and Witness: The Quaker Tradition*. Maryknoll, NY: Orbis Books, 2004.

Bottorff, J Douglas. *A Practical Guide to Meditation and Prayer*. Unity Village, MO: Unity Books, 1995.

Bowker, John. *World Religions: The Great Faiths Explored and Explained*. London, U.K.: DK Publishing, 2006.

Boyce, Frank Cottrell. *God on Trial*. Public Broadcasting System, aired November 9, 2008, http://www.pbs.org/wgbh/greatpiece/godontrial/synopsis.html.

Brattston, David. "The Medicine of Immortality," in *Spectrum Magazine* online edition, September 26, 2010, http://spectrummagazine.org/authors/david-brattston.

Brodd, Jeffrey. *Primary Source Readings in World Religions*. Winona, MN: Saint Mary's Press, 2009.

Brother Lawrence. *The Practice of the Presence of God*. E.M. Blaiklock, transl. Nashville, TN: Thomas Nelson Publishers, 1982.

Brumet, Robert. *Birthing a Greater Reality*. Unity Village, MO: Unity Books, 2010.

Butterworth, Eric. "The Truth in a Nutshell." Butterworth Collection website: http://www.ericbutterworth.com/truth-nutshell.html.

Carvalho, Nirmala. AsiaNews.it, October 4, 2011, http://www. asianews.it/news-en/Mumbai:-a-special-blessing-for-animals-owned-by-Hindus,-Parsees-and-Christians-22810.html.

Chalmers, Joseph, O. Carm. "Lectio Divina Bible Meditation," British Province of Carmelite Friars, http://www.carmelite.org/index.php?nuc=content&id=72.

Chaundy, Bob. "The Burning Times," *BBC News Magazine*, October 30, 2009. http://news.bbc.co.uk/2/hi/uk_news/magazine/8334055.stm.

Chidester, David. *Christianity, A Global Perspective*. NY: HarperCollins, 2000.

"Cherokee Prayer Blessing." *Pearls of Wisdom: Awakening Personal and Global Consciousness* website, http://www.sapphyr.net/natam/quotes-nativeamerican.htm.

Chryssavgis, John. *Light Through Darkness: The Orthodox Tradition*. Maryknoll, NY: Orbis Books, 2004.

Church of Christ website. Bethlehem, Pennsylvania. "The Evils of Denominationalism." www.churchofchristbethlehempa.org/FAQs/THE%20EVILS%20OF%20DENOMINATIONALISM.htm.

Colombe. "Yule Prayer Song," http://www.wicca-spirituality.com/yule-prayer.html.

Cott, Jonathan. "The Cosmos." *Rolling Stone Magazine*. Dec. 25, 1980– Jan. 8, 1981.

Crisp, Melinda. "Neopaganism vs. Wicca," http://melinda-crisp.deviantart.com/art/Neopaganism-vs-Wicca-171633387.

Cunnius, Barbara. "Spiritualism Is New Dimension of Life, Dr. Marcus Bach Claims." *Reading Eagle,* October 8, 1980.

Curtis, Ken. "Martin Luther: Monumental Reformer." *Christianity. com* website, source: http://www.christianity.com/ChurchHistory/11629922/.

Daily Om. "Leave a Positive Footprint: Blessing Space." http://www.dailyom.com/articles/2007/7907.html.

Davis, Wade. "Other Cultures" poster, Northern Sun Products, http://www. Northernsun.com/Other-Cultures-Wade-Davis-Poster-(4450).

Delio, Ilia. *Franciscan Prayer*. Cincinnati, OH: St. Anthony Messenger Press, 2004.

Deloria, Vine, Jr. *God Is Red: A Native View of Religion*. Golden, CO: Fulcrum Publishing, 1994.

Doerr, Edd. "Humanism Unmodified." *The Humanist Magazine*, November/December 2002, http://www.thehumanist.org/humanist/articles/DoerrND02.htm.

Dunwich, Gerina. *Exploring Spellcraft: How to Create and Cast Effective Spells*. Franklin Lakes, NJ: Career Press, 2001.

Dysinger, Luke, O.S.B. "How to Practice Lectio Divina—A Step-by-Step Guide to Praying the Bible," http://www.beliefnet.com/Faiths/Catholic/2000/08/How-To-Practice-Lectio-Divina.aspx.

Egyptian Book of the Dead. "The Negative Confession," http://www.philae.nu/akhet/ Confession.html.

Ehrman, Bart D. *Lost Christianities: The Battles for Scripture and the Faiths We Never Knew*. New York: Oxford University Press, 2003.

Fernando, Anthony With Leonard Swidler. *Buddhism Made Plain: An Introduction for Christians and Jews*. Maryknoll, NY: Orbis Books, 1993.

Fillmore, Charles and Fillmore, Cora. *Teach Us to Pray*. Unity Village, MO: Unity School of Christianity, 1941.

Fillmore, Charles. *Atom-Smashing Power of Mind*. Unity Village, MO: Unity Books, 1949.

Fillmore, Connie. "Five Basic Unity Principles," from *Keys to the Kingdom*, http://content.unity.org/association/aboutUs/what WeBelieve/unityPrinciples.html.

Fillmore, Myrtle. *Myrtle Fillmore's Healing Letters*. Unity Village, MO: Unity Books, 1954.

"First Fruits." *Jewish Virtual Library*. http://www.jewishvirtuallibrary.org/jsource/judaica/ejud_0002_0007_0_06495.html.

Fischer, William L. *Alternatives*. Unity Village, MO: Unity Books, 1980.

"The Five Daily Prayers." Movement for the Propagation of Islam, http://aaiil.org/text/books/mali/muslimprayerbook/fivedailyprayers.shtml.

Fox, Emmett. "The Golden Key," http://www.soberrecovery.com/forums/spirituality/187423-scientific-prayer-little-emmet-fox.html.

The Free Dictionary. "Modalism," http://www.thefreedictionary.com/modalism.

Freeman, James Dillet. "I Am There," http://www.unity.org/resources/articles/i-am-there. _____. "Prayer for Protection," http://www.unity.org/resources/articles/prayer-protection.

Gibran, Kahlil. *The Prophet.* http://www.allgreatquotes.com/kahlil_gibran_quotes3.shtml.

Glasser, William. *"Positive Addiction," Journal of Extension, May/June 1977.*

Griffin, David Ray. *God and Religion in the Postmodern World: Essays in Postmodern Theology.* Albany, NY: SUNY Press, 1989.

Griffin, Emilie and Steele, Douglas V., eds. *Quaker Spirituality: Selected Writings.* NY: HarperCollins, 2005.

Gurge, Anura. "Benedict XVI's Latin Mass 'Summorum Pontificum' Given More Muscle." *Popes and the Papacy* website, http://popes-and-papacy.com/wordpress.

Hanh, Thich Nhat. *Living Buddha, Living Christ.* NY: Riverhead Books, 1995.

Harkness, Georgia. *Prayer and the Common Life.* Nashville, TN: Abingdon Press, 2005.

Harland, Phil. "Breaking News: Early Christians Were Impious Atheists," *Religions of the Ancient Mediterranean,* http://www.philipharland.com/Blog.

Harris, Sam. *Letter to a Christian Nation.* NY: Vintage Books, 2008.

Hasselbeck, Paul. *Heart-Centered Metaphysics.* Unity Village, MO: Unity Books, 2010.

Herbal Musings website. "Beltane," http://herbalmusings.com/beltane.htm.

Hertz, Joseph H. *Pirke Aboth: The Sayings of the Fathers.* NY: Behrman House, 1945.

Horton, Paul B. and Hunt, Chester L. *Sociology.* NY: McGraw-Hill, 1964.

Howell, Nancy. "Chimpanzees, Bonobos, and the Future of Theological Reflection." Paper delivered at Lyceum 2008, Unity Institute.

"Humanist Manifesto I." American Humanist Association. Originally issued 1933. http://www.americanhumanist.org/Humanism/Humanist_Manifesto_I.

"Humpback Whale Song." *Whale Trust,* http://www.whaletrust.org/whales/whale_ song.shtml.

Internet Encyclopedia of Philosophy, http://www.iep.utm.edu.

Isola, Kelli. "Answering the Call of World Day of Prayer," Kelli Isola blog for 7-31-12, http://www.kellyisola.com/answering-the-call-of-world-day-of-prayer/.

Jeremias, Joachim. *The Prayers of Jesus.* Eugene, OE: Wipf and Stock Publishers, 2006.

Joelle's Sacred Grove, http://www.joellessacredgrove.com/Holidays/sabbats.html.

Keating, Thomas. *Centering Prayer in Daily Life and Ministry.* Gustave Reininger, ed. NY: Continuum, 2003.

King, Barbara J. *Evolving God.* New York: Random House Digital, 2007.

Kohaus, Hannah More. "The Prayer of Faith," http://content.unity.org/prayer/prayersAffirmations/prayerOfFaith.html.

Kotic, Elvira et al., "Glossolalia," College of Anthropology. 29 (2005) 1: 307–313, http://www.psihijatrija.com/bibliografija/radovi/Koic%20E%20GLOSSOLALIA%20COLLEGIUM.pdf.

Lakota Indian Vision Quest, "Crying for a Vision." The Wild West website, Native American Religion, http://www.thewildwest.org/nativeamericans/nativeamericanreligion/103-lakotaindiansthevisionquest.html.

Lape, Herb. "A Case for Eldering and Dicsipline." *Friends Journal,* Earlham School of Religion, http://www.friendsjournal.org/case-eldering-and-discipline.

Lavine, T.Z. *From Socrates to Sartre: The Philosophic Quest.* NY: Bantam Books, 1984.

Lewis, Jone Johnson. "Aimee Semple McPherson." Women's History, About.com. http://womenshistory.about.com/od/protestant/a/aimee_mcpherson.htm.

Lonsdale, David. *Eyes to See, Ears to Hear.* Maryknoll, NY: Orbis Books, 2000.

Malik, Prerna. "What Is Right Effort in the Eightfold Path of Buddhism?" http://suite101.com.

Marleaux, Bryan. Grace World Mission, http://www.graceworldmission.org/.

Marriott, Alice and Rachlin, Carol K. *Plains Indian Mythology.* NY: Mentor Books, 1975.

Marshall, George N. *Challenge of a Liberal Faith, Third Edition.* Boston: Skinner House Books, 1988.

Martella-Whitsett, Linda. *How to Pray Without Talking to God.* Charlottesville, VA: Hampton Roads Publishing Company, 2011.

Martin, Thomas F., OSA. *Our Restless Heart: The Augustinian Tradition.* Maryknoll, NY: Orbis Books, 2003.

Marty, Martin. "Our Religio-Secular World." *Daedalus*: Summer, 2003.

Mass, Robin and O'Donnell, Gabriel, O.P., eds. *Spiritual Traditions for the Contemporary Church.* Nashville, TN: Abingdon Press, 1990.

McGiffert, Arthur Cushman. *A History of Christian Thought, Vol. I.* New York: Charles Scribner's Sons, 1932.

_____. *A History of Christian Thought, Vol. II*, 1933.

McGreal, Wilfrid, OCarm. *At the Fountain of Elijah: The Carmelite Tradition.* Maryknoll, NY: Orbis Books, 1999.

McGuckin, John Anthony. *Standing in God's Holy Fire: The Byzantine Tradition.* Maryknoll, NY: Orbis Books, 2001.

Moravian Church in North America website, http://www.moravian.org/the-moravian-church/the-moravian-church/history.html.

Mother Teresa of Calcutta and Brother Roger of Taizé. *Mary: Mother of Reconciliations.* Oxford, UK: A.R. Mobray and Company, 1987.

New Revised Standard Version of the Bible. Nashville, TN: Abindgon Press, 2010.

Nichols, Mike. "Beltane: Celebration of May Day." http://deoxy.org/time/sabbats/05-04.htm.

Nouwen, Henri, S.J. *The Way of the Heart: Desert Spirituality and Contemporary Ministry.* NY: Seabury Press, 1981.

_____. *Intimacy.* NY: HarperSanFrancisco, 1969.

O'Connor, Flannery. Commen on Eucharist, at the *Shameless Popery* (Pro-Catholic) website, http://catholicdefense.blogspot.com/2012/04/flannery-oconnor-on-eucharist-and.html.

Om Sakthi. "The Meaning of Om," http://www.omsakthi.org/worship/mantra.html.

Onah, Godfrey Igwebuike. "The Meaning of Peace in African Traditional Religion and Culture." Pontifical Urban University, Rome. http://www.afrikaworld.net/afrel/goddionah.htm#_ftn22.

O'Neil, Dennis. "Common Elements of Religion," http://anthro.palomar.edu/religion/rel_2.htm.

Overseas Missionary Fellowship-Cambodia. http://www.omf.org/omf/cambodia/about_cambodia/animism_profile.

Pennington, Basil. "Centering Prayer—A Gift From the Desert," in *Centering Prayer,* http://www.kyrie.com/cp/a_gift_from_the_desert.htm.

_____. "Introduction," in *Centering Prayer in Daily Life and Ministry,* Gustave Reininger, ed. NY: Continuum, 2003.

Phillips, J.B. *Your God Is Too Small.* NY: MacMillan Publishing Co., 1961.

Ponder, Catherine. *Open Your Mind to Prosperity.* Martina del Rey, CA: DeVorss, 1983.

Pritchard, James B., ed. *The Ancient Near East—Volume 1: An Anthology of Texts and Pictures.* Princeton, New Jersey: Princeton University Press, 1958.

"The Quaker Way." Friends General Conference website, http://www.fgcquaker.org/explore/quaker-way.

Raggio, Nora. "Pre-Columbian Sacrifices." San Jose State University School of Art and Design, http://gallery.sjsu.edu/sacrifice/precolumbian.html.

Rahtjen, Bruce D. *Paul and His World,* Audio Cassette lecture. Unity Village, MO: Unity School of Christianity, 1978.

Rahula, Wapola. *What the Buddha Taught.* Second ed. NY: Grove Press, 1974.

Roberts, Dalton. "My Sunday Journal." Email newsletter, 6-3-12.

Robinson, Bruce A. "Is Wicca a Form of Satanism?" ReligiousToler-ance.org website, http://www.religioustolerance.org/wic_sata.htm/.

Robinson, John A.T. *Honest to God*, 40th Anniversary Edition. Louis-ville, KY: Westminster John Knox Press, 2002.

Russell, Michael F. and Wall, A. "Denominationalism." Netplaces web-site: http://www.netplaces.com/christianity/the-new-world/denominationalism.htm.

Russell, Pamela. "The Palaeolithic Mother-Goddess: Fact or Fiction?" *Reader in Gender Archaeology,* Kelley Hays-Gilpin and David S. Whitley, ed. NY: Routledge, 1998.

Sadiki, Larbi. "Libya: Testing tolerance." Al-Jazeera News Ser-vice, 9-04-12. http://www.aljazeera.com/indepth/opinion/2012/09/201291125110843653.html.

Sagan, Carl. *The Demon-Haunted World: Science as a Candle in the Dark-ness.* NY: Ballantine Books, 1996.

Saint Teresa of Avila. "Bookmark of St. Teresa of Avila." Carmel, CA: Carmelite Sisters by the Sea, http://www.carmelitesistersbythe-sea.net/meditations.htm.

Santa Barbara Sacred Spaces website. "What Is a Sacred Space?" http://www.sacred-spaces.info/sba/index.html.

Satipatthana Sutta. *The Foundations of Mindfulness.* Nyanasatta Thera, trans., http://www.accesstoinsight.org/lib/authors/nyana satta/wheel019.html.

Schmid, Randolph E. "Humans Flirted With Extinction 70,000 Years Ago," *USA Today*, http://www.usatoday.com/tech/science/2008-04-24-human-extinction_N.htm.

Scott, Donald. "Evangelicalism, Revivalism, and the Second Great Awakening." Web-published essay, Queens College/City Uni-versity of New York; TeacherServe website of the National Humanities Center, http://nationalhumanitiescenter.org /tserve/nineteen/nkeyinfo/nevanrev.htm.

Seton, Ernest Thompson and Seton, Julia M., compilers. *The Gospel of the Redman: A Way of Life.* Santa Fe, NM: Seton Village, 1966.

Sheikh Ali Al-Timimi. Lecture on "Islam—Elevation of Women's Status." *Islam for Today,* http://www.islamfortoday.com/womensstatus.htm.

Sheldrake, Phillip. *A Brief History of Spirituality.* Oxford, U.K.: Blackwell Publishing, 2007.

Shepherd, Thomas W. *Friends in High Places,* Third edition. Lincoln, NE: iUniverse Books.

_____. *Jesus 2.1.* Unity Village, MO: Unity Books, 2010.

_____. *Good Questions.* Unity Village, MO: Unity Books, 2009.

Smith, Maurizio G. "American Indian Vision Quest." http://www.theosophy-nw.org/theosnw/world/america/am-smit.htm.

"The Spiritual Exercises of St. Ignatius," Society of Jesus, Oregon Province. http://www.nwjesuits.org/JesuitSpirituality/SpiritualExercises.html.

Spong, John Shelby. *Why Christianity Must Change or Die: A Bishop Speaks to Believers in Exile.* NY: HarperCollins, 1999.

_____. *Jesus for the Non-Religious: Recovering the Divine at the Heart of the* Human. NY: HarperSanFrancisco, 2007.

Stanford Encyclopedia of Philosophy, http://plato.stanford.edu.

Staniforth, Maxwel trans. *Meditations of Marcus Aurelius.* London: Penguin Books, 1964.

Steer, Douglas V., ed. *Quaker Spirituality: Selected Writings.* NY: Paulist Press, 1984.

Stewart, Columbia, OSB. *Prayer and Community: The Benedictine Tradition.* Maryknoll, NY: Orbis Books, 1998.

Stewart, Tom. "St. Patrick: The Trinity and the Shamrock." *What Saith the Scripture* website, http://www.whatsaiththescripture.com/ Fellowship/Edit_Trinity.and. Shamrock.html.

Sueler, John. "Empty Your Cup," http://users.rider.edu/~suler/zenstory/emptycup.html.

Svoboda, Sister Melannie, S.N.D. "Five Steps to Better Prayer." *Catholic Religious Vocation Network* website: http://www.vocationnetwork.org/articles/show/75.

Swami Sivananda Saraswati Maharaj. "Meditation on Sri Krishna," in "Five Prayers for All Occasions," About.com website, http://hinduism.about.com/od/prayersmantras/a/5prayers.htm.

Symmes, Patrick. "History in the Remaking." *Newsweek* online, 2-18-2010, http://www.thedailybeast.com/newsweek/2010/02/18/history-in-the-remaking.

"Terminology: Neo-Paganism, Wicca, Witchcraft. " Article at Religionfacts.com, http://www.religionfacts.com/neopaganism/terminology.htm.

Thomas, Mark. "Why Atheism," http://www.godlessgeeks.com/WhyAtheism.htm.

Tillich, Paul. *The Courage to Be.* New Haven, CT: Yale University Press, 1952.

_____. *A History of Christian Thought.* NY: Touchstone, 1968.

Underhill, Evelyn, ed. *The Cloud of Unknowing.* http://www.sacred-texts.com/ch/cou/cou03.htm.

Valiente, Doreen. "Invocation of the Moon Goddess," Pagan Songs, Chants, and Prayers, http://www.squidoo.com/paganchants.

Venerable Henepola Gunaratana. *Mindfulness in Plain English.* http://www.vipassana.com/meditation/mindfulness_in_plain_english_5.php.

Vivekananda, Swami. "Dualism or Monism?" http://www.eaglespace.com/spirit/workbeforeus1a.php.

Wall, Kathleen and Ferguson, Gary. *Rites of Passage: Celebrating Life's Changes.* Hillsboro, OR: Beyond Words Publishing, Inc., 1998.

Wallace, Anthony F.C. *Religion: An Anthropological View.* New York: Random House, 1966.

Wallace, B. Alan. "A Mindful Balance," www.alanwallace.org/spr08wallace_comp.pdf.

Ward, Benedicta. *The Desert Fathers: Saying of the Early Christian Monks.* London, UK: Penguin Books, 2003.

Weatherhead, Leslie. *The Christian Agnostic.* Nashville, TN: Abingdon Press, 1965.

"What Is Sufism?" Nimatullahi Sufi order, http://www.nimatullahi.org/what-is-sufism/.

Wigington, Patti. "The Role of Prayer in Paganism." About.com, http://paganwiccan.about.com/od/prayersandincantations/a/Role_of_Prayer.htm.

Will, George F. "Address to University of Miami Class of 2005," Steven Shapiro's 24/7 Innovation website, http://www.steveshapiro.com/2005/06/19/george-will-certitude-2/.

Wimala, Bhante Y. *Lessons of the Lotus.* Colombo, Sri Lanka: Bhante Y. Wimala, 2009.

Woodling, Myth. "Balance in a Pluralistic faith." http://www.jesterbear.com/Wicca/Pluralistic.html.

Woods, Richard, OP. *Mysticism and Prophecy: The Dominican Tradition.* London, U.K.: Darton, Longman and Todd, 1998.

Yogananda, Paramhansa. *Autobiography of a Yogi,* 13th edition. Los Angeles, CA: Self-Realization Fellowship, 2010.

Zender, Tom. *One-Minute Meditations at Work.* Bloomington, IN: Balboa Press, 2011.

_____. *The Restless Spirit.* Online newsletter, August 2012. http://www.tomzender.com/newsletter-archive.

Zydek, Fredrick. *Dreaming on the Other Side of Time.* Omaha, NE: Holmes House, 2002.

_____. *The Conception Abbey Poems.* Third Ed.. Vernon, CT: Winthrop Press, 2011.

ENDNOTES

Invocation

[1] Charles and Cora Fillmore, *Teach Us to Pray* (Unity Village, MO: Unity School of Christianity, 1941), 36-37.

Chapter 1

[1] George F. Will, "Address to University of Miami Class of 2005," excerpted by Steven Shapiro's 24/7 Innovation website; online source: http://www.steveshapiro.com/2005/06/19/george-will-certitude-2/ (accessed 08-02-12).

[2] Wade Davis, "Other Cultures" poster, Northern Sun Products, http://www.northernsun.com/Other-Cultures-Wade-Davis-Poster-(4450) (accessed 07-11-12).

[3] Matthew 7:7.

[4] "U.S. Envoy Dies in Benghazi Consulate Attack," Al-Jazeera News Service online, September 12, 2012; online source: http://www.aljazeera.com/news/middleeast/2012/09/20129112108737726.html (accessed 09-12-12).

[5] "Libya: Testing Tolerance," by Dr. Larbi Sadiki, Al-Jazeera News Service online, September 4, 2012; source: http://www.aljazeera.com/indepth/opinion/2012/09/201291125110843653.html (accessed 09-12-12).

[6] George F. Will, "Address to University of Miami Class of 2005."

[7] "The Evils of Denominationalism," Bethlehem, Pennsylvania, Church of Christ website: www.churchofchrist-bethlehempa.org/FAQs/THE%20EVILS%20OF%20DENOMINATIONALISM.htm (accessed 08-21-12).

[8] Bart D. Ehrman, *Lost Christianities: The Battles for Scripture and the Faiths We Never Knew* (New York: Oxford University Press, 2003.)

[9] "Denominationalism," Michael F. Russell and Amy Wall; http://www.netplaces.com/christianity/the-new-world/denominationalism.htm (accessed 09-16-12).

[10] The spiritual guardian assigned to editors is Saint John Bosco. See "Patron Saints of Professions" website, http://www.catho-

lic-saints.info/patron-saints/patron-saints-professions.htm   (accessed 05-08-12).

11 Dalton Roberts, "My Sunday Journal" email newsletter for 6-3-12. Used by permission.

12 Based on an anecdote repeated by many speakers, origin unknown. Here is a link to a version by atheist author Richard Dawkins.   http://www.spiked-online.com/index.php/site/article/2503/ (accessed 04-21-12).

13 Anthony F.C. Wallace, *Religion: An Anthropological View* (New York: Random House, 1966), 72.

14 *All About Philosophy* website, "Cultural Relativism," http://www.allaboutphilosophy.org/cultural-relativism.htm (accessed 09-16-12). The site manager(s) offer a rather thoughtful, critical response to Cultural Relativism from a moderate Christian perspective, which is a helpful counterbalance.

15 "God Is One," Reproduced under the Fair Use Copyright Extension, permission by Baha'i Library Online site, online source: http://bahai-library.com/compilation_bahai_songs#29 (accessed 07-05-12).

16 *All About Philosophy* website.

17 "Humpback Whale Song," *Whale Trust* website: http://www.whaletrust.org/whales/whale_song.shtml (accessed 07-12-12).

18 *Stanford Encyclopedia of Philosophy*, online source: http://plato.stanford.edu/entries/dualism/ (accessed 07-10-12).

19 Swami Vivekananda, "Dualism or Monism?" http://www.eaglespace.com/spirit/workbeforeus1a.php (accessed 09-11-12).

20 23rd Psalm.

21 Ibid.

22 Charles Fillmore, *Atom-Smashing Power of Mind* (Unity Village, MO: Unity Books, 1949), 12.

23 Myrtle Fillmore, *Myrtle Fillmore's Healing Letters* (Unity Village, MO: Unity Books, 1954), 20.

24 Myrtle Page Fillmore, to Charles Fillmore, dated September 1, 1878, transcript in the hand of Myrtle Page, Unity School of Christianity Archives, Unity Village, Missouri.

25 Baha'u'llah, *The Gems of Divine Mysteries* (Haifa, Israel: Baha'i World Center, 2002), line 43.

Chapter 2

1 St. Teresa of Avila, "Bookmark of St. Teresa of Avila," Carmelite Sisters by the Sea, Carmel, CA, Meditation Page; http://www.carmelitesistersbythesea.net/meditations.htm (accessed 08-18-12).

2 "Why do people clap their hands at Shinto shrines?" Some Shintoists today call hand clapping a ritual. http://lang-8.com/113203/journals/1002476/Why-do-people-clap-their-hands-at-Shinto-shrines%253F (accessed 07-06-12).

3 Ken Curtis, Ph.D., "Martin Luther: Monumental Reformer," article published at *Christianity.com* website. Online source: http://www.christianity.com/ChurchHistory/11629922/ (accessed 07-07-12).

4 David Chidester, *Christianity, A Global Perspective* (New York: HarperCollins, 2000), 312.

5 Bryan Marleaux, "Martin Luther and the Reformation," Grace World Mission website, http://www.graceworldmission.org/martinluthervideopg.html (accessed 09-16-12).

6 Swami Vivekananda, "Dualism or Monism?" http://www.eaglespace.com/spirit/workbeforeus1a.php (accessed 09-11-12). Swami Vivekananda (1863–1902) is credited with bringing Vedanta and Yoga to the West, establishing Hinduism as a world religion, and raising interfaith awareness.

7 1 Corinthians 6:19.

8 Romans 8:26-27.

9 Eric Butterworth, "The Truth in a Nutshell," essay reproduced online at The Butterworth Collection website; online source: http://www.ericbutterworth.com/truth-nutshell.html (accessed 09-16-12).

10 Linda Martella-Whitsett, *How to Pray Without Talking to God* (Charlottesville, VA: Hampton Roads Publishing Company, 2011), 3.

11 Ibid., 4-5.

12 Thomas J.J. Altizer's 1966 book (Westminster Press) was revised in 2002 and rereleased by The Davies Group Publishers as *The New Gospel of Christian Atheism*. Altizer is currently in his mid-80s; he is still writing.

[13] Paul Tillich, *The Courage to Be* (New Haven, CT: Yale University Press, 1952), 184.

[14] John A.T. Robinson, *Honest to God*, 40th Anniversary Edition (Louisville, KY: Westminster John Knox Press, 2002), 11-13.

[15] Martella-Whitsett, 3.

[16] Ibid., 29.

[17] Ibid.

[18] Tom Stewart, "St. Patrick: The Trinity and the Shamrock," essay at *What Saith the Scripture* website; source: http://www.whatsaith-thescripture.com/Fellowship/Edit_Trinity.and.Shamrock.html (accessed 07-09-12).

[19] Definition of modalism, *The Free Dictionary*. Source: http://www.thefreedictionary.com/modalism (accessed 07-09-12).

[20] "Five Basic Unity Principles," adapted from Connie Fillmore's "Keys to the Kingdom," by Unity Worldwide Ministries: http://content.unity.org/association/aboutUs/whatWeBelieve/unityPrinciples.html (accessed 07-09-12).

[21] Hannah More Kohaus, "The Prayer of Faith," available online at *unity.org* website. Source: http://content.unity.org/prayer/prayersAffirmations/prayerOfFaith.html (accessed 07-09-12).

Chapter 3

[1] Confucius, *The Analects (Selected Sayings) of Confucius*; online excerpts at City University of New York website: http://academic.brooklyn.cuny.edu/core9/phalsall/texts/analects.html (accessed 08-16-12).

[2] This is a complex question. Like all living faiths, Buddhism has schools of thought. Although most Buddhists reject the idea of a Supreme Being, some find it helpful to meditate on the divine nature within them by veneration of the Buddha. See: http://kadampa.org/en/buddhism/prayer-to-buddha (accessed 05-05-12).

[3] Paul B. Horton and Chester L. Hunt, *Sociology* (New York: McGraw-Hill. 1964), 94.

[4] http://history-world.org/canaanite_culture_and_religion.htm (accessed 09-14-12). The Greek historian Herodotus is usually cited as the source of the sacred prostitute rituals, but in fairness to the Canaanites, some recent studies have cast doubt on the histo-

ricity of this information. The jury is still out on the question.

5 Barbara J. King, *Evolving God* (New York: Random House Digital, 2007), 21-22.

6 Nancy Howell, "Chimpanzees, Bonobos, and the Future of Theological Reflection," paper delivered at Lyceum 2008, Unity Institute.

7 "Research in Religion at Linköping University" Sweden, http://www.liu.se/forskning/kultur/religion?l=en (accessed 03-18-12).

8 Patrick Symmes, "History in the Remaking," *Newsweek* online, 02-18-2010, source: http://www.thedailybeast.com/newsweek/2010/02/18/history-in-the-remaking.html (accessed 03-18-12).

9 Ibid.

10 Klaus Schmidt, in Patrick Symmes, "History in the Remaking," *Newsweek* online, 02-18-10.

11 Ibid., Symmes.

12 Ibid.

13 http://timothystephany.com/Göbekli .html.

14 Psalm 130:1-2.

15 Psalm 126:1-3.

16 Martin Marty, "Our Religio-Secular World," *Daedalus*: (Summer, 2003), 42.

Chapter 4

1 Fredrick Zydek, "Praying Into the Mystery," from *The Conception Abbey Poems*, Third Edition (Vernon, CT: Winthrop Press, 2011), 17.

2 Max Ehrman, "Desiderata," All Poetry website http://allpoetry.com/poem/8574007-Desiderata_-_Words_for_Life-by-Max_Ehrmann (accessed 08-18-12).

3 Marcus Aurelius, *Meditations*, Book Five, paragraph 27, Maxwell Staniforth, trans., (London: Penguin Books, 1964), 87.

4 Dennis O'Neil, "Common Elements of Religion," website established for Behavioral Sciences Department, Palomar College, San Marcos, California: http://anthro.palomar.edu/religion/rel_2.htm (accessed 04-22-12).

[5] International Movie Database, http://www.imdb.com/title/tt0076759/quotes (accessed 04-22-12).

[6] Not related to the heavenly food provided to Israel in the wilderness.

[7] O'Neil; parenthesis in the original.

[8] Clark, Keith, Capuchin, *Make Space, Make Symbols: A Personal Journey Into Prayer* (Notre Dame, IN: Ave Maria Press, 1970), 16-17.

[9] Unsigned essay, "What Is Animatism?" at http://animatism.com/2011/09/22/hello-world/#more-1 (accessed 04-28-12).

[10] Overseas Missionary Fellowship-Cambodia website: http://www.omf.org/omf/cambodia/about_ cambodia/animism_profile (accessed 05-01-12).

[11] Ibid.

[12] *Japan Times* article, quoted by George William Gilmore, *Animism* (1919), available online at http://www.sacred-texts.com/sha/anim/ (accessed 04-28-12).

[13] Unsigned selection, "Polytheism—Modern World," Polytheism website, http://www.polytheism.net/ (accessed 04-29-12).

[14] Gregory S. Aldrete, *Daily Life in the Roman City* (Norman, OK, University of Oklahoma Press, 2008), 142.

[15] World Religions Professor, "Shinto Gods: The Kami," online at http://www.world-religions-professor.com/shintogods.html (accessed 04-30-12).

[16] Ibid.

[17] Ibid.

[18] "Stoicism," Stanford University Encyclopedia of Philosophy, website: http://plato.stanford.edu/entries/ stoicism/ (accessed 04-30-12).

[19] Aldrete, 146.

[20] Ibid., 141.

[21] Ibid., 144.

Chapter 5

[1] "The Cult of the Sun God and Akhenaten's Monotheism," based on Library of Congress information, found at About.com website:

http://ancienthistory.about.com/cs/egypt/a/locegyptmonothe.htm (accessed 05-01-12).

2 James B. Pritchard, ed., *The Ancient Near East—Volume 1: An Anthology of Texts and Pictures*, (Princeton, NJ: Princeton University Press, 1958), 227-230.

3 Psalm 132: 7-9, 13-14.

4 Exodus 20:1-3.

5 Jeremiah 44:16-17.

6 Psalm 82:1-7.

7 John 10:34-36.

8 Genesis 1:26.

9 Ibid., 3:22-23.

10 Ibid., 6:1-4.

11 Psalm 96:1-5.

12 Hinduism: The Basics, website: http://www.himalayanacademy.com/basics/tenq/tenq_1.html (accessed 05-05-12).

13 Rudolph Otto's terms described by Dr. Chuck Shaw's online notes for Religion 201-B01, Greenville Technical College. http://shawcss.tripod.com/REL101/sacred/otto.htm (accessed 05-28-12).

14 Baha'u'llah, quoted at Baha'i website: http://www.bcca.org/bahaivision/prayers/20.html (accessed 07-02-12).

15 http://plato.stanford.edu/entries/pantheism/.

16 Acts 17:22-23, 27-28.

17 C. Alan Anderson and Deborah G. Whitehouse, *New Thought: A Practical American Spirituality* (New York: Crossroad Publishing Company, 1995), 89.

18 http://plato.stanford.edu/entries/panentheism/ (accessed 05-07-12).

Chapter 6

1 John Shelby Spong, *Why Christianity Must Change or Die: A Bishop Speaks to Believers in Exile* (New York: Harpercollins, 1999), 144.

2 David Ray Griffin, *God and Religion in the Postmodern World: Essays*

in Postmodern Theology (Albany, NY: SUNY Press, 1989), 77.

3 George N. Marshall, *Challenge of a Liberal Faith, Third Edition* (Boston: Skinner House Books, 1988), 131.

4 Jonathan Cott, "The Cosmos," (*Rolling Stone Magazine*: December 25, 1980-January 8, 1981).

5 Carl Sagan, http://www.skyimagelab.com/pale-blue-dot.html. Excerpted from a commencement address delivered May 11, 1996. Sagan is referring to the image of the earth from Voyager 1, photographed 1990.

6 Dictionary.com. Online source: http://dictionary.reference.com/browse/science (accessed 05-27-12).

7 Ibid, http://dictionary.reference.com/browse/agnosticism?s=t (accessed 05-27-12).

8 Sagan, quoted at http://www.antireligion.com/wordpress/?page_id=14 (accessed 05-28-12).

9 Sagan, quoted in "God and Carl Sagan: Is the Cosmos Big Enough for Both of Them?" by Edward Wakin, *US Catholic*, May 1981, 19-24.

10 *Nasadiya Sukta*, Hindu creation hymn from the *Rig Veda*, online source Deep Spirits website: http://www.deepspirits.com/spirituality/agnosticism/ (accessed 05-28-12).

11 Protagoras, online source Deep Spirits website: http://www.deepspirits.com/spirituality/agnosticism/ (accessed 05-28-12).

12 Ecclesiastes 3:19-22.

13 "Book of Ecclesiastes—Placement in the Canon," unsigned article in *New World Encyclopedia*; online source: http://www.newworldencyclopedia.org/entry/Ecclesiastes,_Book_of (accessed 06-01-12).

14 David Plotz, "Blogging the Bible", Slate Newsletter, "The Complete Book of Ecclesiastes, Entry 2; posted 04-26-07. Plotz effectively raises agnosticism through the "pie in the sky" cliché. Online source: http://www.slate.com/articles/news_and_politics/blogging_the_bible/features/2007/the_complete_book_of_ecclesiastes/its_godless_weird_and_beautiful.html (accessed 06-01-12).

15 Leslie Weatherhead, *The Christian Agnostic* (Nashville, TN: Abingdon Press, 1965), 27.

[16] Lucretius, quoted at *Internet Encyclopedia of Philosophy*. Sometimes he approaches naturalistic theism in his rhapsodies on nature, but a thoroughgoing skepticism about spiritual realities pervades his work. Online source: http://www.iep.utm.edu/lucretiu/ (accessed 05-29-12).

[17] Mark Thomas, "Why Atheism," http://www.godlessgeeks.com/WhyAtheism.htm (accessed 09-14-12).

[18] Phil Harland, "Breaking News: Early Christians Were Impious Atheists," *Religions of the Ancient Mediterranean* website, posted 11-09-07; http://www.philipharland.com/Blog/2007/11/09/breaking-news-early-christians-were-impious-atheists/ (accessed 06-01-12).

[19] Thomas, website: http://www.godlessgeeks.com/WhyAtheism.htm (accessed 09-14-12).

[20] Sam Harris, *Letter to a Christian Nation* (New York: Vintage Books, 2008), 114.

[21] Bill Mahr and Piers Morgan, Transcript of Interview on *Piers Morgan Tonight*, originally aired July 11, 2011. Online source: http://transcripts.cnn.com/TRANSCRIPTS/1107/11/pmt.01.html (accessed 09-10-12).

[22] Harris, *The Sam Harris Blog*, "In Defense of 'Spiritual,'" dated 06-27-12 (accessed 01-12-13).

[23] Unsigned article, "Atheist Spirituality," *Atheist Revolution* blog site, posted 01-22-08. Online Source: http://www.atheistrev.com/2008/01/atheist-spirituality.html (accessed 06-01-12).

[24] Ibid.

[25] Marshall, 131.

[26] Edd Doerr, "Humanism Unmodified," *The Humanist Magazine*, November/December 2002. Online source: http://www.thehumanist.org/humanist/articles/DoerrND02.htm (accessed 06-01-12).

[27] The influence of Emerson and the Transcendentalists on Unity cannot be overstated. When Charles and Myrtle Fillmore called their first son *Lowell*, after the Transcendentalist author James Russell Lowell, and their second *Waldo* Rickert, they were signaling more than an affinity with the sound of the names.

[28] The expression has been around at least since the mid-20th cen-

tury. I never heard it said without a smile. http://www.infidels. org/library/modern/edwin_wilson/manifesto/preface.html (accessed 06-01-12).

29 Unitarian Universalist Association of Congregations website, "Are My Beliefs Welcome in Unitarian Universalism?" Online source: http://www.uua.org/beliefs/welcome/index.shtml (accessed 06-92-12).

30 American Humanist Association, Humanist Manifesto I, issued in 1933; online source: http://www.americanhumanist.org/Humanism/Humanist_Manifesto_I (accessed 06-02-12).

31 Spiritual Humanist website, online source: http://spiritualhumanist.info/ (accessed 06-03-12).

32 Ibid.

33 "Imagine by John Lennon," article at website of the Socialist party of Great Britain., online source: http://www.worldsocialism. org/spgb/education/depth-articles/society-and-culture/imagine-john-lennon (accessed 09-12-12). Lennon denied he was a socialist, saying he had too much money, but the parallel between his lyrics and Karl Marx is hardly coincidental. Was that the pun songwriter-performer Don McClean was going for in his allegorical hit "American Pie"? (*And while Lenin read a book on Marx, / The quartet practiced in the park / And we sang dirges in the dark /The day the music died."*)

Chapter 7

1 Buddha, *Success Consciousness* website: http://www.successconsciousness.com/buddha_quotes.htm (accessed 07-27-12).

2 In Zen Buddhism, perhaps the best known Buddhist tradition in the West, enlightenment only arises when the individual overcomes all dualism and realizes it is not an individual at all but an expression of the Oneness.

3 Jesse Tanner, Ph.D., Unity Institute scholar with a Ph.D. from the University of the West, a Buddhist University in Rosemead, California. Interviewed by author.

4 Jeffrey Brodd, *Primary Source Readings in World Religions,* excerpt from *The Dhammapada, XIV:187* (Winona, MN: Saint Mary's Press, 2009), 74.

5 BBC Website *Religions,* unsigned article on the "Four Noble Truths,"

to include Noble Eightfold Path; online source: http://www.bbc.co.uk/religion/religions/buddhism/beliefs/fournobletruths_1.shtml#h5 (accessed 09-17-12).

6 Prerna Malik, essay on "What Is Right Effort in the Eightfold Path of Buddhism?" online source: http://suite101.com/article/what-is-right-effort-in-the-eightfold-path-of-buddhism-a275537 (accessed 06-18-12).

7 James 2:15-17.

8 Abdu'l Baha, *Divine Philosophy,* online source: http://www.earth2844.net/2.5Work.htm (accessed 06-18-12).

9 Unsigned article, *The Big View* website. Source; http://www.the-bigview.com/buddhism/eightfoldpath.html (accessed 06-17-12).

10 Ibid.

11 Ibid.

12 Bhante Wimala, unpublished Lecture attended by the author, Colombo, Sri Lanka, February 25, 2009.

13 *The Big View* website.

14 Ibid.

15 Satipatthana Sutta, *The Foundations of Mindfulness,* translated by Nyanasatta Thera. Online source: http://www.accesstoinsight.org/lib/authors/nyanasatta/wheel019.html (accessed 06-26-12).

16 Thich Nhat Hanh, *Living Buddha, Living Christ* (New York: Riverhead Books, 1995), 204.

17 Thich Nhat Hanh, online source: http://thinkexist.com/quotes/thich_nhat_hanh/ (accessed 06-30-12).

18 B. Alan Wallace, "A Mindful Balance," online source: www.alanwallace.org/spr08wallace_comp.pdf.

19 Unsigned article, *The Big View* website (accessed 06-27-12).

20 Sign at Vishva Niketan, photographed by the author, February 23, 2009.

21 Website http://tibettech.com/cart/about-prayer-wheels "His Holiness Jigdal Dagchen Sakya, one of the revered Tibetan Buddhist leaders, is the inspiration for Tibet Tech prayer wheels. He oversaw the design and construction of the prayer wheels" (accessed 06-30-12).

22 John Noss, unpublished lecture at Lancaster Theological Semi-

nary, 1976, attended by the author.

[23] Bhante Y. Wimala, *Lessons of the Lotus* (Colombo, Sri Lanka: Bhante Y. Wimala, 2009), 202-203.

Chapter 8

[1] Zydek, "Praying Into the Living Center," *The Conception Abbey Poems, 20.*

[2] Edward James Olmos, "Olmos on Fire," interview by Julia Reynolds, *El Andar*, Winter 1998. Online source: http://www.elandar.com/back/winter98/stories/olmos.html (accessed 07-14-12).

[3] Sheikh Ali Al-Timimi, "Islam—Elevation of Women's Status", transcript of lecture given at McGill University, Montreal, Canada, *Islam for Today* website; http://www.islamfortoday.com/womensstatus.htm (accessed 07-14-12).

[4] Quran: 59:22-23, http://www.al-islam.org/godattributes/quran.htm (accessed 07-21-12).

[5] *"A Brief Illustrated Guide to Understanding Islam,"* online source: http://www.islam-guide.com/frm-ch3-16.htm (accessed 07-16-12).

[6] World Wide Prayer Times website: http://www.islamicity.com/PrayerTimes (accessed 10-28-12).

[7] Hamid Zarrabi-Zadeh, "Prayer Times Calculation" website: http://praytimes.org/calculation/ (accessed 07-14-12).

[8] "Do Priests Have to Say Mass Every Day?" Catholic Exchange: http://catholicexchange.com/do-priests-have-to-say-mass-every-day/.

[9] Essay on "The Five Daily Prayers," features at "Movement for the Propagation of Islam" website: http://aaiil.org/text/books/mali/muslimprayerbook/fivedailyprayers.shtml (accessed 07-16-12).

[10] "What Is Sufism?" online essay at http://www.nimatullahi.org/what-is-sufism/ (accessed 07-16-12).

[11] Anura Gurge, "Benedict XVI's Latin Mass 'Summorum Pontificum' Given More Muscle," *Popes and the Papacy* website; online source: http://popes-and-papacy.com/wordpress/ (accessed 07-21-12).

[12] Cody Pentecostal Holiness Church, Monticello, FL: http://www.

codyphc.org/custompage1.php (accessed 07-16-12).

[13] Rev. Gary Osborne, "What's Wrong With the Full Gospel, Part 2." Online source: http://www.biblical-pentecostals.org/full_gospel_2.htm (accessed 07-176-12), Rev. Osborne writes: "Let us, as Pentecostals, stand for *all* the truth in God's holy Word! Thus, in answer to my question, *'What's wrong with the full gospel?'* I am happy to report—absolutely nothing! I for one am proud to be a Biblical Pentecostal Christian!!" (Punctuation unedited.)

[14] Laurence A. Justice, "Should a Baptist Church Embrace Pentecostalism?" Online source: http://www.pbministries.org/Theology/Laurence%20Justice/embrace_pentecostalism.htm (accessed 07-16-12). Justice writes: "We could mention many things that are wrong with Pentecostalism. We could mention the divisiveness it seems to bring in a church. We could mention the circus-like atmosphere it creates in the worship services … May God give us the grace and the knowledge of His Word and the strength of character and the honesty to stand against this great error!"

[15] Samuel 10:10-13.

[16] Elvira Kotic, et al., "Glossolalia," scholarly article, Coll. Antropol. 29 (2005) 1: 307-313, online source: http://www.psihijatrija.com/bibliografija/radovi/Koic%20E%20GLOSSOLALIA%20COLLEGIUM.pdf (accessed 07-21-12). List is not exhaustive.

[17] Donald Scott, "Evangelicalism, Revivalism, and the Second Great Awakening," web-published essay, Queens College / City University of New York; TeacherServe website of the National Humanities Center; online source: http://nationalhumanitiescenter.org/tserve/nineteen/nkeyinfo/nevanrev.htm (accessed 07-31-12).

[18] Jone Johnson Lewis, "Aimee Semple McPherson," Women's History, About.com website; online source: http://womenshistory.about.com/od/protestant/a/aimee_mcpherson.htm (accessed 07-31-12).

[19] 1 Corinthians 14:15.

[20] Matthew 15:31.

[21] "The Meaning of Om," Om Sakthi website: http://www.omsakthi.org/worship/mantra.html (accessed 07-17-12).

[22] Barbara Cunnius, "Spiritualism Is New Dimension of Life, Dr.

Marcus Bach Claims," October 8, 1980, *Reading Eagle*, p. 33.

23 Hulda, *About.com Guide.* "Islamic Prayer Timings: At What Time Do Daily Prayers Occur?" Online source: http://islam.about.com/cs/prayer/a/prayer_times.htm (accessed 09-13-12).

Chapter 9

1 Doreen Valiente, "Invocation of the Moon Goddess," Pagan Songs, Chants, and Prayers website; online source: http://www.squidoo.com/paganchants (accessed 07-28-12).

2 "Terminology: Neo-Paganism, WiccaWitchcraft." ReligionFacts.com, http://www.religionfacts.com/neopaganism/terminology.htm (accessed 07-19-12).

3 Melinda Crisp, "Neopaganism vs. Wicca," http://melinda-crisp.deviantart.com/art/Neopaganism-vs-Wicca-171633387 (accessed 09-18-12).

4 Patti Wigington, "The Role of Prayer in Paganism," About.com. http://paganwiccan.about.com/od/prayersandincantations/a/Role_of_Prayer.htm (accessed 07-19-12).

5 Myth Woodling, "Balance in a Pluralistic Faith"; source: http://www.jesterbear.com/Wicca/Pluralistic.html (accessed 07-19-12).

6 Revenna Angelline, personal email to author, (07-27-12).

7 Woodling, "Balance in a Pluralistic Faith."

8 Wigington, "The Role of Prayer in Paganism."

9 Joelle's Sacred Grove website; source: http://www.joellessacredgrove.com/Holidays/sabbats.html (accessed 07-20-12).

10 Ibid.

11 Galen Gillotte, *Book of Hours: Prayers to the Goddess* (St. Paul, MN: Lewellyn Publications, 2001), 42-43; 45-46. When contacting Gillotte for permission to use his verses, he replied by email: "I do give permission to quote the work ... However, I must tell you that I had an experience from Spirit, and have since returned to the Catholic Church. I don't know if that will make a difference to your using the work; I see my Pagan path as bringing me home again." From my encounters with the affirmative, inclusive nature of Neo-paganism, I am certain they would be happy to hear of any seeker who finds the way home.

12 http://www.joellessacredgrove.com/Holidays/sabbats.html

(accessed 07-20-12).

13 Colombe, "Yule Prayer Song," http://www.wicca-spirituality. com/yule-prayer.html (accessed 07-20-12).

14 Ibid.

15 Christina Aubin, "Beltane—Holiday Details and History," *Popular Pagan Holidays* website, online source: http://www.witchvox. com/va/dt_va.html?a=usma&c=holidays&id=2765 (accessed 07-21-12).

16 Mike Nichols, "Beltane: Celebration of May Day," online source: http://deoxy.org/time/sabbats/05-04.htm (accessed 07-20-12).

17 Gerina Dunwich, *Exploring Spellcraft: How to Create and Cast Effective Spells* (Franklin Lakes, NJ: Career Press, 2001), 112-113.

18 "Beltane—May 1st" from *Herbal Musings* website: http://herbalmusings.com/beltane.htm (accessed 07-21-12).

19 Bob Chaundy, "The Burning Times," *BBC News Magazine*, October 30, 2009; online edition: http://news.bbc.co.uk/2/hi/uk_news/ magazine/8334055.stm (accessed 07-21-12).

20 Bruce A. Robinson, "Is Wicca a Form of Satanism?" Religious Tolerance.org website, http://www.religioustolerance.org/wic_ sata.htm/ (accessed 09-17-12). In the cited biblical passage, Exodus 32, Moses talks Yahweh down before the Creator can smite the Golden Calf partygoers in the valley below.

Chapter 10

1 Exodus 3:4-5.

2 "What Is a Sacred Space?" Santa Barbara Sacred Spaces website; online source: http://www.sacred-spaces.info/sba/index.html (accessed 07-23-12).

3 Psalm 46:10.

4 "What Is a Sacred Space?"

5 "Sacred Space," Minnesota Episcopal Environmental Stewardship Commission website; online source: http://www.env-steward.com/reflect/space.htm (accessed 07-23-12).

6 Santa Barbara Sacred Spaces, (accessed 08-03-12).

7 Habakkuk 2:20.

8 1 Kings 19:11-12.

9 Joseph H. Hertz, *The Sayings of the Fathers: Pirke Aboth* (New York: Behrman House, 1945), 12.

10 *Pirke Avoth (The Wisdom of the Fathers),* 3:13. The Chabad Library. Online source: http://www.chabad.org/library/article_cdo/aid/2019/jewish/Chapter-Three.htm (accessed 08-20-11).

11 Eckhart Tolle in "The Awakening of Eckhart Tolle," interview by Paula Coppel, *Unity Magazine,* Eckhart Tolle's website. Online source: http://www.eckharttolle.com/article/Spiritual-Awakening-Of-Eckhart-Tolle/ (accessed 08-20-11).

12 Henri Nouwen, S.J., *The Way of the Heart: Desert Spirituality and Contemporary Ministry* (NY: Seabury Press, 1981), 59.

13 Unsigned Internet article. http://websitejudge.com/internet/webdesign/monkeymind.net (accessed 08-20-11).

14 Michael L. Birkel, *Silence and Witness: The Quaker Tradition* (Maryknoll, NY: Orbis Books, 2004), 40.

15 "The Quaker Way," Friends General Conference website: http://www.fgcquaker.org/explore/quaker-way (accessed 07-23-12).

16 Herb Lape, "A Case for Eldering and Discipline," *Friends Journal,* Earlham School of Religion, online source: http://www.friendsjournal.org/case-eldering-and-discipline (accessed 07-23-12).

17 Birkel, 18.

18 Douglas V. Steer, ed., *Quaker Spirituality: Selected Writings* (New York: Paulist Press, 1984), 26.

19 J. Brent Bill, *Holy Silence: The Gift of Quaker Spirituality* (Brewster, MA: Paraclete Press, 2006), 90-91.

20 George Fox, in *Quaker Spirituality: Selected Writings,* Emilie Griffin and Douglas V. Steele, eds. (New York: HarperCollins, 2005), 12.

21 Birkel, 42. Italics added.

22 David Lonsdale, *Eyes to See, Ears to Hear* (NY: Orbis Books, 2000), 74.

23 Birkel, 47

24 Ibid., 41.

25 Bill, 2.

26 Ibid, 3-5.

27 James Dillet Freeman, "I Am There," online source: http://www.
unity.org/resources/articles/i-am-there (accessed 07-23-12).

28 Pseudo-Dionysius the Areopagite, in Arthur Cushman McGiffert,
A History of Christian Thought, Vol. I. New York: Charles Scribner's
Sons, 1932.

29 Thomas W. Shepherd, *Friends in High Places,* Third edition (Lincoln, NE: iUniverse Books, 2006), 55.

30 Khalil Gibran, *The Prophet,* "On Children," All Great Quotes website, http://www.allgreatquotes.com/kahlil_gibran_quotes3.
shtml (accessed 07-25-12).

31 Anonymous, ThinkExist.com website, online source: http://
thinkexist.com/quotation/one_of_life-s_greatest_mysteries_is_
how_the_boy/149191.html (accessed 07-26-12).

32 Marcus Bach, *The Unity Way of Life* (Kansas City, MO: Unity
Books, 1962), 24.

33 Ibid., 25.

34 Buddha, quoted at http://www.buddhist-tourism.com/bud-
dhism/buddha-quotes.html (accessed 08-28-11).

Chapter 11

1 Henry Alford, "Come Ye Thankful People Come," http://www.
hymnsite.com/lyrics/umh694.sht (accessed 07-28-12).

2 Randolph E. Schmid, Associated Press, "Humans Flirted With Extinction 70,000 Years Ago," *USA Today,* 4/24/2008; online source:
http://www.usatoday.com/tech/science/2008-04-24-human-
extinction_N.htm (accessed 07-28-12).

3 Pamela Russell, "The Palaeolithic Mother-Goddess: Fact or Fiction?" *Reader in Gender Archaeology,* Kelley Hays-Gilpin and David
S. Whitley, ed. (New York: Routledge, 1998), 261.

4 Ibid., 267.

5 Ibid.

6 Godfrey Igwebuike Onah, "The Meaning of Peace in African Traditional Religion and Culture," Pontifical Urban University, Rome;
published at Chidi Denis Isizoh's website: http://www.afrika-
world.net/afrel/goddionah.htm#_ftn22 (accessed 07-28-12).

7 Nora Raggio, "Pre-Columbian Sacrifices," online essay at San Jose

State University School of Art and Design Website: http://gallery.sjsu.edu/sacrifice/precolumbian.html (accessed 07-29-12).

8 "First Fruits," Jewish Virtual Library; online source: http://www.jewishvirtuallibrary.org/jsource/judaica/ejud_0002_0007_0_06495.html (accessed 08-02-12).

9 Ibid.

10 Shepherd, *Jesus 2.1: An Upgrade for the 21st Century* (Unity Village, MO: Unity Books, 2010), 112.

11 1 Corinthians 10:30-33.

12 Ibid., 27:15-18.

13 Genesis 27:38.

14 "Leave a Positive Footprint: Blessing Space," *Daily Om* message for April 18, 2007; online source: http://www.dailyom.com/articles/2007/7907.html (accessed 07-30-12).

15 "Cherokee Prayer Blessing" at Pearls of Wisdom: Awakening Personal and Global Consciousness website; online source: http://www.sapphyr.net/natam/quotes-nativeamerican.htm (accessed 07-30-12).

16 "The Blessing of Animals," unsigned article at tourism website of Ibiza, Spain: http://www.ibizaa-z.com/ibiza.php?name=Feb%20-%20Santa%20Gertrudis&section=fiestas (accessed 08-01-12).

17 Nirmala Carvalho, "Mumbai: a Special Blessing for Animals Owned by Hindus, Parsees, and Christians," AsiaNews.it, October 4, 2011, http://www.asianews.it/news-en/Mumbai:-a-special-blessing-for-animals-owned-by-Hindus,-Parsees-and-Christians-22810.html.

18 James Morrison, "Petition the Lord With Prayer," in *The Soft Parade*, the Doors' fourth studio album; http://www.lyricsfreak.com/d/doors/the+soft+parade_20042755.html (accessed 08-26-12).

19 Frank Cottrell Boyce, *God on Trial*, Public Broadcasting System, aired November 9, 2008; online site; http://www.pbs.org/wgbh/greatpiece/godontrial/synopsis.html (accessed 08-01-12).

20 Robert Brumet, *Birthing a Greater Reality* (Unity Village, MO: Unity Books, 2010).

21 Kelli Isola, "Answering the Call of World Day of Prayer," Kelli

Isola blog for 07-31-12, online source: http://www.kellyisola. com/answering-the-call-of-world-day-of-prayer/ (accessed 08-03-12).

22 "What Is Sacred Space?" Santa Barbara Sacred Spaces; http:// www.sacred-spaces.info/sba/index.html (accessed 08-03-12).

23 "Reservation of the Blessed Sacrament," *New Advent Home Catholic Encyclopedia;* online source: http://www.newadvent.org/cathen/12784b.htm (accessed 08-03-12).

24 Bishop John Shelby Spong, John Shelby Spong Weekly Column, 11-05-09; online source: "http://johnshelbyspong. com/2009/11/05/the-origins-of-the-new-testamentpart-v-interpreting-the-life-of-paul/ (accessed 08-03-12).

25 St. Augustine, quoted in essay by Rev. Ken Collins, "What Is a Sacrament?" Online source: http://www.kencollins.com/sacraments/sacrament-02.htm (accessed 08-07-12).

26 St. Augustine, *De Peccatorum Remissione et de Baptismo Parvulorum,* 412 C.E., quoted by David Bennett, "The Eucharist," at the Ancient and Future Catholics website; online source: http://www. ancient-future.net/eucharist.html (accessed 08-07-12).

27 Bishop Ignatius, in David Brattston, "The Medicine of Immortality," in *Spectrum Magazine* online edition, September 26, 2010. Source: http://spectrummagazine.org/authors/david-brattston (accessed 08-09-12).

28 Paul Tillich, *A History of Christian Thought* (New York: Touchstone, 1968), 261.

29 Flannery O'Connor and the Eucharist and Church History, Shameless Popery website (pro-Catholic site), posted 04-20-12; online http://catholicdefense.blogspot.com/2012/04/flannery-oconnor-on-eucharist-and.html (accessed 08-07-12).

30 Paramhansa Yogananda, *Autobiography of a Yogi,* 13th edition (Los Angeles, CA: Self-Realization Fellowship, 2010), 152.

31 Ibid., 153.

32 Ibid., 155.

33 Ibid.

34 Kathleen Wall and Gary Ferguson, *Rites of Passage: Celebrating Life's Changes* (Hillsboro, OR: Beyond Words Publishing, Inc.,

1998), xiii.

35 Birth Rites-Islam, BBC-Religions. http://www.bbc.co.uk/religion/religions/islam/ritesrituals/birth.shtml (accessed 08-08-12).

36 Childhood website, "Modern Western Conception of Childhood," unsigned article; online source: http://family.jrank.org/pages/232/Childhood-Modern-Western-Conception-Childhood.html (accessed 08-08-12).

37 Ibid.

38 "A Jewish boy automatically becomes a bar mitzvah upon reaching the age of 13 years, and a girl upon reaching the age of 12 years. No ceremony is needed to confer these rights and obligations. The popular bar mitzvah ceremony is not required, and does not fulfill any commandment." Judaism 101 website: http://www.jewfaq.org/barmitz.htm (accessed 08-08-12).

39 U.S. Conference of Catholic Bishops website: http://old.usccb.org/movies/q/quinceanera.shtml (accessed 09-06-12).

40 "Bendición Al Cumplir Quince Años," ("Order for the Blessing on the Fifteenth Birthday"), U.S. Conference of Catholic Bishops, Decree of Publication, issued July 26, 2007; online source: http://www.fwdioc.org/worship/Documents/quince_anos_eng.pdf (accessed 09-06-12).

41 "Ten Bizarre Rites of Passage;" http://listverse.com/2009/12/28/10-bizarre-rites-of-passage/ (accessed 08-08-12).

Chapter 12

1 Zydek, "Getting to the Still Center," *Conception Abbey Poems*, 9.

2 Jeffrey Brodd, *Primary Source Readings in World Religions*, excerpt from *The Dhammapada, XIV:187* (Winona, MN: Saint Mary's Press, 2009), 95.

3 The Báb, "Remover of Difficulties," Baha'i Faith website: http://www.bahai.com/Bahaullah/prayers.htm (accessed 08-28-12).

4 His Holiness Sri Swami Sivananda Saraswati Maharaj, "Meditation on Sri Krishna," in "Five Prayers for All Occasions," About.com website: http://hinduism.about.com/od/prayersmantras/a/5prayers.htm (accessed 08-28-12).

5 Psalm 8:3-4.

6 Psalm 68:28.

7 Genesis 1:26.

8 John 4:23-24.

9 Unity of Omaha website: http://www.unityomaha.org/weddings.htm (accessed 08-24-122).

10 Shepherd, *Good Questions: Answering Letters From the Edge of Doubt* (Unity Village, MO: Unity Books, 2009), 31.

11 Unity of Dayton website: http://www.unityofdayton.org/aboutus.html (accessed 08-21-12). *Modern Thought* is today known as *Unity Magazine*.

12 "How May We Pray With You?" *Unity.org* website: http://www.unity.org/prayer (accessed 08-21-12).

13 "Affirmative Prayer," *Unity—A Positive Path for Spiritual Living*, Unity School of Christianity website: www.unity.org/prayer/inspirationalArticles/affirmativePrayer.html (accessed 08-26-12).

14 Ibid.

15 Morrison, www.lyricsfreak.com/d/doors/the+soft+parade_20042755.html (accessed 08-26-12).

16 "What Is Affirmative Prayer?" *Unity.org* website: http://www.unity.org/prayer/what-affirmative-prayer (accessed 08-21-12).

17 "The Negative Confession," *Egyptian Book of the Dead*, http://www.philae.nu/akhet/Confession.html (accessed 08-24-12).

18 Online Medical Dictionary, *McGraw-Hill Concise Dictionary of Modern Medicine* (The McGraw-Hill Companies, Inc., 2002) http://medical-dictionary.thefreedictionary.com/in+denial (accessed 08-24-12).

19 John Suler, Ph.D., "Empty Your Cup," http://users.rider.edu/~suler/zenstory/emptycup.html (accessed 08-24-12).

20 Catherine Ponder, *Open Your Mind to Prosperity* (Martina del Rey, CA: DeVorss, 1983), 27.

21 Matthew 12:43-45.

22 Rev. Todd Nelson, blog entry, First United Methodist Church of Andover, MA. Website: http://1stumcandover.blogspot.com/2012/01/devotional-for-1252012-matthew-1243-45.html (accessed 04-27-12).

23 William Glasser, *"Positive Addiction,"* Journal of Extension, May/June 1977.

24 Psalm 23:1-4.

25 Fillmore, *Atom-Smashing Power of Mind,* 72.

26 J Douglas Bottorff, *A Practical Guide to Meditation and Prayer* (Unity Village, MO: Unity Books, 1995), 79. Available online at "Consciousness, Denial and Affirmation," *Independent Unity Blog,* 09-29-11; http://dougbottorff.com/2011/09/29/consciousness-denial-and-affirmation/?like=1 (accessed 08-26-12).

27 H. Emilie Cady, *Lessons in Truth* (Kansas City, MO: Unity Books, 1896), 45.

28 James Dillet Freeman, "Prayer for Protection," from *Unity Magazine;* republished online at Unity School of Christianity website: http://www.unity.org/resources/articles/prayer-protection (accessed 08-26-12).

Chapter 13

1 Father Luke Dysinger, O.S.B, "How to Practice Lectio Divina—A Step-by-Step Guide to Praying the Bible," http://www.beliefnet.com/Faiths/Catholic/2000/08/How-To-Practice-Lectio-Divina.aspx (accessed 08-12-12.)

2 1 Kings 22:7-8.

3 1 Kings 13:11-12.

4 Robert M. Seltzer, Bible as Ancient Literature, "Go With Gilgamesh, but Lose the Animal Livers," http://www.myjewishlearning.com/texts/Bible/Origins_of_the_Bible/Other_Ancient_Texts/Bible_as_Ancient_Literature.shtml (accessed 08-17-12).

5 "Urim and Thummin," *New Advent Home Catholic Encyclopedia* website; http://www.newadvent.org/ cathen/15224a.htm (accessed 08-13-12).

6 Bruce D. Rahtjen, *Paul and His World,* audio cassette lecture, (Unity Village, MO: Unity School of Christianity, 1978). Dr. Rahtjen, who tragically drowned in 2010 at the age of 77, was a retired Episcopal priest, former professor of Old Testament Studies at St. Paul School of Theology in Kansas City, and a much-beloved frequent speaker at Unity Village.

7 2 Kings 21:11.

8 2 Kings 21:14-16.

9 John 1:1-5.

10 Joseph Chalmers, O.Carm, "Lectio Divina Bible Meditation," The British Province of Carmelite Friars website; http://www.carmelite.org/index.php?nuc=content&id=72 (accessed 08-18-12). Some sources capitalize (*Lectio Divina*) while others do not. This book regards the spiritual discipline as a proper noun requiring capitals, unless quoting an author who does otherwise.

11 Fr. Gabriel O'Donnell, O.P., "Reading for Holiness: Lectio Divina," in *Spiritual Traditions for the Contemporary Church*, Robin Mass and Gabriel O'Donnell, O.P., eds. (Nashville, TN: Abingdon Press, 1990), 46.

12 Ibid., 47.

13 "Lectio Divina," Argos International website: http://www.agros.org/ag/docs/LectioDivina.pdf (accessed 08-18-12).

14 Joseph Chalmers, O.Carm, "An Introduction to 'Prayer in Secret' and Lectio Divina Meditation on the Scriptures," British Province of Carmelite Friars: http://www.carmelite.org/index.php?nuc=content&id=73 (accessed 08-14-12).

15 Martella-Whitsett, 110.

16 Dysinger, http://www.beliefnet.com/Faiths/Catholic/2000/08/How-To-Practice-Lectio-Divina.aspx (accessed 08-17-12).

17 Maas and O'Donnell, 48.

18 Rumi, quoted at http://www.indranet.com/potpourri/poetry/rumi/rumi.html (accessed 08-17-12).

19 Secret, Sacred Mormon Tabernacle Ceremonies; http://nowscape.com/mormon/mormcr1.htm (accessed 08-20-12).

20 Maas and O'Donnell, 48-49.

21 Joseph Chalmers, O.Carm, "Prayer in Secret," The British Province of Carmelite Friars website; online source: http://www.carmelite.org/index.php?nuc=content&id=73 (accessed 08-18-12).

Chapter 14

1 Thomas Keating, "The Practice of Attention/Intention" in *Centering Prayer in Daily Life and Ministry*, Gustave Reininger, ed. (New York: Continuum, 2003), 13.

2 "Centering," *Mind Tools* website: http://www.mindtools.com/pages/article/newTCS_83.htm (accessed 09-01-12).

3 Basil Pennington, "Centering Prayer—A Gift From the Desert," in *Centering Prayer*, online excerpt: http://www.kyrie.com/cp/a_gift_from_the_desert.htm (accessed 09-01-12).

4 "About Contemplative Outreach," Centering Prayer NY: http://www.centeringprayerny.com/about-contemplative-outreach/ (accessed 08-29-12).

5 Basil Pennington, "Introduction," in *Centering Prayer in Daily Life and Ministry*, Gustave Reininger, ed. (New York: Continuum, 2003), 10.

6 Matthew 6:7-8, KJV.

7 Matthew 6:7-8.

8 Shepherd, *Friends in High Places*, 86.

9 "Reciting the Most Beautiful Names of Allah," *Islamic Path* website: http://islamicpath.org/dua_names.html (accessed 08-29-12).

10 Baha'u'llah, quoted by Shoghi Effendi in *God Passes By*, cited at official Baha'i Faith website: http://www.bahai-library.com/writings/shoghieffendi/gpb/116-120.html. This is the very quote read to me at a Baha'i meeting when I was 18 years old.

11 Carly Simon, "You're So Vain," www.lyricsfreak.com/c/carly+simon/you+are+so+vain_20354877.html (accessed 08-29-12).

12 Amos 5:21-24.

13 Sign posted at Vishva Niketan Buddhist Retreat Center, Colombo, Sri Lanka.

14 Sister Melannie Svoboda, S.N.D., "Five Steps to Better Prayer," *Catholic Religious Vocation Network* website: http://www.vocationnetwork.org/articles/show/75 (accessed 08-30-12).

15 Maltbie Davenport Babcock (1858-1901); traditional English melody, "This Is My Father's World," http://www.hymnsite.com/lyrics/umh144.sht (accessed 08-30-12). Shamelessly anthropomorphic, gender insensitive and yet magnificently peaceful lines I have loved all my life.

16 Keating, 13.

17 Keating, "The Method of Centering Prayer," in Reininger, *Center-*

ing Prayer, 131.

18 Matthew 6:6 (KJV, NRSV).

19 Keating, 131.

20 Ibid., 132.

21 Ibid.

22 *The Cloud of Unknowing,* author unknown, Evelyn Underhill, ed., 1922 edition; online source: http://www.sacred-texts.com/chr/cou/cou03.htm (accessed 09-05-12).

23 Christa Tippett, "The Maasai Creed," *On Being* website: http://www.onbeing.org/program/need-creeds/feature/maasai-creed/1295 (accessed 09-05-12).

Chapter 15

1 Emmett Fox, "The Golden Key," http://www.soberrecovery.com/forums/spirituality/187423-scientific-prayer-little-emmet-fox.html (accessed 09-06-12). Some versions truncate the first sentence to omit the opening words "Scientific prayer." The editorial changes, to a work written early in the 20th century, might represent a desire to make the essay sound more reasonable, less New Agey.

2 Ibid.

3 Ibid.

4 Ibid.

5 Thomas W. Shepherd, "A Golden Key for Private Franklin," abridged version of an article first published in Unity booklet *Seasons of Change—Seasons of Hope,* July 2007, and reproduced in excerpt form at http://content.unity.org/homepageArchive/features/aGoldenKey.html (accessed 09-06-12).

Chapter 16

1 The Venerable Henepola Gunaratana, *Mindfulness in Plain English,* Chapter 3, "What Meditation Is," online excerpt at http://www.vipassana.com/meditation/mindfulness_in_plain_english_5.php (accessed 09-04-12).

2 "Meditation in the Christian Tradition," Blog of Rideau Park United Church, Ottawa, Ontario, Canada, 01-11-11, source: http://rideauparkspirituality.blogspot.com/2011/01/meditation-in-christian-tradition.html (accessed 09-04-12).

3 Josh Davis, "Two Types of Meditation," source: http://www.de-droidify.com/meditation.htm (accessed 09-04-12).

4 "Saint Ignatius of Loyola," EWTN online library; http://www.ewtn.com/library/MARY/IGNAITU2.HTM (accessed 09-08-12).

5 "Brief Biography of St. Ignatius of Loyola," http://norprov.org/spirituality/lifeofignatius.htm (accessed 09-08-12).

6 "The Spiritual Exercises of St. Ignatius," Society of Jesus, Oregon Province; online source: http://www.nwjesuits.org/JesuitSpirituality/SpiritualExercises.html (accessed 09-08-12).

7 Ibid.

8 Tom Zender, *The Restless Spirit* online newsletter, August 2012, available in *RS* archives 09-01-2012: http://www.tomzender.com/newsletter-archive. (Accessed in subscription format: 08-15-12.)

9 Zender, *One-Minute Meditations at Work* (Bloomington, IN: Balboa Press, 2011), xiii.

10 Maurizio G. Smith, "American Indian Vision Quest," lecture delivered at Theosophical Library Center, Altadena, CA, 04-18-86; online source: http://www.theosophy-nw.org/theosnw/world/america/am-smit.htm (accessed 09-07-12).

11 Lakota Indian Vision Quest, "Crying for a Vision," The Wild West website, Native American Religion; online source: http://www.thewildwest.org/nativeamericans/nativeamericanreligion/103-lakotaindiansthevisionquest.html (accessed 09-07-12).

12 Black Elk, quoted at http://www.thewildrose.net/sweat.html (accessed 09-07-12).

13 Aesop's Fable, "The Fox and the Grapes," at *The Phrase Finder* "Sour Grapes" definition; website: http://www.phrases.org.uk/meanings/sour-grapes.html (accessed 09-09-12).

14 Robert Green Ingersoll; http://www.entwagon.com/cgi-bin/quotes/quotes.pl?cat=Visualization&id=2 (accessed 09-09-12).

Chapter 17

1 Based on notes of conversation with the Venerable Bhante Y. Wimala, Spring, 2012.

2 See Chapter 1.

3 "Alfie," by Burt Bacharach and Hal David; http://www.lyricsmode.com/lyrics/b/burt_bacharach/alfie.html (accessed 09-09-12).

4 "Jefferson Davis Quotes on Slavery," The Confederate Partisan website (filled with religious language): http://www.csapartisan.com/jefferson_davis_quotes.html (accessed 09-11-12).

5 Abraham Lincoln, Speech at Springfield, IL: http://www.stolaf.edu/people/fitz/COURSES/debates.htm (accessed 09-10-12).

6 The Moravian Church in North America website: http://www.moravian.org/the-moravian-church/the-moravian-church/history.html (accessed 09-10-12).

7 Carl Sagan, "Extraordinary Claims Require Extraordinary Evidence," online essay by Matt Slick, Christian Apologetics and Research Ministry website, http://carm.org/extraordinary-claims-require-extraordinary-evidence.

8 Harry Emerson Fosdick, Quotes.net website, http://www.quotes.net/quote/77.

Benediction

1 Myrtle Fillmore, from *Myrtle Fillmore's Healing Letters,* (Unity Village, MO: Unity Books, 1954), unnumbered introductory pages. Frances W. Foulks wrote in that same introduction: "The preparation of these pages for your perusal has been a service of love undertaken in appreciation of a great soul. It has been like being again in her presence and receiving instruction and inspiration from the Christ Mind that spoke so freely through her; like receiving a benediction from her."

APPENDIX

Affirmation of Inclusive Christianity in a Multifaith World*

I believe in God, One Presence and One Power,
   Who speaks to me
personally, as a still, small voice within,
   impersonally, as the power of Omnipotent Goodness, and
   historically, through teachers and prophets of all faiths
wherever consciousness arises in God's vast Cosmos.
I believe in Jesus the Christ,
   understood and reinterpreted through time as
the man of Nazareth and Way Shower,
Who calls us to serve all the children of the Universe
with compassion,
   And in Christ Jesus, the crucified and risen Lord,
   Who demonstrates the mystery of life eternal
   and points to the imago Dei in every sentient being.
I believe in the Holy Spirit,
   Which empowers the Cosmos to be,
   inspires creativity and understanding,
   and leads people by holy wisdom
   to discover their path to spiritual truth.
I believe in the equality of all God's children,
   in the rich diversity of ethnic and cultural backgrounds,
in the differing physical and intellectual expressions,
and in the varieties of orientations which shape a healthy life.
I believe in our unity of purpose
   as a gathered community of faith, in the community of world faiths,
which knows the power of affirmative prayer;
I believe in the communion of spiritual growth
And the eternal possibility for Oneness in God
   through an endless, innovative union of joy and love.
Blessings and peace, divine order and refreshing inspiration, healing
power and demonstrated prosperity, wholeness of life and love eternal
will accompany me now and forevermore, through the power of the
Christ within. Amen

   —Thomas W. Shepherd, D.Min.

*The above is a personal statement, not intended as the official viewpoint of any organiza-
tion or religious body. It is offered to promote discussion about inclusive Christianity in a
multifaith world.

ACKNOWLEDGEMENTS

I have been blessed in this work with energetic research assistants and knowledgeable coworkers. Several colleagues at Unity Institute provided a sounding board for the ideas as they developed, notably Robert Brumet, Theodore Collins, Paula Coppel, Claudell Hefner-County, Mark Fuss, Paul Hasselbeck, Carla McClellan, Camille O'Brien, Eric Page, and Tom Thorpe—none of whom should be held accountable for the sometimes-controversial final product. Research assistants, who provided great assistance in the background materials of so many cultural groups and supportive theological reflection, including Jeanmarie Eck, Brandon Nagel, Marilyn Schoenfelder, Michael Schoonover, William Shepherd, Lindsey Shepherd, Emily Shepherd, and Jesse Tanner. Also, the technical/creative support from Unity Books found human expression in the good work of Lila S. Herrmann, Terry Newell, Sharon Sartin, Ryan Gibbs, and many others.

Special thanks to the Venerable Bhante Y. Wimala for his intellectually cogent, deeply spiritual remarks on Buddhism. I am also grateful to Unity Books editor Stephanie Stokes Oliver, who prodded me with deadlines, and the "Profits and Scribes" writers' group that meets at the Unity Village Bookstore—especially Dave County, Ed Frownfelter, and Don Rogers. Add to the list my bimonthly congregation at Unity of the Lakes, Warsaw, Missouri, on whom I foisted some of these ideas during the writing process.

Finally, I must thank my wife, Carol-Jean, who guarded my writing time from intruders and encouraged every step of the process. (See Proverbs 31:29.) And belated thanks to our primordial ancestors, who first looked up at the stars and wondered what life was about. The journey will never end, but I like the path so far …

ABOUT THE AUTHOR

Rev. Dr. Thomas W. Shepherd is an ordained Unity minister and retired U.S. Army Chaplain who teaches Historical and Theological Studies at Unity Institute and Seminary, Unity Village, Missouri. Although best known for his popular Q&A column "That's a Good Question" in *Unity Magazine*, "Dr. Tom" (as students call him) has authored several books, including *Jesus 2.1: An Upgrade for the 21st Century, Glimpses of Truth, Good Questions*, and *Friends in High Places*.

Shepherd served in Vietnam with the U.S. Army as a medical evacuation helicopter pilot, where he was awarded two Distinguished Flying Crosses, Air Medal, Purple Heart, and the Vietnamese Cross of Gallantry. After Vietnam he left the Army, graduated college and seminary, and returned to duty as a military chaplain, completing 20 years' active service in 1988. Shepherd holds a B.S. Ed. from the University of Idaho, Master of Divinity from Lancaster Theological Seminary, and a Doctor of Ministry degree from St. Paul School of Theology in Kansas City. Dr. Shepherd speaks conversational German, Japanese, and Spanish, and has studied the Greek, Latin, and Vietnamese languages.

In addition to Unity, Dr. Tom holds ministerial credentials with the Unitarian Universalist Association and the National Association of Congregational Christian Churches, and worked as Assistant Executive Director/Theologian in Residence for the Universal Foundation for Better Living. He served Unity Churches in Georgia, South Carolina, and California before accepting a post on the faculty of Unity Institute in 2005. Dr. Tom received the 2011 Charles Fillmore Award from Unity Worldwide Ministries. His controversial *Theo-Blog* can be found at *http://revtom-theo-blog.blogspot.com/*.

Printed in the U.S.A.

B0194